East Meets West in Dance

Voices in the Cross-Cultural Dialogue

Edited by

Ruth Solomon

and

John Solomon

harwood academic publishers
Australia • Canada • China • France • Germany • India • Japan
Luxembourg • Malaysia • The Netherlands • Russia • Singapore
Switzerland • Thailand • United Kingdom

First published 1995
Second printing 1997

Amsteldijk 166
1st Floor
1079 LH Amsterdam
The Netherlands

British Library Cataloguing in Publication Data

East Meets West in Dance: Voices in a
Cross Cultural Dialogue. – (Choreography
& Dance Studies, ISSN 1053-380X; Vol. 9)
  I. Solomon, Ruth   II. Solomon, John
  III. Series
  792.8

  ISBN 3-7186-5604-3

This book is dedicated to
Carl Wolz
to whom everyone involved in the
dance exchange between East and West
owes a debt of gratitude

Contents

Part VIII   Taiwan

Introduction to the Series

Choreography and Dance Studies is a book series of special interest to dancers, dance teachers and choreographers. Focusing on dance composition, its techniques and training, the series will also cover the relationship of choreography to other components of dance performance such as music, lighting and the training of dancers.

In addition, *Choreography and Dance Studies* will seek to publish new works and provide translations of works not previously published in English, as well as publish reprints of currently unavailable books of outstanding value to the dance community.

Robert P. Cohan

Acknowledgements

The editors gratefully acknowledge grants from the Pacific Rim Research Program of the University of California, and the Academic Senate and Arts Division Research Committees, University of California, Santa Cruz; the invaluable work of Zoe Sodja and Cheryl Van De Veer in all phases of manuscript preparation; Muriel Topaz's expert editorial assistance; and the unfailing generosity of the thirty-five contributors to this book.

List of Illustrations

Cover photo: Dance Forum Taipei dancers in *Pearls Roll Away*

    Choreographer: Renée Wadleigh

    Photographer: Liu Zhen-xiang

About the Editors

Ruth Solomon

As a performer Ruth Solomon has appeared on and off Broadway, on television, and in concerts throughout the United States and Canada. She was for many years a permanent member and solo dancer with the Jean Erdman Dance Theater.

Ms. Solomon has created more than fifty works in her unique version of the modern dance idiom, in addition to staging and choreographing such diverse musical/dramatic productions as Euripides' *Hecuba,* Stravinsky's *L'Histoire du Soldat,* and Brecht's *Three Penny Opera.*

From 1967 to 1970 she was assistant director of the dance program at New York University School of the Arts. Since 1970 she has headed the dance program which she established at the University of California, Santa Cruz, where she is Professor of Theater Arts/Dance. Her highly successful teaching technique has been documented in an hour-long video, "Anatomy As a Master Image in Training Dancers."

Other aspects of Ms. Solomon's multifaceted career are represented by her publications. Her articles on dance performance, administration, and pedagogy have appeared in all major dance periodicals, and her research in dance medicine has produced publications in various medical journals. She was invited to speak at the Olympic Scientific Congress in Seoul, Korea(1988), and has subsequently taught in China, Hong Kong, Taiwan and Japan. Her most recent publications are *Preventing Dance Injuries: An Interdisciplinary Perspective* (1990), *Soviet-American Dance Medicine 1990* (1991), and "The New Faces of Dance Scholarship," a monograph of her Scholars' Lecture as the National Dance Association's Scholar of the Year for 1992.

John Solomon

John Solomon, M.A. (Columbia University) and Ph.D. (Indiana University) in American Literature, served on the faculty and administrative staff of several universities, including the University of Hawaii and the University of California, Santa Cruz. Since 1983 he has devoted himself primarily to freelance editing. His recent dance-related publications are: *Preventing Dance Injuries: An Interdisciplinary Perspective* (1990), *Soviet-American Dance Medicine 1990* (1991), and "Dance in a Global Perspective: The 5th Hong Kong International Dance Conference" (*Journal of Physical Education, Recreation and Dance,* Nov.-Dec., 1991).

Introduction

For quite some time Americans in virtually all walks of life have been telling one another that "Multi-culturalism is the wave of the future" and "The twenty-first century will be the Age of Asia." Now, suddenly, the future is upon us. This book offers a first-of-its-kind assessment of how the unfolding of these interrelated predictions is affecting the world of dance.

No dance person today can afford to ignore what is happening in the countries of Asia and the Pacific Rim. Most notably, state-sponsored academies, public schools, and private studios there are training world-class dancers at a great rate. Professional companies throughout the area are touring internationally, and thereby establishing reputations. Dance concerts in all genres regularly attract full-house audiences, eager to be exposed to what is new. Conferences are promoting the cause of scholarship. As surely as our private lives in the West have adjusted to the importation of products, and populations, and processes from Asia and the Pacific, our professional lives as dancers are being impacted by developments in that part of the world.

Much of what is happening in the East is being fueled by Western dancers/chorcographers/teachers, usually hired short-term to perform, create new works, set existing repertory, serve on faculties, and provide classes or workshops. Simultaneously, their Asian counterparts are coming to the United States and to Europe in ever-increasing numbers, mainly to study technique, gain performing experience, or achieve the advanced degrees that are not yet available in their national universities but are required for professional advancement in those and other institutions. Most of these visitors take what they have learned back home (although some do stay on), thereby enhancing the cross-cultural pollination. Further, in the Pacific Rim countries there is a growing network of arts organizations and freelance producers that is facilitating exchange not only with the West, but also among themselves.

Asian-Pacific exposure to Western dance certainly pre-dates this recent surge in activity: ballet has been widely known there throughout the twentieth century; the pioneer Denishawn modern dance company toured the region in the 1920s, and the companies of José Limón, Merce Cunningham, and Martha Graham were there as early as the 1950s (Miss Graham recruited the first in an illustrious line of Japanese dancers to her company at that time). Our personal involvement in this bit of history

1

dates to the summer of 1963, when Ruth Solomon was hired to teach at the International Artists Center in Tokyo along with Rod Alexander in jazz and Rudolf Nureyev in ballet (who also performed that summer in Tokyo with Margot Fonteyn, as part of their world tour). What had been sporadic contact began dramatically to coalesce during the 1980s, however, with the creation of new dance academies and programs, or the expansion of existing ones to include Western dance, in China, Hong Kong, Indonesia, Japan, the Philippines, Korea, and Taiwan.

Our method for describing how this cross-cultural exchange came about and exploring its implications on both sides of the Pacific has been to invite many of the people most involved in it to tell their stories. Much to our delight, virtually everyone we asked to the party accepted. Almost immediately, however, it became apparent that this task we were setting ourselves and our contributors was anything but simple. Very few of these people have written extensively for publication, and for many English is, at best, a second language. All are extremely busy in the pursuit of their dance careers, and communications were further complicated by distance and different cultural imperatives, where correspondence is concerned.

The solution to these problems was to arrange face-to-face meetings whenever possible. This was facilitated by travel grants to present papers at conferences, and appointments to teach at various venues, throughout the Pacific Rim. Hence, more than half of the following chapters are the result of interviews tape recorded in hotel rooms, or studios, or over tea, and later transcribed and edited. We have found that the business of cross-cultural exchange is often conducted in cumbersome ways. Nonetheless, the enthusiasm and eloquence demonstrated by the contributors to this book have made it seem, in this case at least, well worthwhile.

Some of these contributors are teacher/performers, others are dance administrators, and some do both. In soliciting material for the book we formulated two lists of topics, one for Eastern administrators and one for Western teachers, that were intended to suggest approaches to the subject of cross-cultural exchange that seemed to us particularly germane. These same topics were often raised in the interviews, thereby establishing something of a thematic structure for the book as a whole. Of the administrators we asked, for example, about the goals of their programs in general, and specifically how they utilize cross-cultural teaching; with whom they coordinate in furthering the cause of cross-cultural exchange; and what problems they, their teachers, and their students have experienced. The questions for the teachers encouraged them to consider in various ways why they had been asked to teach in the Pacific Rim countries, whether these assignments made unusual demands on them, and what they felt had been accomplished. We asked both groups for their thoughts about the future of the enterprise.

The reader should not, however, expect rigid adherence to any predetermined outline. In fact, each contributor has very unique things to offer; everyone essentially gave us more than we asked for, and we went willingly with the flow. The teachers seemed especially liberated by the opportunity to talk/write about how they approach their work.

Each also had a wealth of anecdotal knowledge to draw upon in describing the experience of living temporarily in a different culture. One rich source of information we had not originally anticipated was the observations of the Easterners who had lived and studied in the United States. The administrators, for the most part, took it upon themselves to place their work in the context of local history, traditions, and customs.

The importance to East-West relations in dance of one organization in the United States, the American Dance Festival, can hardly be overstated. ADF has long been recognized as an outstanding summer program, but since the early '80s its operations have expanded to include year-round preeminence as a power broker on the international dance exchange. Hence, we begin with complementary chapters by two of ADF's principal officers, Stephanie Reinhart and Martha Myers, which transcend national boundaries and provide something of an overview. Thereafter the chapters are arranged by nationality. This allows for an accumulation of information about each country; it also lets readers with an interest in specific countries reference them quickly. For the total picture, of course, it is necessary to read all the way through, as each chapter adds its own pieces to the puzzle.

This book is intended to serve two functions: it deals in quasi-anthropological fashion with the issues involved in transplanting an art form (Western dance) from one culture to another, and it provides practical guidance for those who might want to participate in this endeavor. As a guide to the organizational structure of East-West dance it gathers together a body of information that is presently available only from widely scattered sources, and often in languages other than English. In its more general function, as an exploration of the problems and rewards inherent in multi-culturalism, it should be of interest to people in all fields, who will find in the burgeoning attempts of dance to organize itself on an international scale suggestions that are widely applicable.

East and West definitely have experienced both problems and rewards as a result of this exchange. Dancers in the countries of Asia and the Pacific have received a sudden jolt into prominence that promises new opportunities both for themselves and for their communities. Like most cultural disjunctions, however, this one raises the divisive needs to preserve what is traditional on the one hand and to assimilate what is new on the other. This dilemma is much in evidence throughout the region, and there are signs of a backlash effect. In their chapters many of our Eastern contributors express a new-found appreciation for their own cultural roots, which has been achieved through exposure to Western influences. Once those influences have served their purpose, however—providing tools and perspectives with which to confront the realities of contemporary life—there is a nagging sense that they must be resisted for the sake of getting back to what matters in the long haul.

The Westerners have discovered a whole new market for their wares. It pays them well, causes them to feel needed, energizes them with the spirit of adventure, and affords them the opportunity to work with students who "can do anything" and are not yet jaded enough to take for granted what they have to offer. On the other hand, for most of them teaching abroad means essentially taking time out from the activities on which their career development has been based. It also means enduring some degree of isolation in places where the languages and customs are very different indeed. Despite the unfailing considerateness and generosity of their hosts, very few of the Westerners have cracked the inner circle of the countries in which they have taught. There would seem to be, in fact, a tacit understanding on both sides that the relationships formed in the early stages of this exchange are transitory in nature.

If multi-culturalism in dance has so far been something of a mixed blessing, it is nonetheless here to stay. As the world shrinks around us, it is increasingly necessary to visualize dance in a global perspective. This book takes a first, admittedly limited step in that direction; we were regrettably unable to involve all of the people who might have contributed to it. We trust that as the dialogue continues they will find other opportunities to make their voices heard.

Ruth Solomon
John Solomon

Part I:

An Overview

Chapter One:
The American Dance Festival's International Projects: Invention and Implementation, I

Stephanie Reinhart

Stephanie Reinhart has worked as an arts administrator since 1969, when she joined the staff of the National Endowment for the Arts. Her association with the American Dance Festival dates to 1977, and she became its Associate Director in 1982 and Co-Director in 1993. She has traveled world-wide lecturing on American modern dance and arts administration (most recently in Prague, St. Petersburg, and Moscow), and generally promoting the cause of international exchange in dance. She was instrumental in opening communications with dance officials in Japan, Korea and Indonesia, and introducing French modern dance to American audiences. Ms. Reinhart serves as panelist, consultant, and board member to many arts organizations, and is a recent Fulbright Fellow.

The international network which the American Dance Festival (ADF) has woven began in 1979, when Charles Reinhart, Director of ADF, Lisa Booth, ADF's then-Administrative Director, and myself, at that time Director of Planning and Development, received a grant from the Japan-US Friendship Commission to explore the possibility of an ADF residency in Japan, and to inform ourselves of the state of Japanese modern dance. ADF was not without international connections before '79; Charles Reinhart had traveled extensively in Asia in the 1960s as manager of The Paul Taylor Dance Company, for the State Department organizing its Cultural Presentations Program, and representing Isadora Bennett, the legendary press agent and founder of the Asia Society Performing Arts Program. He therefore knew first hand the significance of dance in Asian cultures. It was that trip in '79, however, that really launched our international interests.

We didn't have any idea what we would find when we wrote that first grant to the Friendship Commission. In retrospect, I think a kind of naive optimism informed our early explorations, along with a basic pragmatism. Like the surfers in the 1960s film *The Endless Summer*, we were following an intuitive bent—looking for the big wave:

7

new talent in modern dance. It has taken us into "new territory," and since 1979 we have visited over 30 countries. Both administratively and artistically our international projects have expanded our vision of reality, and, by extension, that of the artists and audiences we serve. It is important to note, though, that these projects have been assimilated organically into a general expansion of creative activity in dance. They have evolved within the context of ADF's original mission since its founding in 1934—to support choreographers, to find wider audiences for their work, and to provide training for dancers.

Our 1979 Japan trip was aided immensely by the Japanese dance critic and historian Miyabi Ichikawa, who set up a rigorous schedule for us to see as wide a range of Japanese modern dance as possible. We saw (in the words of Martha Graham) good and bad dance! There were modern dances built on traditional forms, and those apparently influenced by US and German modern dance. The best came last—a memorable mountaintop performance in Kyoto by the remarkable Dairakudakan. Sitting outdoors in 30° weather, with no shoes, our feet in plastic bags and blankets wrapped around us against the chill, we discovered *Butoh*, which we introduced to US audiences in 1982.

We presented four companies from Japan in 1982: Bonjin Atsugi, Miyako Kato and Dancers, the Waka Dance Company (led by the much honored Shigeka Hanayagi) and Akaji Maro's Dairakudakan, presenting the shocking and grotesque underbelly of Japanese society. The four companies admirably reflected the wide range of creativity occurring in Japanese modern dance at that time.

Their performances at ADF were accompanied by a public panel entitled "Dances and Their People." In this forum choreographers, critics and historians explored the development of Japanese modern dance and, using dance as a window on culture, its wider implications for Japanese society. The panel was part of a humanities project begun in 1979 with the assistance of philosophy professor Dr. Gerald Myers. A primary goal of subsequent humanities projects over the last decade has been to explore how people and their cultures can be seen through dance, and how the dances created are a reflection of the attitudes, mores, myths, beliefs, and values (religious, philosophical, sexual) that comprise the ecology of a culture. These projects have been a vehicle for giving voice to the disparate cultural identities and political realities encountered in our international work.

"Four From Japan" paved the way for our historic rerooting of ADF in 1984 and 1986 for month-long residencies in Japan. Both of these mini-ADFs included classes by a distinguished faculty (1984: Betty Jones, Martha Myers, Bella Lewitzky, Ruby Shang, and Ralf Haze; 1986: Martha Myers, Betty Jones, Ruby Shang, Yuriko Kimura, Clarence Teeters and Pooh Kaye), and performances by Martha Clarke's Crowsnest and Laura Dean Dancers and Musicians in 1984, and Pooh Kaye/ Eccentric Motions and Bill T. Jones/Arnie Zane & Company in 1986. Ruby Shang created a spectacular site-specific work, *The Tokyo Event*, in a Japanese park, using Japanese dancers from her classes.

The classes were enormously successful, attracting students from across Japan. They offered to Japanese dancers a revolutionary concept—studying simultaneously with a range of master teachers. In Japan one ordinarily studies with one teacher for life. In fact, the head of the Japanese dance educator's organization bowed deeply to me at a reception and congratulated me on the success of our residency—apologizing for her original skepticism. Our ADF-Japan project certainly broke the rules, but the young Japanese dancers loved it, and, since then, ADF-Durham continues to receive significant groups of Japanese dancers each summer.

The big step forward in our international programming occurred in 1983, when we began thinking about ADF's upcoming 1984 50th anniversary. We convinced USIA's then-Director of Arts America, Juliet Antunes, to send us around the world to look for companies to be part of what was to be ADF's First International Modern Dance Festival. In exchange, as "ACULPECS" (American Cultural Specialists Abroad), we gave lectures on modern dance and arts administration. "Around the world" meant we had to choose which direction to start: we went East, on a two-month voyage visiting Japan, The Philippines (during the Makati riots against

Figure 1   Students at ADF-Tokyo in 1986 performing
Ruby Shang's site-specific piece *The Tokyo Event*. Photo: Jay Anderson

Marcos), Indonesia, India, Israel, France and England. Packing and unpacking 50 times was painful, but the journey was remarkable.

Our 50th anniversary celebration featured companies selected from the many we saw. They ranged from Uday Shankar's 1930s groundbreaking modern dance depiction of man versus the machine, to Astad Deboo's (Bombay, India) bizarre solo *Asylum*, to Dance Indonesia's (Jakarta Institute of the Arts) presentation of a Muslim, martial arts, ritualistic Sumatranese modern dance, *HHHHHUUUUU...* Accompanying the '84 performing season was a series of humanities panels directed by Dr. Myers, who also edited *The Aesthetic and Cultural Significance of Modern Dance,* a collection of commissioned essays by dance experts from India, Indonesia, The Philippines and Great Britain.

Nineteen eighty-four marked the establishment of our trailblazing International Choreographers Workshop (ICW), heralded by *Newsweek* as "a decided success." This was perhaps one of the most significant undertakings of ADF in the 1980s, and it has proven one of the most personally moving aspects of my work as an arts administrator. Each year as the choreographers arrive at ADF from their disparate countries and gather in a circle on our summer office porch surrounded by the blossoming magnolia trees I am full of emotion. It is sharing the common language of dance that has brought together these individuals, yet each retains an enormous respect for his or her cultural distinctions. I am always reminded of the words of the great Robin Howard, founder of the modern dance movement in Great Britain, when he spoke of dance as a tool for world peace, and of the spirit which informs Anna Halprin's communal *Circle the Earth* dances.

With initial funding from USIA, which led to a subsequent partnership with the Rockefeller Foundation and significant support from the Asian Cultural Council and the Trust for Mutual Understanding, we conceived the idea of celebrating what we sensed was a global phenomenon. We saw that modern dance was developing in countries around the world, and we hoped to give international choreographers the opportunity to share their dance and to deepen their knowledge and experience of American modern dance. What began as the ICW program has evolved organically to the development of a four-tiered international format which now includes:

- International Choreographers Workshop (ICW)
- International Choreographers Commissioning Program (ICCP)
- Institutional Linkages Program (ILP)
- Mini-ADF's

INTERNATIONAL CHOREOGRAPHERS WORKSHOP

That first year, relying on a network of US Embassy cultural affairs officers and our own contacts in the field, we brought 13 choreographers from China, Hong Kong, Malaysia, Mexico, Senegal, France, Korea, India and Indonesia to ADF for three weeks during our summer season. The program was extended to the full six weeks of ADF in 1986, and continues to offer the participants the opportunity to take classes, see performances, and experience an intensive period of experimentation and in-depth exchange with artists from around the world. The choreographers can present their work in an informal showing and give a master class. They also have discussions and seminars with composers, scholars, choreographers, educators, and musicians in residence at ADF. The project is a special kind of sabbatical for the participants, who represent a range of experience and power. Some are leaders of established modern dance institutions in their country, while others work in relative isolation. One choreographer from Rwanda asked at an initial meeting, "How did you ever find me?" To date 195 choreographers/dancers from 68 countries have participated in the workshop.

INTERNATIONAL CHOREOGRAPHERS COMMISSIONING PROGRAM

> It is a greenhouse. It is like being in a closed place. You are protected. You are given everything—food, room, space, dancers. You don't have to worry about the things you have to in your normal life. You just dance, just do what you love to do. It is an unreal, ideal situation.[1]

> It is exciting and a privilege, an honor to have 20 dancers to work with and to have everything provided. I don't have to worry if a dancer will get home that night or have enough to eat or get back for the next rehearsal. In Ecuador it is very difficult to get a work past a certain level ... because of the uncertainties of getting everyone to regular rehearsals.[2]

For this program, established in 1987, each year we invite three or four previous ICW participants to come back for a six-week residency. During the residency they experiment in a laboratory environment with a group of dancers auditioned specifically for this purpose. They develop new dances, share their differing aesthetics with other choreographers, and are offered the opportunity for the work to be showcased before an international audience. The brilliant fusion of modern dance forms and traditional Indonesian dance exhibited in *Circle of Bliss,* created as part of the program in 1991 by Sukarji Sriman, was the perfect blending of two worlds, and an absolute representation of the program's underlying philosophy.

INSTITUTIONAL LINKAGES PROGRAM

It was Dr. Christopher (Kit) Paddack, Acting Chief of the Creative Arts Division at USIA, who advised and guided us in the early stages of building the ICW and its

---

1. Anat Daniely, Israel, 1992 ICCP, unpublished interview with Alta Lu Townes, Summer, 1992.
2. Susana Reyes, Ecuador, 1992 ICCP, unpublished interview with Alta Lu Townes, Summer, 1992.

Figure 2   Sukarji Sriman's *Circle of Bliss,* commissioned by ADF in 1991.
Photo: Jay Anderson

extension to the third aspect of our international programming, the "Linkages." Consisting of a series of exchange projects between ADF and dance institutions world-wide, and developed in collaboration with previous ICW's, the Linkages range from sending choreographers/teachers abroad for 2-4 weeks, to setting works on US or international companies, to mini-ADF's offering classes and performances (Japan: 1984, 1986; Korea: 1990, 1991, 1992; India: 1990; Moscow: 1992). They have often been supported by USIA, in partnership with the Rockefeller Foundation.

The first linkage, a pilot program, was with China. It began in Guangzhou in 1987, in conjunction with the Guangdong Dance Academy. The project started rather simply with a provocative question from Yang Mei-qi (ICW '86), Director of the Academy. Mei-qi came into Charles Reinhart's office one summer afternoon and asked why in the Limón technique the dancers drop to the floor (the principle of Fall and Recovery). Charles answered, "Why not?" Mei-qi took that in, then quietly asked if she could come back to see Charles in a few days. She returned with a request and a plan to help her start a modern dance program, China's first, in her Academy. Charles committed himself to helping her; then we had to find the funds.

Dancers from all over China were auditioned and brought to Guangzhou for a three-year course. From the beginning the goal was for this group to become a company. We agreed to send choreographers/teachers to help forge a modern dance based on Chinese traditions and culture. By sending teachers gifted in composition/improvisation and a variety of techniques we encouraged the Chinese dancers to make their own dances. Five US teachers went over for three-month residencies during the first three years: Sarah Stackhouse, Ruby Shang, Doug Nielsen, Lucas Hoving, and Lynda Davis. Although Tiananmen Square in June, 1989 and the continuing government crackdown prevented us from sending a teacher in the fall of '89, our commitment to the project continued, and since 1990 four more ADF teachers have been sent for residencies ranging from 1-2 months: David Hochoy, Claudia Gitelman, Stuart Hodes, and Chiang Ching. It was Chiang Ching who actually recommended we bring her former classmate, Mei-qi, to ADF as an ICW because, as Ching said, she could make things happen!

In the six years of the linkage we resisted requests to send over US dances that the group could simply "put on." Our project was never about sending *Swan Lake* abroad, and that has been its strength. Charles Reinhart believed that in order for modern dance to flower in China it must be based on Chinese culture. The training we offered was often difficult for the dancers, who were being asked to think and move by their own instincts and intuition, and in essence to challenge the authoritarian Chinese educational system. Ultimately, they produced some wonderfully original works—dances about the repression of women, the power of the people, personal freedom, etc. They made dances with Chinese themes and with enough ambiguity to get past the censors. It is only now, in 1993, following the teaching residency of Stuart Hodes, that we have finally agreed to send a teacher to set a classic American modern dance work on the company so they can "know that these dances they are making are good. . . . They have no international standard to measure them against."[3]

*   *   *   *   *

All along the way we have been asked "What is modern dance?" We have held to the tenet that modern dance is a way of thinking; a system of belief which allows for the creation of new work based on individual expression. It is not a vehicle for American cultural imperialism. As Stuart Hodes has said: "Modern dance takes the shape of the people who create it. It's like pasta. Pasta has no flavor without the sauce. There are many different sauces."[4] Longa Fo Eye Oto, a choreographer who is Associate Director of the National Institute for the Arts in Kinshasa, said that "Dance is like water. When you put it in a cup it takes the shape of the cup. It's the same in the cup of my country. If I ask where this water is from you cannot tell that it is from the US."[5]

It is in the training of modern dancers that individual creativity is nourished, relying on composition and improvisation. This has proved threatening to the establishment in some countries—both artistically and politically—as modern dance artists continue to break down barriers and create new visions. In some parts of the world, particularly those with strongly entrenched traditional arts, there is a good deal of tension between the traditional and the new:

> What American modern dance has achieved is what all others need. I know the traditional dances at home, which are becoming like museum pieces. In fact, we have not been traditional enough—people created dances in the past, and we need to create anew. Modern dance epitomizes a dance of the world. It is movement of the body that knows no boundaries. What I take home is not American modern dance, it is movement compatible with mine.[6]

We have always stressed that it is not a question of either/or; one must preserve the traditional, but also allow for and nurture the new. In its broadest political sense, modern dance is democratic as it allows for individual freedom and creativity. Yet, of course, it is autocratic as well. What we are witnessing around the world is choreographers creating modern dance works based on the rich dance traditions of their particular cultures.

We wanted to show this fusion of old and new to our audiences. Thus, we selected Deddy Luthan and Tom Ibnur's *Awan Bailau* (1982) as one of the works to be performed by Dance Indonesia at ADF in 1984 and again in 1986. Evolved from the dance traditions of Minang-kabau (West Sumatra), the dance is a blend of *Penca-silat* (traditional martial arts) and *Bakaba* (traditional poetry recitation). It

---

3. Stuart Hodes, unpublished interview with Alta Lu Townes, Summer, 1992.
4. *Ibid.*
5. Longa Fo Eye Oto, *The New York Times*, July 15, 1990, Sec. II, p. 31.
6. Francis Nii-Yartey (Artistic Director, The National Dance Company of Ghana), *The New York Times*, July 15, 1990, Sec. II, p. 8.

is also, however, a study of young Minangs facing the hard realities of life in modern Jakarta.

Some of the same political and economic considerations are informing the globalization of modern dance as those affecting the evolution of bi-national corporations. There is the conflict between nationalism and isolationism on the one hand, and the economic need and artistic impulse to forge international partnerships on the other. ADF has responded to this elemental issue:

> The ADF is badly needed, and not only by Americans. It has truly international importance as a kind of coordinating center for the development of modern choreography in today's world.[7]

Jingoistic sentiments emerged in some quarters in the late 1980s, but we were concerned only with where the talent was; if our border crossings resulted in substantially changing the profile of ADF's population, this seemed more of an enriching element than a problem. How do we evaluate the impact of these international exchanges? If we look only at the simplest of our objectives—to promote and stimulate cross-cultural exchange, to nurture creativity, and to act as a catalyst in relieving choreographers of their isolation—then, by and large, we have clearly succeeded. The long term ramifications of the program are perhaps best left to the future to evaluate. We can say with some certainty, however, that to many we have given a sense of hope, encouraged new ways of thinking, and "illuminated the burst of experimental activity in dance abroad."[8]

7. Marina Dolganova-Balenko (dance critic for Moscow's *Sovetskaya Kultura*), *The New York Times,* July 29, 1990, Sec. II, p. 23.
8. Anna Kisselgoff, *The New York Times,* July 15, 1990, Sec. II, p. 8.

Chapter Two:
The American Dance Festival's International Projects: Invention and Implementation, II

Martha Myers

Martha Myers is Dean of the American Dance Festival and Professor of Dance at Connecticut College. As teacher, dancer, choreographer, television performer, author and dance/movement consultant she is one of this country's best known and most widely acclaimed personalities. At ADF she directs and teaches in the Center for Professional Dance Training and Education, which presents workshops on the body therapies, dance medicine, choreography, and the Professional Dancer's Update. She has taught and lectured across this country and in Europe, Japan, China, Hong Kong, Australia, and South America. Ms. Myers' articles on dance training have appeared in numerous publications—including a classic series on the body therapies in **Dance Magazine**—*and as chapters in several books on dance science. Her series of nine television programs,* **A Time to Dance,** *has been shown on PBS in this country and abroad.*

In a little over a decade the Directors of the American Dance Festival, Charles and Stephanie Reinhart, have built, piece by piece, an amazing global exchange, the first of its kind in dance, that now takes place throughout the year on several continents. As Stephanie Reinhart describes in the preceding chapter, there are four individual but integrated components to this exchange: the International Choreographers Workshop and the International Choreographers Commissioning Project (ICCP) bring recognized dance choreographers/directors from around the world into the classes and onto the stages of this country; the Institutional Linkages Program and the Mini-ADF's send our dance artists abroad. In my dual capacities as ADF Dean and faculty member I have had the privilege of contributing to these programs in different ways and degrees. What follows are reflections on some of the issues raised by my experiences.

FACULTY AND CURRICULUM

Many factors are entwined in selecting faculty for ADF international projects. We begin from the pool of outstanding artist/teachers who have been at ADF and whose work, therefore, we know through personal observation and student feedback. We seek a mixture of classical approaches to modern dance, together with new and divergent styles and developments in the field. Foreign hosts also make suggestions concerning particular teachers, styles, or companies they think would be attractive to their students and contribute meaningfully to their needs. A group in one country may have never been exposed to modern dance or to only one style (such as Graham technique, which became known early and well in the Pacific Rim). Another group may want a teacher from a "third generation" company such as Trisha Brown or Pilobolus. We have also sent teachers who incorporate body work (e.g., Alexander, Feldenkrais, Deep Muscle Therapy, or Laban Movement Analysis) into their teaching. Especially in Japan and Korea, our host presenters have proven to be well-informed about American modern dance artist/teachers.

The curriculum for Mini-ADF's is modeled on that of the ADF six week school schedule, but instead of 56 daily classes there are 15 to 18, depending on the number of faculty involved. It includes modern, jazz, and African-American techniques, as well as composition, improvisation, and repertory. These are "core" courses. Enrichment studies may include one or more of the following classes which are offered in the Durham six week schedule: Music and Dancers, Injury Prevention, Deep Muscle Therapy, Performance Coaching, Partnering, and Dance Conditioning. Additionally, as at ADF-Durham, informal "showings" of class work may be held at the end of a residency if requested by hosts or students and deemed appropriate by faculty. Faculty may also choose to offer a brief concert of their own work.

Institutional Linkages Program residencies most often involve only one or two faculty, for stays of two weeks to a month, with the exception of the first China residencies, which were three month visits. We always try to match faculty expertise with host country needs or requests. Also, as our faculty are representing ADF and the United States—whether by intention or not they are our ambassadors—their agenda in accepting a residency must go beyond "doing a good job" or "having a nice trip." We take this factor into account in the selection process. We are fortunate to have engaged a group of warm, gifted artists to work with in these projects, and the feedback from host countries has been uniformly enthusiastic, with requests for return visits of many participating teachers. Residencies are evaluated in writing by both participating faculty and host country.

WORKING AND LIVING CONDITIONS

Despite detailed planning in advance, each residency or tour presents new administrative as well as artistic challenges. At ADF-Durham placement classes are held to determine skill levels for technique classes, and class size is calculated in relation to available space and appropriate time of day. We have developed registration protocols to assure a smooth beginning to classes which we try to duplicate on our tours, though flexibility is essential as quick adjustments are often called for. On our first trip to Korea, for instance, 500 students showed up instead of the 300 expected. We were aware that many of them had traveled from all parts of the country and greatly anticipated this workshop, so we quickly rearranged and added classes. On that occasion some studios more resembled schools of salmon than dancers in brightly colored leotards, but we left few applicants in tears. Despite these difficulties, *The Korea Times* reported that: "The opening of the ADF at the Sejong Cultural Center in Seoul on July 30-Aug. 11 is said to be the most significant event in the history of Korean dance society."[1]

There is no universal norm for determining class size. What seems impossibly large to one teacher, or in one culture, seems normal to another. At ADF we have had teachers who encourage large technique classes, happily accepting 40 in a class (given an appropriately sized studio), while others want no more than 25. The ballet guru Maggie Black is renowned for her New York classes that have been filled with as many as a hundred or so professionals from the city's major companies. Cultures, too, vary in their sense of what feels "crowded." A well known choreographer recently writing to me on his return from Tokyo remarked on his relief to be home in New York City, away from the "crowded conditions" he had experienced there. On my frequent trips to New York from a small town in Connecticut I have the same response on a different scale; the crowds and stimuli of the "Big Apple" seem ferocious. At ADF we are sensitive to these many considerations in our goal of providing an optimal learning/teaching environment both on our travels and at home.

As an essentially non-profit art form dance "lives lean," its budget as trim as its practitioners' bodies. In most of the countries we visit, as in New York, modern dancers have no Lincoln Center studios to welcome us, and no Ritz-Carlton. In Korea we *did* work in the state-of-the-art Sejong Cultural Center, but more often working and living conditions that in the country visited are above average can still be lower than the US standard (even when the "standard" is that of New York's Soho, where so many dance artists live and perform). I have returned from overseas (Russia in particular) feeling spoiled, privileged, and deeply saddened by the deprivation experienced by many of my dance colleagues in other parts of the world. Living and working on tour calls for personal flexibility and ingenuity. I have been impressed watching members of our group—highly respected professionals at home—quietly and effectively get to work teaching a technique or composition class in a cramped theater drawing room with varnished parquet floors (an historical theater, beautifully romantic, but sticky floors nonetheless). Living accommodations can require not only ingenuity, but a degree of stoicism. Nonetheless, I personally feel I have "lived

---

1. *The Korea Times*, July 12, 1990.

well" wherever I have been, and I have certainly always been treated with respect and appreciation by our hosts.

Translation is a crucial component of teaching abroad. As dance is often thought of as "non-verbal," the particular difficulties involved may not be apparent until one is faced with trying to communicate without a common language. Classes involving subtle concepts and specialized vocabulary, such as composition/ improvisation or anatomy and muscle therapy, present problems comparable to other verbal disciplines; dance, including technique classes, is every bit as dense with concepts as literature, drama, or music. There is the additional handicap in teaching dance science of an esoteric vocabulary, or in Laban Analysis of an idiosyncratic use of language.

In Japan I first learned what has been corroborated on subsequent trips to other parts of the world: that at least one student in class always speaks English as well as or better than the translator, and many understand English even if they lack confidence in their speaking skills. However, in my experience, relying on surrogate translators can be tricky. "Prompting" from students can be seen by some translators as a threat to their status and authority. In Japan and Korea students only volunteered when specifically called upon, and then hesitantly. In Russia, on the other hand, the "volunteer" translators got a bit out of hand, vying with the professional assigned to this position.

We have for the most part been fortunate in the skills of our translators. When there is a problem it is usually due to lack of specific acquaintance with dance, or the particular area of dance being taught. I have been surprised when a direction in a somatics class, such as "imagine your bones sinking into the floor," produced a perplexed look on some students' faces, and giggles from those who knew English. I was told later the translation was "imagine your bones disintegrating or decaying on the floor."

Perhaps the most disconcerting aspect of translation is that you never really know what is being said—only that words have a strange and strong power. It takes a few classes to create a harmonious rhythm between translator and teacher; no matter how excellent the translation, the process is still time-consuming. It alters the pace of a class. What one dreams of in a translator is a specialist in one's subject and a super linguist, such as the young man who worked with me in somatics classes in Korea having recently returned with his Ph.D. in somatic education from Ohio State University. Failing that, there is of course "dance language" (posture/gesture and signs), which communicates mountains without words.

Shorthand explanations, simple images rather than complex metaphors, have proven effective for me, even though one knows there is a depth of meaning in the material left unsaid. Dance is akin to poetry with respect to its resistance to pedantic translation. One reads meaning in the spaces between words. Thus Baudelaire in French is a substantially different experience from an English version. As the Chinese-American novelist Fae-myenne Ng has noted: "I have a whole different vocabulary of feeling in English than in Chinese, and not everything can be translated."[2]

DANCE SCIENCE AND SOMATICS

The dancers in countries we have visited have had (at the time of our residency) little or no experience with dance science—i.e., anatomical/kinesiological principles of movement, prevention of injury, and the basics of injury diagnosis and care. Nor were they familiar with somatics as an aid in analyzing movement, altering neuromuscular patterning, and moderating and extending the range of movement options. Often, they have learned what they know by rote—by copying and memorizing. Much dance in the United States is also presented in this way, and copying/memorizing is a time-honored method of learning all physical skills. However, what we now know about the learning process and individual learning styles makes this approach seem rather rudimentary. New methods can make dance study far more effective and less frustrating, and extend the span of performance. In all of the places I have toured I have found amazing receptivity to these new ideas. Students respond bravely to explorations of movement that must seem "foreign" to them, not only different and difficult, but even "bizarre."

In Japan in 1984 and Korea in 1990, when I was teaching injury prevention and somatics, I was told by my students that there were no sports/dance medical specialists available to them. They had no access to physical therapy or to doctors who could treat their problems with skill and understanding. In Tokyo they seemed to think that the major ballet companies might have access to such expertise, but as is often the case in the United States, the non-traditional/non-established performers were less fortunate. In both countries and in China, where I visited but did not teach, dancers tended to turn to traditional Eastern medicines, which were often effective according to their reports.

I have enjoyed discussion with a few Japanese and Chinese medical practitioners, and especially with a physician to the Beijing Opera Ballet. This physician, Dr. Wen Rang-wan, visited ADF for several days in the mid-eighties, attending one of our Dance Science/Body Therapy workshops. She also worked with me privately on a back problem, using massage and "moxibustion" technique.* These experiences have left me with the impression that neither Eastern nor Western medicine is likely to have the complete answer to maintaining health and "curing" illness; the important thing is to have access to the full range of choices. We are fortunate in the West to

2. Fae-myenne Ng, *The Village Voice*, February 9, 1993, Supplement, p. 5.

* "Moxibustion" is a technique using compressed, flammable "wands" containing herbs. These, when ignited at one end, produce heat and smoke, rather like incense. The wand is then held just above the skin of the patient at the point of inflammation/pain, or at the appropriate accupressure point in the body.

have the resources of contemporary sports/dance medicine, but there is also increasing interest in adjunctive therapy and traditional folk remedies, with research now at the national level (NIH) to validate the effectiveness of these modalities. This reflects cross-cultural exchange of a potentially very important nature indeed.

COMPOSITION AND AESTHETICS

I always preface my composition classes by emphasizing that aesthetic attitudes and tastes are highly complex and infinitely disputable. They are conditioned by history, culture, personal experience, and even by our individual chemistry (no two olfactory or tasting mechanisms, visual, aural, or cognitive perceptions, are the same). This brings up a key point with regard to the philosophy and purpose of the exchanges in which ADF has been involved. I share the Reinharts' conviction—and mission— regarding the expectation of taking American modern dance abroad. We in no way wish to impose Western aesthetics, styles of dance, etc., on another culture. Rather, we hope to extend mutual creative and aesthetic options by sharing modern dance artistic credos with our compatriots in other cultures, and in turn learning theirs. How can their ethnic dance forms and ours be extended or transformed, our perceptions heightened, our imaginations made richer, by this exchange?

I try, in going abroad, to maintain as clear and clean a perceptional slate as possible—to learn about the culture before I go, and deepen this understanding experientially during the visit. I particularly explore what I can of its arts and medicine, and its approach to dance training and choreography. In turn, I hope to share with students and colleagues my own experiences and knowledge of dance performance, composition, science and somatics. The imparting of information, from them to me, from me to them, I see as a resource for mutual exploration and growth, not an exchange of knowledge "chips" which are to be hoarded and systematized.

On the other hand, our work is not "value free." Our group (ADF) is brought to a country to share what we know, what we do. This constitutes, loosely, a body of principles about technique and aesthetics. The very principles are, however, in flux, accounting for the development of wildly different styles and approaches to modern dance. If telling students that they can make dances in new ways, as *they* want, and urging them to discover meaningful resources in their own lives, cultures, history and dreams is "imposing," I guess we're guilty. Even in suggesting to students that there is more to "dig out," maybe a richer lore some levels down in their material, I give them room to decide to leave it where it is, or to dig in different directions than I might have suggested. Sometimes, I tell them, you may have to stop at the brink— to accept where you *are* before daring to tread on more dangerous ground. Students need to feel comfortable in making this choice.

The hunger for new ideas and creative challenges is expressed in a UPI report on our Moscow Mini-ADF in 1992: "Even though Russia has been prying open its doors to the West for some time, Russian modern dance enthusiasts flocking to the festival found their first opportunity to take American contemporary dance classes. Students traveled thousands of miles, from as far away as the Russian Pacific Coast, paying more than a month's salary for a chance at seeing and learning modern dance styles from the West. Hundreds of dancers, choreographers and students came to the festival seeking lessons, knowing that after auditions only 80 would make the cut. Still, the risk was worth it in a country with no modern dance instructors."

JAPAN, KOREA, CHINA, AND AFTERWARD

Our first Mini-ADF (1984) was to Japan for one month. We worked first in the southern islands, then in Osaka and Tokyo. I still have strong images of the lush, tidy green rice paddies covering the countryside, extending to the very edge of the cities. I also recall the elderly men and women walking on the roads, their spines bent double, like small half-moons. They had developed painful spinal deformations (kyphoses) from working in the fields.

On that "maiden voyage" the faculty included three quite different modern dancers—Betty Jones, Bella Lewitzky, and Ruby Shang—in addition to Ralf Haze (Jazz) and myself (Body Therapy and Injury Prevention). At ADF we don't identify ourselves with a particular modern dance "school" or company (such as "Graham," Limón," or "Cunningham"); seasoned modern dance artists tend to have integrated their training and performing experience anyway, making their own creative amalgam from many sources. Students can deduce from reading each teacher's biography the primary influences on his/her work. Since ADF is a modern dance festival, our general emphasis is always on this genre.

In both Japan and Korea students varied with respect to age, dance experience, and body knowledge. It was gratifying to work with teachers and more experienced professionals as well as aspiring students. From my functional anatomy class in Tokyo emerged a small "anatomy club," organized by a group of women who stayed together after our visit to continue their study and movement exploration. Their work eventually produced an anatomy manual, using Japanese and translated English references, plus their own class experiences. The group called themselves the "Martha Myers Club." One of the beguiling aspects of teaching in Asia is that our students have made us feel very needed—and honored.

Another gratifying aspect of our trips is the opportunity to attend performances of dance and theater. We have been fortunate to see a good deal of other cultural resources as well—museums, shrines, and historic places. Our interest in and acquaintance with the national culture of the countries we visit provides meaningful references for teaching. It is important to our students and hosts that we appreciate their art and absorb something of the milieu in which they live and work. This loudly makes the point that our interest is in ex*change*, not imposition or usurpation.

Figure 3   Dancers of the Guangdong Modern Dance Company in
Situation (1991), by Zhang Yi and Zhang Li. Photo: Jay Anderson

In 1990 Charles Reinhart and I traveled to Guangzhou, China, to participate in the ceremonies marking the first Modern Dance graduating class of the Guangdong Academy. The official debut of the Guangdong Modern Dance Company followed the graduation. It was a milestone event, and for us a very moving one. The Chinese government sent two puzzled and somewhat suspicious "cultural representatives" from Beijing to oversee the political correctness of this fledgling company. The threat of censorship that our artists have recently felt in this country, from Washington and the NEA, is a reality in China. The gentlemen from Beijing quizzed me politely but pointedly about the content of several pieces on the concert. It was disconcerting, even frightening, to think that I might, through misinterpretation or ineptness of a phrase, jeopardize this beautiful company and its dancers. In answering their questions I weighed my words very carefully! Afterward there was a wonderful banquet, a special tour of Guangzhou, and a disco party complete with flashing strobe lights, deafening rock music, and spectacular dancing, all washed down with plates full of poached eggs and cups of punch that silently appeared on our tables as we danced the night away.

When companies like Guangdong and others in our exchange projects return to ADF to perform *their* work, revealing their special creative explorations in the modern dance idiom, the full impact of these programs comes home to me. As Harvey Lichtenstein, Director of the Brooklyn Academy of Music, said in a recent *Dance*

Magazine article describing the international offerings on BAM's schedule: "For us, it's almost like looking at experimental Western work. It may take time to assimilate…, but art from outside our customary environment has an important social and political aspect—it allows us to communicate with other cultures."[3]

Modern dancers in the United States will have to listen ever more intently to their own inner voices, and perhaps also to John Cage's admonition to "pay careful attention to all things at all times," in order to find and maintain their creative authenticity. Although what we hope for in exchange is constant revitalization of our art form, it would be sad to find, as Joseph Mazo recently wrote of an international jazz festival, "that the most innovative work in this quintessential American dance form is coming from Helsinki and Nagoya!"[4] The aesthetic choice of working at the "cutting edge" is both challenging and exhilarating, and the pace quickens in a global community.

3. Harvey Lichtenstein, "BAM! You're Avant-Garde!" *Dance Magazine*, March 1993, pp. 60-64.
4. Joseph Mazo, "Jazz Dance: The State of the Art—Part II," *Dance Magazine*, February 1993, pp. 78-79.

Part II:

China

Chapter Three:
From 'Beasts' to 'Flowers': Modern Dance in China

Ou Jian-ping

> ***Ou Jian-ping** was one of the first recipients of the M.A. in Dance degree in China, and he has also studied dance technique and criticism in the United States and Germany with the aid of grants from the Asian Cultural Council and the German government. He is currently Associate Research Fellow and Founding Director of the Foreign Dance Study Section of the Dance Research Institute under the auspices of the China National Arts Academy, and guest teacher in the Modern Dance Major of the Beijing Dance Academy. Mr. Ou is a widely published author in both English and Chinese, and a frequent contributor to **Dance Magazine** and **The International Encyclopedia of Dance** in the US, and the UK's **World Ballet and Dance** and **International Dictionary of Ballet.** His international dance experience has given rise to a course, Modern Dance Creative Experience, which he has taught with great success throughout China.*

I. AN INTRODUCTORY LOOK AT BALLET AND MODERN DANCE IN CHINA

Ballet, which officially came into China via the so-called "Socialist Camp" headed by the Soviet Union "Big Brother" in the 1950s, was an instant success. Sino-Soviet friendship was just then at its peak, which naturally led to the enthusiastic, absolute, and essentially blind acceptance of this pure crystallization of Western civilization by both the Chinese State leadership and the professional dance community. By 1954 this influence had been institutionalized in the Beijing Dance School, the first official school for theatrical dance in China. Founded under the monopolistic direction, and even hand-to-hand and heart-to-heart guidance of the Soviet ballet experts, the Beijing Dance School quickly developed a Ballet Department with its own major program (alongside a major in Chinese Classical Dance, which drew its material from the Beijing Opera, Kunqu Opera, and other traditional Chinese operas).

Conversely, modern dance, another purely Western import, faced sharp rejection in this country that had just rid itself of the imperialism of various colonialist countries and was reveling in its hard-won independence. Modern dance became associated with the fear of American imperialism; since the founding of the People's Republic of China in 1949 it was nervously equated with "fierce floods and savage beasts." Particularly during the Cultural Revolution (1966-1976), and even for several years before and after that ten-year disaster when Leftist politics and ideology dominated the whole country, modern dance suffered from heavy attacks and even a complete prohibition by the Central Government before 1980.

From my point of view US modern and post-modern dance achieved peaks of prosperity during the 1940s and 1960s, which unfortunately coincided with a period during which China was first suffering through its War of Resistance Against Japan (1937-1945) and its Civil War (1945-1949), and then fighting a Cold War with the United States (1949-1972). Only when the Central Government wisely and bravely adopted a "Reform and Open" policy after 1980 did relations with the US thaw sufficiently to provide a foothold for modern dance.

II. GERMAN ROOTS: THE INCEPTION OF MODERN DANCE IN CHINA

History records that the Empress Ci Xi of the late Qing Dynasty (1875-1909) witnessed Isadora Duncan's *Greek Dance* in her royal palace as performed by Isadora's sole Chinese student, Yu Rong-ling, the daughter of a Chinese ambassador to France who studied with Isadora in Paris in 1902. Denishawn and Irma Duncan, with her Russian students, visited China in 1925 and 1928 respectively, and made warm impressions on this aged feudal country. At present the dance audience in China knows and likes American modern dance, and is willing to pay high prices on the black market for its tickets; the US style of modern dance has clearly influenced this country a great deal over the last ten years. Nonetheless, it was German modern dance that first sowed the seeds for acceptance of the art form in this Eastern country in the 1930s. This was due largely to the efforts of Mr. Wu Xiao-bang (1906-), whose career as dancer, choreographer and teacher started with Western ballet and flourished with German modern dance.

As the adopted son of a rich family, Mr. Wu graduated from college as a non-arts major, went to study music in Japan in 1929, and changed his first and second names from Zu-pei (meaning "nurtured by his ancestor") to Xiao-bang (a Chinese homonym for Chopin), as he so much admired Chopin's patriotism. By chance, while in Japan he witnessed a creative and stirring dance called *A Host of Ghosts* by a group of college students, suggestive of all kinds of people in society struggling for life. This moved him so deeply that he made up his mind to devote his life to dance, which was so penetrating and touching to his heart that no other art could match it in his feelings. At that time he also attended performances by the Japanese modern dancer Baku Ishii, and even a recital by Ishii's Korean student Choi Sung-hui.

In the winter of 1929 Mr. Wu entered the Dance Institute of Masao Takada, where he studied ballet for almost two years. After the "September 18 Incident," when the Japanese began to invade China, he returned to his homeland and opened the first Chinese theatrical dance school in Shanghai, which roused great interest in the art circles. However, the venture ran into trouble because no male dancer had ever done this kind of theater dance before. Soon the school met with bankruptcy, and Mr. Wu had to go back to Japan to study more in the Takada Dance Institute. Mrs. Takada, who was now the ballet teacher, had once studied with Isadora Duncan in Paris, as a result of which she emphasized naturalness even in her ballet teaching, and encouraged independent creativity in the students. Two years later Mr. Wu went back to Shanghai, and opened his own Xiao-bang Dance Institute. The next year (1935) he gave his first recital, which attracted only one ticket buyer, a Polish lady who was interested in three dances choreographed to Chopin's music. This failure forced him to go back to Japan for a third time, and it was during this stay that he studied German modern dance with both Takaya Eguchi and Misako Miya, his former classmates in ballet. They did only a summer workshop, but that completely opened new doors for Mr. Wu. Thus began his life-long career as the founder of Chinese modern dance, which he called "New Dance." This was the same term as the Germans had used from the very beginning, but it had different connotations for him—"new" as distinguished from the feudalistic dances of old China.

The War of Resistance Against Japan gave Mr. Wu a chance to make full use of the German modern dance he had studied in Japan. His large number of patriotic solos, particularly *March of the Volunteers* (the music of which became the national anthem when the republic was established in 1949), *To Beat and Kill the Traitors, Broadsword Dance*, and *The Song of the Guerrillas*, became very popular on the front lines. During the Civil War he again choreographed many solo dances, including *The Hungry Fire* and *The Ugly Flattery*, exposing the dark side of the old China. He also did some ensemble dances and dance dramas, such as *A Marching Dance*, to encourage the revolutionary soldiers to liberate the whole of China. During this time he was teaching his modern dance concepts and methods to many students who later became the backbone of the New China's dance world.

After the New China was born in 1949, Mr. Wu continued his experimental work in combining Western modern dance concepts and methods with Chinese themes and classical music through his own dance company, Heavenly Horse Dance Studio. He was especially concerned with filming religious dances in the Taoist and Confucian temples, but he failed to continue this effort for long because the Cultural Revolution was approaching. When the Cultural Revolution finally ended in 1976 Mr. Wu was already seventy years old. By that time he was Chairman of the China National Dance Artists Association and Founding Director of the Dance Research Institute, as well as the first instructor for the M.A. Degree in Dance in China. He kept traveling all over China and teaching his modern dance theory and practice for years, and published five books, but he was too old to do all the energy consuming dance experiments of his earlier years, which is a great pity not only for himself but also for his country.

Another Chinese dance pioneer, Madam Dai Ai-lian (1916-), ten years younger than Mr. Wu, came back to China from London to join the War of Resistance Against Japan, and created a large number of patriotic dances, such as *The Story of the Guerrillas* and *Air Raid*. Having studied ballet with Anton Dolin and Margaret Craske first, and then German modern dance at the Mary Wigman School and the Jooss-Leeder School, both located in London, Madam Dai also made great contributions to the theatrical staging of the new Chinese dance. For whatever reasons, Madam Dai's interest after 1949 was mainly concentrated on ballet (although occasionally she choreographed some excellent Chinese folk-style dances, such as *The Lotus Flower Dance*). That is why she was appointed the first principal of the Beijing Dance School, where ballet has been a major course since 1954—a position which was totally rejected by Mr. Wu, who refused to help the Russian ballet experts dominate this first theatrical dance school in China. He preferred to let the school go its own (Chinese) way, with some help from German modern dance, which could effectively teach students to create something of their own. However, Madam Dai did borrow one useful thing from German modern dance, namely Labanotation, with which she and the student members of her Chinese Labanotation Society recorded many Chinese folk and ancient dances.

Virtually everyone in the dance world of China today traces their origins, directly or indirectly, to Mr. Wu and Madam Dai, and to the German influence they brought into the country. To its great credit, the Central Government has treated them well (except for periods when Leftist politics were dominant), and given them much of the credit they so richly deserve. Two prominent successors, Mr. Guo Ming-da (1916-) and Mr. Wang Lian-cheng (1931-), who studied the Americanized German modern dance of Alwin Nikolais in the 1950s and 1980s respectively, have also had an impact. Nonetheless, Western modern dance did not take deep root in China's soil until the Guangdong Modern Dance Company was officially established in 1992. This was the culmination of four year's of hard work, with the continuous help of Mr. Charles Reinhart and the American Dance Festival, and Mr. Ralph Samuelson at the Asian Cultural Council. Only then was Western modern dance included in the "one hundred flowers" that Mao Ze-dong said would symbolize the many styles of Chinese art.

III. WHY DID IT TAKE SO LONG?

To my mind there are numerous reasons why it has taken China over half a century to assimilate Western modern dance. We have already discussed some of the political reasons. Others fall under the following headings:

A. Economic: The best soil for Western modern dance, particularly for pure dance, is provided by a highly developed productive society. In the old China even such trivial items as matches, candles, and nails had to be imported.

B. Social: Western modern dance is the product of capitalist societies, while ballet was born out of feudal societies; in short, the two art forms belong to different historical periods and social systems. China had a long history of feudalism—over two thousand years—so it was not socially receptive to modern dance. The real issue does not lie in the difference between capitalism, which dominates the US and most of the European countries, and communism, which predominates in China and some other countries in Asia and Latin America, but in the difference between capitalism and feudalism. That explains the Chinese empathy for ballet: though aesthetically it may be against the authentic Chinese tradition, ideologically, with its highly developed form which requires absolute unity of thinking and moving, ballet met the needs of Mao Ze-dong, who intended to maintain strong control over China.

C. Ideological: Confucianism, and particularly its doctrine of the mean, has dominated the majority Han population of China for the last two thousand years. Thus, there has been very little democratic tradition in this country, at least before the Western democracy-and-science inspired "May 4 Students Movement" of 1919. Again, an established taste for democracy is required for the cultivation of modern dance.

D. Educational: Sharp contrasts exist between China and America regarding the purposes of education. In China, from ancient times to the present, all children have received a "collectivist" education, and "Be a good boy (or girl)" is the phrase on every parent's or teacher's lips. In this context "good" always means "well-tamed." On the other hand, "The general end of education in America ... is the fullest development of the individual within the framework of our present industrialized democratic society."[1] Obviously, the concepts and practices of American individualism have been emphasized, and these are key factors in the development of modern dance. Anna Sokolow, the American modern dancer and choreographer, has given us a typical modern dance credo in her much quoted essay *The Rebel and the Bourgeois:* "Go ahead and be a bastard. Then you can be an artist."[2]

E. Aesthetic: Much as in France and Russia, where classical traditions were so deeply rooted that it was absolutely impossible to generate a native modern dance, so China has had to import the art form from the outside. In this sense the United States (and, to a lesser extent, Germany) has the "advantage" of less well established traditions.

The Russian's socialist and anti-formalist ideology of 1930-1950 dominated the "Liberated Areas" of China in the 1940s, and all of the New China until 1980, when many other ideologies besides Marxism and Leninism came into this country from

---

1. Alma M. Hawkins, *Modern Dance in Higher Education,* CORD, Inc. 1982, Dance Research Special.
2. Anna Sokolow, quoted from Selma Jeanne Cohen, ed., *The Modern Dance: Seven Statements of Belief,* Middletown, CT, Wesleyan University Press, 1966.

the West to enrich the intellectual climate. Hence the inclination to think of art as form and medium which exist only for the purpose of expressing content. This tendency is, of course, antithetical to any sense of pure form, which is one of the most valued aspects of Western modern dance.

F. Technical: The pioneers of Chinese modern dance did not master much technique. For example, Mr. Wu Xiao-bang studied German modern dance in Japan for only three weeks in the 1930s, and what he learned was already more Japanese than German. For that matter, German modern dance has never been as systematically developed as the American Graham, Cunningham, or Limón techniques, which naturally has been an obstacle to its effective dissemination around the world. Madam Dai Ai-lian invested herself primarily in ballet and the popularization of Labanotation. When finally there was someone from China, Mr. Guo Ming-da, who was in America for eight years in the 1950s and studied US modern dance, the style to which he was exposed was the highly Germanic one of Alwin Nikolais. Tragically, when he came back to China in 1956 he fell victim to the anti-American fever of the times, being sent to Guizhou Province, a remote place far from Beijing, the cultural center of China. During the Cultural Revolution he was actually called back to Beijing and forced to give misinformation about Western modern dance, criticizing it as "decadent and crazy style," "pessimistic dispirited mysticism representing the no-way-out and hopeless struggle of the American reactionary ruling class," etc. Another Chinese folk dance teacher from the Beijing Dance School, Mr. Wang Lian-cheng, studied with Nikolais in the 1980s, and came back with a lot of useful Nikolais techniques, which through his teaching aroused much interest in many different cities in China. Unfortunately, his career was cut short by a cerebral hemorrhage.

In conclusion, China has been slow to accept Western modern dance for a variety of reasons, but with the easing of political pressures after 1980 we begin to see signs of a new openness. Recently I was approached by a number of Central Government officials who had seen some modern dance abroad and had occasion to compare it with the highly formalized ballet at international competitions. In the process of inviting me to be chief judge at the all-China preliminary contest for the International Modern Dance Competitions in Nagoya and Paris they told me that, as non-dance professionals, they loved the fresh and varied modern dance simply because it was so much more interesting to look at than the always repetitious ballet. Now we need to find more dance people with good training both technically and theoretically who are willing to work hard for many years in order to take advantage of the opportunities available in this kind of atmosphere. Two developments are particularly promising: 1. We finally have our own company, The Guangdong Modern Dance Company, which is well on its way to establishing a good reputation both nationally and internationally. In order fully to join the ranks of the world-wide dance community it will need to understand the importance of capturing the attention of the international mass media. As for the education and training of company members, they will need to build on the familiarity with the latest techniques and theories that was initiated through the early sponsorship of the American Dance Festival; 2. In September, 1993, the Beijing Dance Academy (formerly the Beijing Dance School) introduced its Modern Dance Major under the leadership of the Choreography Department. Twenty men and women, most of whom had excelled in Chinese folk or classical dance (similar to those in the Guangdong Modern Dance Company) were chosen by audition to form the first class in this two-year program. They have been taking courses in Modern Dance History and Theory, Graham- and Limón-based technique, Improvisation and Choreography, etc., taught by the program's two faculty members (Mr. Zhang Shou-he, a graduate of the Hong Kong Academy for Performing Arts, and Ms. Wang Mei, a former member of the Guangdong Company), and one guest teacher (currently, this author). At the end of only their first semester the students of this program, presenting themselves as the Beijing Dance Academy/Landtop Modern Dance Company, premiered seven works choreographed by the faculty under the title *Greeting the World* in Wuhan and Beijing. These performances met with very positive critical acclaim. Now the audiences are eager to see dances choreographed by the students themselves, at least at their graduation in the summer of 1995.

Somewhat belatedly, modern dance is assuming its proper place amid the other flowers in the garden of Chinese arts. As I suggested in an interview several years ago, this seems totally appropriate at this point in our history: "Opening up China to avant garde dance forms doesn't hurt socialism, as China is strong enough not to be swallowed up by any outside influences."[3] Rather than fearing fierce floods, the Chinese people and their government have every reason to anticipate from this development the nurturing rain of new ideas.

---

3. Nancy Cacioppo, "Dancing His Way to Peace: An Interview with the Chinese Dance Critic/Scholar Ou Jian-ping" *The Journal-News* , West Nyack, NY, Sept. 30, 1988, p. F3.

Chapter Four:
Bringing Modern Dance to China*

Yang Mei-qi

Yang Mei-qi has been a dance educator for over twenty years. She is currently Principal of the Guangdong Dance School, Guangzhou, China, which was founded in 1959 to train young dancers of high potential. Since 1988 she has provided the impetus for establishing the Guangdong Modern Dance Company. This company, trained with the assistance of staff from the American Dance Festival, is the crowning jewel in China's efforts toward creating a unique style of Chinese modern dance.

Ms. Yang is also Vice-Chairman of the Chinese Dancers Association, Guangdong Division. She is extremely knowledgeable in the major tribal folk and traditional dances of China, and is recognized by her peers as an expert in this field. Her many research papers have been widely published by professional journals. In order further to assist her students in developing their careers, Ms. Yang has visited the United States, the former Soviet Union, Korea and Hong Kong.

In 1985 I was chosen to be the principal of the Guangdong Dance Academy [a high school for training students in classical Chinese dance. Its facilities adjoin those of the Guangdong Modern Dance Company, and Yang Mei-qi serves both institutions, but otherwise they are totally independent]. As a new principal I wanted to examine the state of dance in China at that time from an educational point of view. I already felt that Chinese dance education was in danger of finding itself at a dead end if it were not quickly reformed. That is because for the past 30 years or so every effort had been bent on establishing a uniquely Chinese classical dance vocabulary. The vocabulary was very limited at that time because it was controlled by Russian dancers who came here by special invitation to instruct the local dance workers (the opera artists, etc.), but it didn't have anything in common, really, with the local society. The dance form itself did not derive from a local context; it was strictly an academic study in research,

* EDITORS' NOTE: What follows is the product of several interviews which the editors conducted in Guangzhou, China, January, 1993.

using ballet principles mixed with some movement from the Peking Opera. It was totally lacking in that raw gut-feeling of the native Chinese culture. Also, in the training process itself there was a great deal of emphasis on technical detail, endlessly repeating the same movement in order to perfect that special vocabulary. I felt this kind of training was terribly restrictive; young children coming into the system very active, open and lively had become quite mechanical by the time of graduation— machines repeating the same routine every day. From an educational point of view I thought this was not good.

In China in the old times the emphasis was always on the integration of art and humanity—on trying to cultivate the creative, spiritual side of human nature. Now the educational system was reversing all of that; it was not encouraging the students to explore their creativity, their individuality. It was suppressing the human spirit. For a number of decades—several generations of students—it was just a question of repeating the same old thing over and over. The dance was very dry and predictable; even if you closed your eyes in the middle of a piece you knew what was happening on stage. All the movement was the same. Generally the dancers did not even remember what the dance they were doing was about; they just put on lurid make-up and beautiful costumes and did the movement on stage, following a certain set pattern. It was all a matter of putting on a forced smile and trying to project a pre-determined emotion, which had nothing to do with real life. So, I realized there were lots of problems with dance as a creative art and in dance education at that time, but I couldn't find any way out.

My understanding of the situation was not unique. I had many friends of my own generation who shared the same view. There were lots of people in the dance community who realized that the art form was isolating itself from the public. We knew that dance had alienated its audience, but we didn't know what to do about it.

At the end of 1985, when Mr. Gorbachev first came to power, four dance people from China, myself among them, were chosen to go to Russia as part of an exchange program. I took all of the questions I have enumerated here with me to Russia, hoping to find answers there. I thought that because the classical Chinese dance was developed according to a system devised by the Russians, they would know how to set it right. Since 1956 we had been out of touch with Russia because the advisors had been withdrawn, so I wanted to find out what had developed there during those years. I went to four cities—Moscow, Leningrad, Kiev and Dublinsk—and everywhere I asked my questions of the dancers and educators I met. Everyone was very surprised to find that we were having problems: "Our system," they said, "is perfect." They felt that there could be no need for reformation or change. I was quite disappointed not to have found any answers.

Then, in 1986, the Asian Cultural Council provided a scholarship for Chiang Ching (a beautiful dancer who, after training in Beijing and having had a very successful movie career in Hong Kong, was living and working in New York) to go to China to select some dance workers to participate in the summer program at the American Dance

Festival. She recommended three people: a choreographer, Mun Wen-yuan; a dancer, Zhao Ming; and an educator, myself. It was expensive to make that trip, but fortunately I had relatives who supported me, so I spent more than twenty days in New York, and then went to ADF for two months.

My stay in New York had a very strong effect on me. Because my involvement had been almost exclusively in Chinese folk dance, I did not at that time appreciate modern dance as an art form; its aesthetic was shocking to me. So every time I attended a modern dance concert I asked the question, "Why are they doing this?"— and the answer I always got back was "Why not?" This forced me to re-think my attitudes toward dance and life in general. I especially watched lots of small theater productions, and gradually I became more excited because each time I expected something new; although I often didn't know what was going on, I was looking for something to happen. For perhaps the first time I experienced the freedom provided by the stage—so many possibilities!

I also went to some of the schools in New York, such as Nikolais' choreography workshop, and saw how dance was taught there. It was very liberating; my understanding of what lies at the core of dance was expanded greatly. I saw that dance happens through the body, which is privately owned by a person. So it is the art form for a very private kind of expression. This should not be controlled by any external agency that would direct it one way or another. Especially in dance education it is important to realize that modern training does not emphasize only one source of energy, or the preeminence of one part of the body. It involves a holistic concept of the body in time and space. I found that a modern dance class requires more brain power than physical energy, and that was very rewarding for me. In reviewing the Chinese dance training I saw that there are always only two time elements, fast movement and slow movement. The space element is always frontal, and at the middle level. So at that time it was almost impossible for the Chinese dancers to imagine movement in uneven counts, or shifting focus, or going from rolling on the ground into the air. That was all very eye-opening for me. I realized, as any arts educator should, that the cultivation of creativity is all important, but techniques for doing that were totally lacking in the current Chinese system. I thought that it would be important to expose the students to technique and improvisation classes simultaneously.

In watching Westerners do modern dance I always admired their courage in trying to be different—to explore something new. Even more amazing to me, though, was seeing Orientals do this. I vividly remember a performance by a Korean trio, two women and a man. They had the entire theater painted white, and hung with white draperies. What they tried to present was a traditional Taoist or Buddhist way of seeing the world—its essential emptiness or nothingness, and evanescence. For me it was very Chinese, because the two cultures are quite close, and they were able to make very profound statements by the use of quite contemporary means. For example, the man stood on his head for a long time, and then suddenly stood up and drew three beautiful Chinese brush paintings. The women then used knives to cut them to shreds. At the end the women were bare-chested, with long skirts that covered the whole floor. They danced around the man, who did calligraphy on their bodies and their dresses. Finally, he painted a circle on his own body, and we were reminded in a Taoist way of the oneness of things. The origins of this work were totally Oriental, but within a Western structure. I was very touched. Having always been in love with my own culture—having always known that there are many precious things in China—I wanted to find a way to put those things in touch with contemporary life. I wanted to allow them to express themselves in their own way.

I saw that in China at that time there were really only two ways of conceptualizing dance. The first was to serve a political purpose: to propagandize; to educate people. The other was to bring out the folk elements: to evoke the ethnic characteristics of the Chinese people. Because there were only those two ways of doing things on stage, dance had little to do with human thoughts and emotions. After seeing all the things I did in New York and at ADF I thought there must be a way of changing this, so during my last week in the US I wrote a letter to Charles Reinhart, suggesting a plan to bring modern dance into China, starting with education. I asked that ADF lend its support by sending teachers to provide three years of college-level dance training, followed by one year of practical experience in performance.

That is the curriculum I proposed in 1986. To make such a proposal was considered very bold in China at that time because all modern art was heavily stigmatized as "bourgeois"—as decadent, and therefore not to be practiced in China. However, from my own experience I knew this to be a false concept. I knew that

Figure 4 *Tide,* by Wang Mei (Guangdong Modern Dance Company)

modern dance is not pro or anti any political dogma—that in fact it takes no political stance. It is just a means of self-expression, like literature or the visual arts, to be used in any number of ways. Because of this new understanding I was able to stand firm in talking to the Chinese authorities. Also, at that time a new policy was enacted in Guangdong Province which encouraged the principals of schools to be more responsible than ever before for what was taught in their programs. My superior happened to be a well-educated artist who was quite open to and supportive of my ideas.

Charles Reinhart immediately accepted my plan, and suggested that I apply to the Asian Cultural Council for financial assistance. He phoned Ralph Samuelson at the ACC and made an appointment for me to see him at 3 p.m. on the last day before my visa for staying in America expired. So I left the Festival a day early, took a plane to New York, and rushed to Mr. Samuelson's office before catching the evening plane for China. I remember he asked me if I had the approval of my government, and I said I was 80% sure that I did! I was able to say that because I felt the spirit of the times was leaning in my direction, but I knew I would have at least 20% convincing to do.

That was in August of 1986. Eventually word came from the ACC that they were very interested in my proposal, but would have to discuss it at a meeting to be held in April, 1987. So there began a long period of negotiations that were too complex and tedious to be detailed here. Suffice it to say that after I explained my plan to the Chinese officials, they were unable to accept it because of the emphasis at that time on warding off all bourgeois influences. In January, 1987, Mr. Samuelson came to Beijing, and I went there to talk to him. He told me that things looked good on the ACC side. Then, in February, Zhao Zhi-yang, the Chief Secretary of the Communist Party, made a speech over the Chinese New Year that indicated a relaxation of the Party's line on cross-cultural exchange. So, the provincial government agreed to my plan. However, by that time the economy was such that I had virtually lost any opportunity to raise the necessary funding. I wrote a paper of many pages explaining modern dance and our need of it, and on the basis of that I won the support of the Provincial (State) Cultural Bureau, which passed it on to the more powerful Party Publicity Bureau, where it was "stonewalled" for some months. By the time my plan finally gained all of the necessary approvals there seemed to be no money available anywhere to implement it. Finally, in early May, I found an official in the Financial Bureau who was able to squeeze enough out of his emergency reserve fund to get things started, and we set out to audition dancers. I should make it clear that the money used to establish and maintain the company has all come from the Chinese side; the ACC provided funds only for bringing in Western teachers.

There was also a good deal of initial difficulty in recruiting students. The future of the enterprise was obviously uncertain. In many of the cities we went to, the dancers we might have wanted were already working for other companies, so we had to audition them secretly. Also, the timing was awkward. With its four-year curriculum the program was to yield the equivalent of a college degree, but in May and June it was already too late for high school graduates to take the appropriate entrance examinations. Even if there had been time to take the exam it is probable that many of the students would not have been able to pass it. I went to the Education Bureau to see if they could make a special allowance in this case, but they turned me down. In order to remedy this lack of Chinese certification I finally hit on the idea of having Charles Reinhart award our "graduates" a special certificate from ADF! This may seem strange to Western eyes, but for the Chinese it is very important to have a piece of paper certifying work completed. Ultimately, many more students applied than we could accept (there were 18 in the first group), and we gave them the kind of examination/audition that got them thinking about their creative potential, so that seemed to make a good impression.

Over the brief course of our history we have experienced a number of what I would call "setbacks"—not specific things so much as general problems that we could not easily anticipate and over which we exercise little control. In the political arena, for example, there are always ups and downs. In response to governmental policy we can sometimes be aggressive in pressing our case, while at other times we must be protective. As I indicated a moment ago in describing my quest for funding, one must always walk a line between the Party Bureau and the State Bureau; each is capable of overriding the other, and when something goes awry no one wants to take the responsibility.

I remember one time I was officially informed that an important approval of the company had come through. We were elated. Then, almost immediately afterward, I began to hear that it had been cancelled. So I went into hiding! I refused to take any calls, or anything of that sort. A message was left for me that I could not proceed with formation of the company, but we went ahead as though nothing had happened. When they finally found me I was confronted with a new argument. They were convinced of the artistic merit of what I wanted, they said, but "real world," i.e., political, considerations left no room for doing it. I said to one official: "Listen, I don't even care if my career is jeopardized by doing this. Just let me do it." He said: "*Your* career is one thing. We also have to be concerned about the careers of other officials who give you their support and approval." They tried to convince me that instead of starting a modern dance company I should help with the training of dancers for their commercial Light Music Group. I went to talk to the director of that company, but afterward I was totally depressed and regretful. I couldn't see investing all that I had accomplished so far—arranging to bring in Western teachers, etc.—in that kind of endeavor.

So that is a sample of how things have gone politically: a few steps forward, a few steps back. I could tell many stories of this sort. It has never been easy.

A second set of problems is economic in nature. At one point there was literally no money in the company's coffers. I had to go to the commercial people to try to borrow money. It has always been a question of squeezing out a little here, a little there, just to keep things going.

Figure 5 *Tide*, by Wang Mei (Guangdong Modern Dance Company)

Finally, the dancers themselves have presented problems. Many of them came to Guangzhou in very poor condition. Also, simply coming here and discovering all of the commercial attractions of the city has caused them to be distracted. No longer can they devote themselves purely to their art. It is very difficult to hold them together, to keep them concentrated. This younger generation is at a crossroads. Before, everything was basically one way; now they are opened up to all kinds of alternatives. Each one has different goals, including their material needs and their perception of the self. On the one hand, they want recognition of their individuality; on the other, they refuse to accept responsibility. They have been opened up to new concepts (well known to modern dance) of personal identity. Some have simply used the company as a stepping stone to achieve their own ends.

It was my intention in creating the company to make of it a "safe haven," a shelter, within which a group of pure artists might explore their art form. I must confess that this vision has been somewhat diluted by the political, economic, and psychological setbacks I have described here. The six years of the company's existence have coincided with a period of great upheaval in Chinese history, rendering fulfillment of my original vision virtually impossible. What we often find in the development of history is that although we may have a plan, and pursue it with all of our energy, ultimately things will find their own course, beyond our poor power to predict. These problems I have described may not seem new to artists in the rest of the world, but it seems important to say that we are now going through them here in China as well.

There have also been very great successes. Generally speaking, in the four years the company has been performing throughout China it has exerted a great influence over the direction Chinese dance is taking. During that time we have gone to Beijing twice, and we have put effort into making ourselves known in the dance circles there. And performing outside the country brings a great deal of recognition to ourselves and to China. We are fortunate to have friends in the media who have called attention to us through their critical acclaim.

The first time we went to Beijing (1988) was during the *Taoli Bei* (Peach and Plum Cup), the bi-annual competition of national dance academies from throughout China. We took with us a class demonstration and some small works. Then, in 1990, we went again with two full-evening programs. One was choreographed by Willy Tsao, a jazzy evocation of modern city life. The other was totally created by the students themselves. Everyone of importance was there, including reviewers from the major newspapers. This was shortly after the episode in Tiananmen Square. The arts had been strongly suppressed—nothing was allowed beyond carefully controlled political statements—so no one expected a big explosion from the south, from Guangzhou. What we performed was not just any dance, but something that was new and energetic in ways they were unaccustomed to. It was as though the audience was almost suffocating, and suddenly there was a breath of fresh air. They realized that the people on stage were dancing what they really felt. In all of that explosive movement they saw a reflection of their own longing to express themselves. Suddenly it seemed that everyone, both those in the audience and the dancers on stage, was in tears.

After the performance the Chinese Dancers Association held a big conference especially to discuss it. All of the leaders of the dance groups and artistic directors of companies came. Many of those in attendance were in their 40s and 50s, members of the older generation. Even this normally conservative element was excited; they said that our presentation was a breakthrough, a milestone. They even suggested that a letter be written to the National Cultural Bureau, demanding that this group be protected, that it not be allowed to die. That was important at the time because it was not known whether the government would allow the company to be officially "established."

By now we can say that not only the dance circle but the entire arts community of China sees this company as a symbol of hope for the future. This I consider quite appropriate, as my original concept in bringing modern dance to China encompassed not only dance but modern art itself. I hoped to bring a modernization of perception to our life here. I wanted to open Chinese art beyond the bonds of traditionalism, to allow it to find a place on the international stage. I saw the energy embodied in modern dance swelling out through all aspects of Chinese society, and helping to move it into the modern world.

Obviously, the primary instrument of our development as a training program and as a dance company has been the importation of dance teachers from the West. I would like now to talk about the absorption of this Western influence; how it integrated with our Chinese ways of thinking and concepts of Art. The many great

Figure 6 Wang Mei in *The Long Night* (Guangdong Modern Dance Company)

Western masters who have taught here over the last six years have brought to us many insights and also many questions. This cross-cultural approach to dance education reflects important differences in the ways artists brought up in this part of the world have traditionally conceived of art, beauty, etc. from their counterparts elsewhere. Although our dancers are still quite young (even those who have been with us through all six years), they are already conscious of social problems, and are trying to use dance as a means to express their thoughts about society—about their environment. That makes them different from traditional Chinese dancers. This difference is especially meaningful because, as I have already said, China generally has been undergoing similar changes during this period of time.

Naturally each student has reacted to each teacher in his or her own way. It is my general impression, however, that the first group of teachers made the greatest impression. Sarah Stackhouse had a very clear, refined approach to teaching, which was especially useful when everyone was just beginning. She gave the students a detailed understanding of what she wanted: how to use energy and force; how to live in a clean, unmannered fashion. She helped them reclaim their bodies from the eccentricities of traditional training.

Not only her technical knowledge, but also her devotion impressed the students. She was not young when she came here, but the fact that she stayed on for three months, living and working with them under rather difficult conditions, gave them valuable insight into the life-style of the professional modern dancer. She even showed the students how to roll out and care for the Marley that Willy Tsao had brought for the studio floor. It was winter, and she sewed up a mattress herself and fitted it under the door to ward off the wind. There was one student who was very lazy, often missing classes; she talked to him nine times. Such details were very important to the students. Personally, I felt a particular empathy for Sarah, because I saw in her another person who had sacrificed a great deal for the art form.

The second Western teacher was Ruby Shang. Her technique emphasized the shifting of weight in a relaxed flow. She gave our students a whole new concept of dance: that even things lacking in classical balance and harmony can be beautiful; that shifting of weight helps tremendously in partnering. The classical Chinese dance considered *pas de deux* boys lifting girls onlystraight up and down, but the shifting of weight suddenly opened all kinds of unexpected possibilities. It showed our students new dimensions in the relationships between human beings.

I especially requested to have Douglas Nielsen come, because I had seen him teach and was impressed by the intricate leg patterns he used. In Chinese dance the leg work is normally very simple; elaboration of movement takes place mostly in the upper body. I thought Douglas' work would be a valuable complement to the early training our students had received. He also created four new works on our students, developed out of his experience in China. After he left we mounted a production of his works.

Lynda Davis was another impressive teacher. One of her teaching techniques involved the use of paintings by Chinese artists. She increased the students' understanding of the relationship between form and quality, and time and space, by analyzing the paintings she chose. Then she encouraged the students to produce small works based on what they had learned from the analyses. The collective work created in her composition class, entitled *Square-Bottomed Bamboo Basket and Bamboo,* was a wonderful example of how she inspired the students to make a very Chinese modern dance piece.

The Western teachers, including those who came later, led our students into a brand new area of art. The students were no longer technical machines. Their creative or imaginative faculties were opened up; they began to find subconscious inspiration. More importantly, they were deeply affected by the teachers' refined personalities and devotion to their art, a gift that would be a lifelong benefit to them.

The events of June, 1989, caused a temporary break: I think the Americans were unsympathetic with the political situation in China and didn't want to come. We did have a husband and wife from Canada, and Helen and John Sky from Australia, and a woman from England, who came by way of the City Contemporary Dance Company in Hong Kong. These people stayed from two weeks to two months. During that time Willy Tsao filled in a great deal; we started work on the first major piece he did for us, *City Romance,* right after June 4, and premiered it in October,

1989. I had met Willy through Chiang Ching who, during her visit here in 1986, recommended him as an "advisor" to the company (there were originally a lot of advisors, including Carl Wolz, Charles Reinhart, and Wong Lin-lu, from UCLA). Of course, Willy has stayed on, and is now Artistic Director to the company and its most important current influence. As the company's personnel changes, the early dancers drifting away and being replaced by those who had no exposure to the American teachers, his influence becomes even greater.

With the later group of Americans an unfortunate pattern developed, despite their good intentions. Ross Parkes came and arranged for one of our boys to go to the States. David Hochoy took another back with him. Then ADF provided two scholarships for our dancers, and neither of them came back. That was definitely a problem with the Americans; they kept telling our people how beautiful they were, and how they would be stars if they went to the States, so naturally they couldn't resist. Once they got to the States the many attractions they found there made it psychologically very difficult, if not impossible, for them to return.

Another unexpected problem stemmed from the fact that Charles Reinhart had apparently instructed all of the teachers he sent specifically *not* to ask the students

Figure 7 *Basket and Bamboo,* choreographed and danced by the Guangdong Modern Dance Company, under the direction of Lynda Davis

to copy their works; rather, they should be encouraged to create their own brand of modern dance. That was clear from the very beginning. The problem was that neither Charles nor I fully appreciated that the dancers here in China have a very narrow perspective on life. Their education is quite limited; at best they have been through the equivalent of junior high in the West. The teachers came for just three months each, and during that time concentrated their whole life experience and threw it at the students. There simply wasn't enough time for effective, efficient communication to take place; also, of course, the language problem prohibited deeper communication. The first month was basically taken up with just learning the students' names. By the time the teachers were ready to start bringing out each student's personality, they were on their way home. The educational structure we created was by its very nature always incomplete.

Every one of the Western teachers remarked on the beauty of the dancers' technique. They were also impressed with the work done in improvisation and composition; they thought it was wonderfully unique, like nothing they had ever seen before. So they left well satisfied. The truth of the matter is, however, that what the students were showing them was just what they had learned in their previous training; we knew there was nothing unique or creative in that at all. So I must admit that what we got from those teachers was really something quite superficial, not something that deeply changed our students' concept of dance. I always felt embarrassed when some older Chinese dancers would come here and ask our students "What is modern dance?" because I knew their answers were not very intelligent.

As Chairman of ADF Charles Reinhart has always shown genuine concern for this newly born Chinese modern dance company. He attended the opening ceremony of the school, examined the progress of the students, came to award our "graduates" their certificates from ADF, and made it possible to bring the group to ADF-Durham in July, 1991. The company owes a great deal to his profound influence, and that of the master teachers sent by ADF.

In sum, I feel that this situation I am describing is a product of history. Because of all the things that accumulatively affected this first generation of Chinese modern dancers, the outcome was inevitably going to be imperfect. We were given this time, this place, these economic and political factors to deal with, and what we produced simply is what it is. We have to accept it on its own terms. If we are able to continue this process into the future we will attempt to learn from the mistakes of the past. We will try to improve the matters of scheduling. Especially, we will have a clearer vision of our own needs, rather than just accepting others' opinions of what we should do. For example, the policy that the American teachers should not impose their ideas on us, well-intentioned as it was, to some extent undercut the learning process. Among other things, teachers like Sarah Stackhouse taught our students pieces from their repertory, but we were not allowed to perform them because we were "not supposed to copy." Hence, our students lost the opportunity to learn by experience what those pieces are really about. We were expected to perform only works created by the students, but their experience was too limited to produce anything that would really hold up. So there was no way for them fully to understand what is worthwhile.

I want now to bring in some very good works, so the dancers can gain experience from performing them. That is not only, I feel, what our dancers need now, but it will also contribute to training an audience. It doesn't matter exactly where the works come from; if they are good, they will speak to the people. Lucas Hoving, when he was preparing to leave, said that what our students need now is to do some good repertory, to learn what quality is, and I hope to follow up on that suggestion. Of course, at the same time we will be creating our own works; we should not have just one diet, because the whole idea of modern dance is opening up. Once you say "Oh, we can't do that," it's no longer modern dance.

We feel a certain loneliness because the whole concept of modern art is not yet well established in China. The government has no tradition of subsidizing modern companies in any of the arts; there is no contemporary institute of music, of painting, etc. Until this company came along all of our artists were classically trained. That is why we are planning to hold a modern arts exhibition and performance week in December, 1993, to bring together those people who have been trying on their own to explore modern forms, and give them an opportunity to present here in Guangzhou, with our company. We will also be bringing in new dancers from the Beijing Dance Academy, where they are setting up a new modern dance section under the direction of Wang Mei, who is a graduate of this school. We hope to develop that connection, and in September we will start a training course of our own for potential company members.

[As previously noted, this text was developed from two interviews with Yang Mei-qi (through Willy Tsao's translation) during a visit to Guangzhou. There was to have been yet a third session, which unfortunately had to be cancelled at the last moment. In that interview we anticipated dealing with Madam Yang's plans for the future of the Guangdong Modern Dance Company, and for herself personally. These she outlined for us as follows:

The first idea is to improve the quality of Chinese modern dancers; to make them devote themselves more whole-heartedly to modern dance.

The second is to create more new works that are original and creative.

Third, to promote the whole system of Chinese culture—the progress and reform of Chinese society—and to help more Chinese understand modern art.

Fourth, to have more cultural exchanges with foreign artists.

Finally, to look for more financial support.

At present we can only dangle this bare-bones skeleton before the reader, with the hope that it may some day be fleshed out.]

Chapter Five:
Some Reflections on Modern Dance in Guangzhou

Claudia Gitelman

*Upon graduation from the University of Wisconsin **Claudia Gitelman** joined the Murray Louis Dance Company. She has also performed concert works of Hanya Holm, Myra Kinch, Don Redlich and others. She was in the original Broadway company of "Camelot," and did regional theater and television before interrupting her performing career to raise a family and earn a Master's degree from Columbia University. Her own choreography has been seen in New York since 1972. She is the recipient of a Fellowship in Choreography from the New York Foundation for the Arts, and two Fulbright Awards. Ms. Gitelman has taught in many important dance centers in this country, five countries in Europe, and in China through the American Dance Festival's Institutional Linkages Program. She joined the faculty of the Mason Gross School of the Arts of Rutgers, the State University of New Jersey, in 1985, and was appointed Associate Professor in 1987. She is also senior faculty member at the Nikolais-Louis Dance Lab in New York City.*

Flying from Seattle in October, 1991, toward an eight-week teaching assignment in China, I was asking myself a rather academic question: "What has been the influence of American modern dance on dance and dancers in the People's Republic?" This line of inquiry was stimulated by the theme of the Society of Dance History Scholars Conference I would address some months hence ("American Dance Abroad: Influence of the United States Experience," University of California, Riverside, February 14-15, 1992). The assignment on which I was embarking, to stimulate and support the creative work of eighteen dancers comprising the Guangdong Modern Dance Company (GMDC), was as a participant in the historic Institutional Linkages Program (ILP) of the American Dance Festival that had sent, over a five-year period, eight American teachers to the only academy in China preparing modern dancers and choreographers.

Like America itself, American modern dance values change, invention, and diversity. It is a sprawling concert art form with no single vocabulary and no common grammar. I wondered how the Chinese artistic community, which treasures virtuosity rather than innovation, was connecting with the American effort. I wondered how the aspirations of China's dance community to enter the international arena of modern concert dance could be accomplished without compromising what is unique to Chinese culture. Further, I pondered whether individual creativity, that ingredient of American modern dance which we prize above all others, isn't a Western ideal, and therefore supposing it to be the cornerstone of a new Chinese art might be supporting, in however well-meaning a way, an evolutionist fantasy. Because modern dance in America developed through individual initiatives and rebellions, is that the evolution to be expected elsewhere?

The architects of ILP wisely aimed at emphasizing theory and method in showing American modern dance to the Chinese. As stated in the ADF program for the Guangdong Company's U S debut in July of 1991: "The goal was not to impose American dance upon Chinese bodies, but to give young dancers the tools with which to create a Chinese modern dance language based on their own traditions and culture." I wondered what tools had been taken up in five years of exposure to Americans, and I proposed to study that question by asking the professional dancers with whom I would work. Their "view from the trenches," and my observations, I reasoned, could be useful to those following me into China, and perhaps to those studying other aspects of social and cultural change in Asia.

My plan to interview the members of GMDC was facilitated even more easily than I naively expected. This ease was attributable to two factors, the friendliness of the Chinese dancers—their willingness to go more than half way to establish rapport—and the skill and sociability of my interpreter, Daniel. After my teaching program was well established we invited individual dancers to lunch with us on a catch-as-catch-can basis (lunching with me was one of Daniel's responsibilities), and I routinely structured the conversation around a series of questions. I asked each dancer why he/she had chosen to participate in China's modern dance experiment. I also wanted to know what each considered the most important things he/she had learned from American teachers. Thirdly, I asked each to predict the future of modern dance in China. Although I did not tape our conversations I made a thorough record of each immediately after it occurred. Out of respect for the privacy and safety of the dancers in reporting my findings I will not attribute histories, descriptions, and opinions to specific individuals.

My question about the dancers' reasons for being where they were elicited "A Chorus Line" of stories. Each had made a decision to audition, and once accepted, each had rearranged her/his life with difficulty and risk. In some cases that meant giving up the prestige and security of an army commission. In some cases the process had involved physical hardship—many days of travel sitting on hard benches in railway cars with no certainty of what lay at journey's end.

All of the dancers, aged 18 to 27, were performing professionals at the time they auditioned. Therefore, they were assigned to work units at locations other than Guangzhou, a city of about seven million situated on the Pearl River, two and one-half hours by train from Hong Kong, and the center of Guangdong Province. In China, changing work units, to which one is connected not only by salary but for housing, health care, and everything that gives one status as a citizen, is no easy matter. In a few cases, work units to which dancers belonged refused to release them for membership in the Guangdong unit. During my stay one dancer travelled to her former city to negotiate a transfer, and returned with news that such a large sum of money was being requested for her release that she would be unable to earn it in her entire lifetime.

Why were the dancers risking their security and causing themselves huge problems to work in a form of dance they knew virtually nothing about (most admitted they had never seen modern dance before they auditioned; two told me they had seen modern dance concerts, but had not understood them at all)? It became clear to me from what the dancers said about their reasons for joining, and from what I saw of their work and their use of leisure time, that push and pull mechanisms were operative in bringing them together. Many told me they wanted the possibility of change. "Chinese dance," one young man said, "is always the same. There is never the possibility for anything different." A woman described how bored she had been in her old company. Another told me she wanted to use her mind as well as her body. Many said simply that they wanted to try something new.

The difference between the movement material the Guangdong dancers are able to work with and the material I saw in traditional Chinese dance performances and in performances of song and dance companies is enormous, and the dancers appreciate that difference. In the studio at Guangdong Academy I saw a thrilling appetite for movement, and in some dancers a fascination with manipulation of their own movement vocabulary. They delighted in conquering every complex coordination and intricate rhythmic problem I could devise for them, and if it involved leaps, turns, extensions, falls, and rushes through space, so much the better. My frustration as a teacher was in getting them to transfer any texture and dynamic nuance I could stimulate in class into their creative work, but that is another story.

If boredom and routine were pushing the dancers from their old affiliations, the opportunity to fulfill themselves physically was not the only thing pulling them to Guangzhou. I learned of other motivations when dancers offered surprising information about each other. "Some dancers are not serious." "Most are here because Guangzhou is a commercial city and there is more chance for moonlighting here." One woman assured me that dancers came to class only because they would be fined if they did not. "They are only interested in the material life of Guangzhou," she said. The remarks of an earnest young man were translated: "All the dancers are here on a personal quest."

Two dancers admitted they wanted to join GMDC to be closer to Western ideas, and to the West. Their move brought them closer to those goals in several ways.

Membership in GMDC has given three men in the company an exit to the United States. Two were brought to the US for study by the ILP. Both managed to prolong indefinitely their visits to the West, and it is assumed in China that the third, who emigrated through the efforts of one of the American teachers, will also find a way to stay.

The threat of emigration is a real problem for ILP and for the administration of GMDC. The company visited the United States in the summer of 1991, and just before embarking director Yang Mei-qi, who claims not to be a religious person, made offerings at a Buddhist temple and prayed that the American premiere would be a success *and* that all the dancers would return. The travel of the company was carefully planned so that dancers would have no opportunity to exploit contacts in the US. One member of the group was left behind in China because, I was told, authorities had reason to believe he was connected to a Tiananmen Square demonstrator.

Guangzhou, the most prosperous city in China, also brings the dancers closer to the West through their contact with Western fashion and pop culture. Western style music is everywhere; crooners perform with song and dance companies, before sports events, and at all of the spectacles the Chinese are so clever at staging. Becoming a popular singer is one of the most coveted routes of upward mobility for young Chinese; modeling clothes is another. Dancers vie for night jobs as back-up dancers in night clubs, or better yet, on music video tapes that are produced in significant numbers for closed circuit viewing in restaurants.

One wonders if the fragile new concert art form will survive the influence of an international commercial entertainment industry. GMDC's most successful program, in terms of audience appeal, is a complete evening of jazz dance created by a Hong Kong choreographer with close ties to the company. The songs of Madonna, the leather jackets, the hip movements usually taboo in China, are irresistible to local audiences; there is no critical community in China to guide the taste of audiences and of the young dancers.

My questions to the dancers about the most important things learned from the Americans elicited answers that were interesting for what they said and did not say. When the word "devotion" was translated twice by Daniel I let it go as sweet flattery of me and the other Americans, but the third and succeeding times I challenged it. I was told that the fact that the American teachers showed up for every class they were scheduled to teach was remarkable, and that the concentration and involvement of the teachers with the learning of the class was something these dancers had never experienced. Many spoke of the example the foreign teachers were giving them for living lives as artists. A serious dancer offered that he thought the visits by American teachers must continue. "Now we know something about theory and about choreography, but we need master teachers standing by to guide us," he said.

The Chinese dancers had encountered American teachers not only in Guangzhou, but also at the American Dance Festival for two weeks during the summer of 1991. There they had spent marathon days in as many classes as they could squeeze into their schedules. One of the concerts they saw was the ADF Faculty Concert. Three of the more sensitive women in the company talked glowingly about the variety of the program, and how each teacher produced something with a different personality. Generally, however, the Chinese dancers were not very articulate about what they had learned from the American teachers who had visited them. "Use of breath," "tension and relaxation," and "movement of the torso" were the only specific movement ideas I wrote down after our talks. More abstract things, like "devotion" and "variety," are what they mentioned.

When the dancers made predictions about the future of modern dance in the People's Republic of China they revealed two things about their artistic life and their culture that astounded me. Every single dancer, though their ultimate predictions were different, disclosed a distrust of other dancers in the company. The dancers were also unanimous in listing "government officials" as a major stumbling block. Government censors must pass on every dance put before the public. I saw this in action on a Saturday afternoon when three uncomfortable young men from government sat through a special run-through of a program intended for an amusement park theater. "The censors are coming Saturday," I had been told in an off-hand way, and I hadn't wanted to miss that. The amusement park program passed, but throughout my stay an aspiring choreographer among the dancers worked very hard to make the necessary "improvements" in a work that had not met with the censors' approval.

Dancers patiently explained to me that the censors would not approve a dance that was seen as too obscure for the masses, nor work that seemed to criticize Chinese culture or the government. One dancer was sensitive to the need to educate an audience through teaching. "We can't even give modern dance classes outside this academy," he lamented, "until the form is officially recognized."

Two dancers, among the most experienced in the group, held out hope. "Officials do care what the outside world thinks, and they are sensitive to the accusation that Chinese dance is always the same," they told me. One reported that he thought dance directors throughout China were hungry for change and would follow the leadership of the Guangdong company if they could. He chuckled conspiratorially when he told me he had seen Western influence in some traditional dance companies. He explained that during a period of openness in the 1970s some overseas Chinese artists had visited the mainland, and that a cadre of young Chinese choreographers who had seen the outsiders or video tapes they left were applying some Western theatrical devices.

With regard to the distrust, one for the other, that the dancers revealed and that I have mentioned earlier, I couldn't refrain from expressing my astonishment to Daniel. Ever philosophical, he quoted an ancient saying: "Chinese are like grains of sand on a plate; they can't stick together." He went on to explain at greater length that the extreme hardship of life in China, century after century, has created a people that, in order to survive, has had to devise intricate means for looking after their own welfare. Working collaboratively is not a strategy that has succeeded for them. Indeed, I had seen this in the studio from the second day. Cooperation became a subtext for some of the exercises

I devised, but that didn't work well; I found the dancers responded best to one-on-one attention from me and to projects in which one dancer had complete authority over others. However, I am straying again into that other story.

These revelations by the dancers about their relationship to the government and to each other brought home to me more than anything else the real dilemma of the ILP and of the dance historians' implied charge to chart the "influence of the US experience abroad." There exists a culture of the body and of the dance studio that can lull one into a belief in complete communication and understanding, but I realized through the dancers' words that they are responding to a culture outside the studio that is virtually incomprehensible to me, and perhaps to most Americans. In his article "Moving from the Inside Out: Modern Dance in Modern China," Roger Copeland described the effects that various freezes and thaws in China's international policy have had on the fortunes of the modern dance experiment.[1] I am innocent of high-level political acumen, but my observations of the dancers and their disclosures to me do lead me to wonder how the arts will use, or be used by, the nascent capitalism that is rampant in Guangdong Province.

The dancers of GMDC, and even cultural officials when they are showing off the company, have learned such phrases as "freedom to use the body in a new way," and "express oneself through dance," and repeat them easily for Western visitors. I found myself asking, after I had been in China for a number of weeks, whether those phrases, from the mouths of Chinese, had a meaning I could connect with. The questions I had pondered during my flight to China were joined by others, not only about the influence of American modern dance in Asia but about my own conceptions, as an American, of modern dance.

The proposition that dancers can be choreographers—"The goal was ... to give the young dancers the tools with which to create a Chinese modern dance language based on their own traditions and culture"—is time-tested in the US, where generation after generation of modern dance choreographers has emerged from companies of other choreographers, who emerged from companies of more senior choreographers. In China the jobs "dancer" and "choreographer" are distinct. Those who hold the latter title receive special training and certification; usually they are incapable of being dancers because of age, health, or ineptitude. Another aspect of American modern dance, an aspect that one can argue has been a curse as well as a blessing, is the room it makes for amateurs. It has been possible for young people with faith in their promise to support themselves as bartenders, word processors, or yoga instructors until grants materialize or full-time dance employment is secured. No extra-institutional art practice exists in China. All theater dancing is done within an institutional framework, and all dance institutions, most especially GMDC, must court government approval in a do-or-die scenario that is unknown to Americans even today.

1. Copeland, Roger (1989) "Moving from the Inside Out: Modern Dance in Modern China," *Dance Theater Journal,* Spring 1989, pp. 10-14.

The first clause of ILP's statement of goals, "not to impose American dance on Chinese bodies," has been honored in an important sense; when the dancers invent they do not borrow idiocyncratic gestures from any American techniques I could recognize. After watching them for a time, and after seeing some other dancing in China, I realized that the dancers were adapting movement from their training in what has come to be called traditional Chinese Dance. Modern dance has given the women permission to do some of the larger, stronger gestures, turns and elevations of the men, and both genders now use the floor much more than previously, I suspect.

How much of the GMDC repertory performed in China is by the dancers is not known to me. American teachers sent by ILP are under pressure from company administration to choreograph, and some do. The company has also invited work from other Americans, as well as from Australians, Canadians, Koreans, and perhaps others. In the eight weeks I was with them the dancers gave two performances. One (as mentioned previously) was all jazz dance, and for the other some modern dance choreographed by the dancers was programmed—partly at my urging, and in my honor, I suspect.

Clearly, ILP and the American agencies that fund it—Rockefeller Foundation, USIS, and the Asian Cultural Council—are sensitive to paternalistic intent. They wish not to transplant an American art form, but to transfer principles that will make possible a new synthesis. If one wishes to transfer principles of change, of renewability, where does one start? One starts in the bodies and hearts of a few of the youths who are capable. It is beyond my poor powers of imagining to predict what will be the aesthetic, to say nothing of the social, consequences of that.

Very recently we had news that GMDC has been recognized as an official company; official recognition was granted and an inaugural concert given on June 6, 1992. If with that recognition goes the establishment of modern dance as an official form, the professional future of the dancers of GMDC may be assured. If the individual who described a cadre of young choreographers ready for experimentation in revising the classical Chinese Dance is correct, there could be an explosion of change in the Chinese dance world.

My mind flies back to one particular lunchtime interview; it was with one of the women especially struck with the variety in the ADF faculty concert. "The danger," she said, "is that modern dance in China will become stereotyped." She described Chinese folk dance as colorful, energetic, and varied; but, she claimed, "When it reaches the stage it becomes stereotyped." Perhaps to that observant dancer, and perhaps to American audiences as well, modern dance in China will seem stereotyped, but it will be achieving its own identity, and evolving with the political, social, aesthetic, and moral structure of a unique culture. Just like in the USA.

Chapter Six:

A Lifetime in Dance, A Moment in Guangzhou

An Interview with Lucas Hoving

Lucas Hoving began dancing in the '30s in his native Holland and went on to work with many of modern dance's pioneers—Kurt Jooss, Rudolf Laban, Agnes de Mille and Martha Graham among them. Today he teaches around the globe and presents a solo concert, Growing Up In Public—An Evening With Lucas Hoving, *in theaters and colleges nation-wide.*

It was in a New York ballet class that Mr. Hoving first met José Limón, and in 1948 formed their now-famous partnership, a duo that changed the character of men's roles in modern dance. Between engagements with the Limón company Hoving and his wife, the dancer Lavina Nielson, toured the country in a duet program.

In the early '60s Mr. Hoving directed opera at the Peabody Institute in Baltimore and formed the Lucas Hoving Dance Company, which performed home seasons in New York and toured internationally for a decade. In 1971, by invitation of the Dutch government, he returned to Holland to reorganize dance education in that country.

Mr. Hoving has taught in Europe, North and South America, and in Asia. He has been the recipient of numerous grants and awards, including several from the National Endowment for the Arts. He now teaches and choreographs both in San Francisco, where he has lived since 1981, and abroad.

Editors: Had you been given any directions concerning what you were to teach before you went to Guangzhou?

Lucas Hoving: No. When I got there and saw the students in a class I couldn't believe it. The technique! Their bodies are a little different from our Western bodies, so it looks a little different, but I immediately realized they had all the technique they needed. So I taught only composition and improvisation. I got the impression this was a little new to them.

E: How long were you there?

LH: Three months.

E: Was this your first experience teaching in that part of the world?

LH: Well, I had taught some master classes. We [the Limón Company] toured there in 1962—in Japan and Korea and Cambodia.

E: Had you talked to any of the teachers who preceded you in Guangzhou? Did you know what you were getting into?

LH: I hadn't talked to anyone, but I felt I had some understanding because of the earlier teaching experience. It was really rather easy, you know, because I had also taught all over Europe and in South America. Oh, I loved it; I absolutely loved it.

E: What we want to know in some detail, of course, is just exactly what it is you "loved."

LH: Well, I love Asian people. My wife (who died some years ago) lived in Japan for several years, and became a Zen Buddhist. She went back to Asia frequently. Also, in Holland, where I grew up, there were lots of Indonesian people (Indonesia was a Dutch colony) so I thought I knew something about the Asian way of thinking. It was not entirely foreign to me.

E: Just in a practical sense, how did you find the living in Guangzhou?

LH: Well, I lived in a college dorm, in a faculty flat on the top floor, and it was quite adequate. The food was a bit dreary—"college food," more primitive than the Chinese food here—but I could always shop for things to supplement it. I had a beautiful time.

E: You had no problem with communication?

LH: Well yes, that's always hard. But I had a nice interpreter, though she was not a dancer. She would also accompany me on some social occasions.

E: What was your schedule like?

LH: I taught two classes a day; I find it hard now to do more than that. I would warm the students up, do some improvisation, and then we choreographed. And they choreographed beautiful pieces. The morning class was an hour and a half, and then in the afternoon it was two hours and on for as long as we felt we needed.

E: You said you did mostly improvisation with the students. Did you feel they had much prior experience with that?

LH: I really don't know. The men were especially slow to join in. They would just sort of sit along the wall and watch. Then gradually they did come in, all except one who remained apart almost to the very end. But you know, when I was preparing to leave, he is the one who wept. He was very much moved by my leaving. There were maybe only about 6 men and 20 women, and I don't remember being so impressed with the men. I think they have trouble getting men into the program there, although they have a wonderful set-up. They even get paid while they are in training.

E: You found the women to be more interesting. How would you describe the difference?

LH: It was as though they were more aware of themselves—free-er—more talented as movers; more sophisticated. They felt much more free to visit me, to invite me to do things with them, to bring their friends and relatives to meet me. And then we would go shopping together for fruits and vegetables in the stalls in the street next to the studio.

E: What do you think was the problem with the men?

LH: I suppose what I was doing was too private for them. They were afraid of exposing too much. You know, it's a different kind of living there; the people are different. Americans are very open, very much more willing to expose themselves, even as compared to Europeans. There is an encouragement of self-examination, of self-awareness.

E: And there was a reluctance to do that kind of thing in China?

LH: Yes: to show their doubts, their fears.

E: Were you able to find things that helped them to do that?

LH: I suppose so. You see the Jooss-Laban school that I come from had techniques for that. We had dance technique of course, but then we also had "choreutics," and all the space things, and then "eukinetics"; those were the really expressive, "quality" things—the moving centrally, peripherally, strong, soft, round, angularly. Marvelous, marvelous; there's really never been anything like it.

E: So you tried to teach from that base in China. Could they respond, because that's rather complex?

LH: Yes, well I would encourage them to go into those things that were not easy for them. Why do they shy away from certain things? Essentially, why do they move the way they do?

E: So you challenged them to explore the unfamiliar.

LH: Oh yes.

E: And how did they do?

LH: Some better than others. I would give them an assignment, and if that happened to be one of the things they shied away from, it was their job to dig into it, to understand it. But the language is a terrible barrier, even if you have a good interpreter. Some of the things I did really freaked them out.

E: Such as?

LH: Well, I use sound. I would have them speak, and of course they spoke in Chinese. So I would have to try to understand their body language. We made progress, but it was very slow. I'm always after the answer to those questions:"Who am I?" "What am I?" In ballet and even in some modern dance techniques such questions don't come into the picture. I keep after them, and I'm not afraid to expose myself to the students. Of course I don't touch everyone. It was very interesting for me, bringing them my totally European based ideas, to see what we could share. I think some of the students were really touched. Dancers have, after all, a way of communicating. I looked into their faces and I thought "they're open; they're right."

E: What do you think they wanted from you as a teacher?

LH: They don't really know what they hope to get out of it. They are just there to get what they can, unlike American dancers, who very much know what they want and are quite judgmental. When I first arrived in Guangzhou I came into the studio and the students were taking class. I sat in the back to watch. When the class was finished they wandered over and sat around me; we talked and just tried to discover one-another. Afterward, there were other occasions to do this kind of thing. For example, six of the male students lived together in a room in the dorm with me—a very spartan life—just some bunk beds by the walls, and a little camp stove in the middle of the room, and that's where they lived and ate.

E: You didn't find them at all distrustful of you, representing a way of life and a dance form that is very much not Chinese?

LH: No, not at all. I never felt that. I only found them open and eager.

E: Were you at all aware of the political situation? Were your relations with the students at all influenced by politics?

LH: No. The thing in Beijing happened while I was there, but that came over the TV as though nothing had happened. I would try to find out more, but I never got anywhere.

E: But you didn't ever feel there was anything you couldn't do or say, because you were in China?

LH: No, nothing I was aware of. I maybe shocked them sometimes, by being outspoken, about sexual matters or whatever. At one point I asked the interpreter, who lived in town, to bring me some books of Western art from the library. There was one book of the surrealists that the students were really taken with. They had never seen anything like that before.

E: Was there any discussion of what you had chosen to teach them? When it became apparent, for example, that you weren't going to teach them technique, did they express any surprise or disappointment?

LH: Well, I did teach some technique, I suppose, but it is the kind of technique that has to do with sensitizing them to movement, not with making them stronger or helping them to raise their legs higher. I have always loved teaching; it's always been a give and take—and especially when you teach improvisation. Teaching technique is a different story. But I like to create a thing in which you never know where you will end up.

E: So you taught them essentially what you would have taught a class, say, in California?

LH: Yes, though of course the Americans are more familiar with the material. To the Chinese it was quite foreign. It was quite foreign to me too when I first encountered it through Jooss and people like Gertrude Heller. I remember coming into the studio expecting to dance, and instead we were made to stand on poles, and having to learn to "give in" to that so it didn't hurt our feet. Sensitizing the body. It's a form of meditation.

E: Do you think the Chinese students, coming from a culture with an established tradition in meditation, might have been particularly receptive to that aspect of the work?

LH: Well, they come to it in a different way. For them there is nothing analytic about it; it's just there. They don't know where it came from.

E: Given the impediments to understanding, to learning, that you have mentioned—the language barrier, the cultural differences, etc.—do you think this idea of trying to teach Western dance to Easterners is worthwhile?

LH: Well, I think it's always good to know about other cultures. For me it's terribly important to know the East.

E: What did you learn there?

LH: Many things. How different we are. But that's always the way it is when you make that kind of journey. We are always having to deal with one another's differences. I remember one time in China I was eating at a big round table the way they do there and I glanced over at the man across the way just as he spat a mouthful of food out right on the table. I turned to the man next to me to say something like "Did you see what he did?" and he was doing the same thing! I realized I wanted to do that too—sometimes when you are eating the vegetables there you come across stuff that you just can't swallow—but of course it wasn't easy for me. It's a different world. One is always coming up against the unexpected.

E: Yes. Speaking of pursuing such questions as "Who am I" through dance, I have noticed among Asian students I have taught, especially in Japan, an inclination to simply mimic what I do. They seem not to want to be individualistic or to do anything that is unexpected. It seems to me that what your approach asks of them is specifically that they "do their own thing." Have you experienced the resistance I describe?

LH: Asian students learn through copying. The subtle little things—the use of hands and such—they learn by imitation, by repetition. It is hard to get at their individuality.

E: And what did you do to try to overcome that?

LH: I'm very much a product of Louis Horst. What he did with *Modern Dance Forms*, especially the psychological component—what he got from Freud about going into the unconscious, the search for self—when I understood what Louis wanted, it was one of the most crucial awakenings of my life. For me everything that Louis did led up to that.

E: And that's what you tried to get at with the students in China?

LH: Yes, because they were so bound by form. That's what Louis was about: go into your subconscious; don't think anymore, let it come out. That is what the dance "forms" are about, and that is how you get beyond the forms.

E: And it's that kind of experience that lies at the core of modern dance?

LH: Yes, I feel that. I learned that in part from Martha Graham, even before I worked with Louis. I was a member of the Graham company for a while. Did you know that? Few people do. I remember Graham was working in class with us one day. She got up from her chair and came and stood behind me—we were doing some sort of repetitive movement—and she said "Now Lucas, all of your ancestors are standing here today, watching you." I tell you, that freaked me out!

E: She knew intuitively how to get to you?

LH: Yes. A great lady! That, to me, is the essence of real teaching, helping someone to open up like that.

E: Did José Limón have that ability?

LH: Oh no. José had terrible trouble expressing himself. He could write beautifully, but he really wasn't very articulate verbally. What I got from José I got by imitating him. There wasn't any psychological component with José; you learned from him physically.

E: And were you able to help your Chinese students reach this deeper level of understanding?

LH: Yes, I think so. Using sound is helpful in that. I always ask my students to connect the movement we do with voice—to sound the movement. I think this helps them to get in touch with the movement and with the self.

Chapter Seven:
Lasting Impressions

Douglas Nielsen

> *Douglas Nielsen studied dance at the California Institute of the Arts under the direction of Donald McKayle and Bella Lewitzky before moving to New York City where he has based his professional career since 1973. A former member of the Gus Solomons, Pearl Lang and Paul Sanasardo dance companies, he has also performed with Betty Jones, Albert Reid and Jeff Slayton, and as a soloist in works by Viola Farber, Beverly Blossom, Anna Sokolow, Murray Louis, and Charles Weidman. His own choreography has been produced in Australia, Canada, China, England, France, Israel, Scotland and throughout the United States. Mr. Nielsen is also known for his professional association with numerous university dance departments, most recently at the University of Arizona. He has received four fellowships from the National Endowment for the Arts, among other awards. The American Dance Festival's Institutional Linkages Program made him its third representative to China in 1988, and first to Czechoslovakia in 1991.*

In the months leading up to my departure for Guangzhou I had become much preoccupied with such matters as getting a parking space close to my office at the university. I am ashamed to admit that after being in China.

I didn't pack until the very last minute. I telephoned the two teachers in New York who had preceded me, and listened to their stories. My experience turned out to be nothing like theirs.

I entered China through Hong Kong, which is a city absolutely mad about money. Everyone in Hong Kong looked as if they were either exchanging currency or thinking about it. Hong Kong reminded me of no other place I have ever been, not even closely comparable to New York City. Innumerable people walked the streets holding cellular telephones to their ears, assuming the attitude of either buying or selling stocks. I didn't understand the implied urgency.

The three hour train ride into China was a trip backward in time (I literally sat in a seat facing opposite the direction the train was going). My first impression of

Guangzhou was bicycles: a bicycle with a big basket of live ducks or a boiled dog, followed by another with a television set fastened over the back wheel. It was all contradictory, a Third World country modernizing for the 21st century.

I have never received a more gracious welcome than that which greeted my arrival in Guangzhou. My appointed interpreter was at the train station along with the academic supervisors from the dance academy, holding a sign with my name on it. I learned later that it took them more than two hours to receive the required clearance to actually meet me in the greeting area inside the depot. Other Chinese were packed behind a fence, straining to catch a glimpse of a relative or friend. A van took us to the academy where all the students were standing outside in the courtyard, waiting patiently as if they had been there for hours, all smiles, waving their arms.

I had a small fourth floor walk-up apartment in a six-story concrete housing complex. From the minute I arrived my height was a topic of conversation. The very first thing they did was have me lie down on the floor next to my bed to measure me, and then the bed. I told them that I don't normally sleep flat out with my arms stretched over my head, but they insisted on making me comfortable. Carpenters were called in, and in a very short time they custom designed a seven foot bed.

My main meals were delivered "hot" to my door from the central kitchen. Imagine, Chinese take-out three times a day! I ate enough rice to satisfy a lifetime need. I had brought along a huge container of Skippy crunchy peanut butter—the industrial size you can buy at the Price Club. I rationed it to last exactly three months, and ate it every day.

The dancers and I worked six days a week (Sundays free), four hours a day, starting at 8:00 am. Every other afternoon I would go into the city either by bus or taxi. The bus cost four cents US and was always packed. I never got a seat and standing was impossible because of my height, so like a giraffe on Noah's ark I would stand where I could stick my head through one of those air vents in the roof of the bus. That way I could see where I was going. It always got laughs and stares; I got used to being stared at in China.

Guangzhou is a very crowded city of over five million people, with some of the worst traffic conditions I have ever seen. New York City is the Emerald City of Oz compared to the congestion of Guangzhou, and the honking is insufferable. It is not unusual to ride in a taxi with the driver honking constantly, in a two-beep mode, from the moment you get in to the moment you get out.

On my first free Sunday I went to Conghua hot springs resort about 50 miles north of Guangzhou. The academy arranged for a driver and private car; it took two hours of non-stop honking before we arrived. On the return trip we passed the usual water buffalo, pedestrians, carts and bicycles on the road, but got caught behind a convoy of a dozen or so big trucks. This was on a two-lane road where passing was suicidal, but my driver couldn't help taking both our lives in his hands by passing the trucks one by one, squeezing back among the convoy always just in time to avoid a head-on collision. Finally, he managed to pass every truck (13, I counted), and without thinking I yelled out in English "Congratulations, you did it!" That startled the driver so much he pulled the car to a stop, jumped out, and opened my door, thinking, no doubt, I wanted to see or do something (he didn't speak a word of English). My heart sank as all 13 trucks passed by. I had to improvise the worst pantomime imaginable to get him back in the car to resume the ride home. I sat with my mouth shut for the rest of the trip, which did indeed include passing all the trucks a second time.

In China all foreigners are usually referred to as Westerners. Considering the flood of tourism in China since the "open door policy," I saw surprisingly few Americans. I was rarely in the parts of town that attract tourists. The dance academy is at the northeast corner of Guangzhou, and the closest tourist attraction is the zoo. I spent one afternoon studying the delicate way the Panda Bear at the zoo ate bamboo, also noticing bus loads of tourists arriving, taking pictures, and disappearing in a matter of minutes. The Panda was obviously a check point on the Westerners' itinerary; I thought it was a pity they could never afford the time to digest what they saw.

The dancers came from cities in Northern China, and were hand-picked from existing traditional and classical dance companies. They were sent to Guangzhou to learn about modern dance—a total of 20, ten men and ten women, ranging in age from 18 to 30, all with strong ballet and Chinese "traditional" dance backgrounds. Some of the men had martial arts training as well. There was always the pending threat that their hometown dance companies would call them back, and that did sometimes happen. None of the dancers spoke English. Being from the North, they spoke Mandarin Chinese; Guangzhou Province speaks Cantonese. My interpreter, Huang Yu-ping, a native of Guangzhou, spoke Cantonese, and therefore had to translate from Mandarin to Cantonese to English.

Fortunately, dance embodies elements of a universal language, at least in so far as body language is more direct than words. When teaching dance, words can get in the way; they can diminish or trivialize an idea. So I felt it was an advantage that I couldn't speak a word of Chinese when I arrived in China. I had Yu-ping by my side constantly, but once I had learned to count and give directions in Chinese I no longer used her in technique class, relying on her only in rehearsals and composition classes, where the teaching was more conceptual. After three months I had grown both to resent and depend upon her. Sometimes I was obviously misunderstood through translation, and sometimes Yu-ping would answer questions I had asked the others without translating what I said. I had to tell her I wasn't talking to her but to them, and it was important that they know what I asked so they would understand my logic and how I was thinking. In a positive way, however, because of the language barrier the dancers paid more attention to how I moved, seeing details far faster than my American students.

In another instance words became useful as a way of adding focus. The assignments I gave in composition ranged from specific limitations to very broad and open structures. It was especially difficult for the dancers to work without music, creating from their own individuality. For instance, I asked them to make a solo in silence without locomotion. They could change levels and directional facings, and explore infinite gestures, but could not move away from one established location. When they showed me their work it was very disappointing: stiff and mechanical, completely devoid of any human quality. I asked them if they were robots; I told them they looked like wind-up toys. The next day I asked them to speak while they danced—to try to give their dancing more dimension, rather than just working mechanically. They were initially distrustful, as though I were trying to trick them, but when the first dancer stepped forward and told a true story about himself while he moved, he clearly performed with more concentration than ever before. While he danced, this is what he said: When he was younger, he and several friends entered an old woman's house and berated her for owning a gold fish. They ordered her to get rid of it, as the Red Guards might have done. He told her raising gold fish was selfish and a politically wrong thing to do. Then he said that when he went home and told his mother what he had done she gave him a good beating. Now, the fact that all of this was totally unrelated to his movement was not a problem. Everyone could see how it changed his performance and gave his dance the irony it lacked before. I sat stunned by the story.

While there I read a lot of wonderful little Chinese fables. One concerned a tiger and a centipede. The tiger asks the centipede, "A hundred legs, how on earth do you walk?" The centipede stopped to think ... and then couldn't walk. That is exactly the philosophy I used while teaching dance in China. I would say "if you stop and think too much you'll freeze." The challenge was to keep working day after day in a process that didn't analyze or paralyze.

The Chinese video taped, notated, or recorded most of what I did or said during the training sessions. I found out toward the end of my residency that the dancers had committed most of my classroom choreography to memory. When I asked them how many phrases they had learned, they said about two hundred. I asked them how many characters there are in the Chinese language; they laughed and said perhaps three to five thousand. I said the same is true of dance, and the ways of putting movement together are infinite. I told them I didn't want them to learn my class by rote. Very often they would say "What is the law?" and I'd simply say "there is no law. I just made it up." This seemed to astound them.

For three months the most asked question, especially by the journalists, was "What is modern dance?" Under the circumstances, that proved to be the hardest thing of all to answer. If dance is truly modern then it is contemporary, and that means it is current and changing. How do you define something so continually creative to a group of people whose traditional culture does not encourage critical thinking or individual freedom?

Abstraction was another difficult thing to teach; having a message without a story doesn't make sense to a lot of people. Basically, if something I said didn't make sense to the Chinese I assumed I was on the right track, because then it was unlike anything else they knew (most people see/understand things only in association or comparison to something they already know). I was teaching the Chinese to do a most uncomfortable thing. I was teaching them to get lost, and, in so doing, to open themselves to a new way of discovery: learning by doing.

One of my most influential teachers in America, Viola Farber, once told me that a good teacher should eventually become unnecessary. When I teach, no matter where, I teach with that in mind. Assuming that I am passing on everything I know, a good student will take what is offered, make it his or her own, and move on. Each generation should surpass the one before, apprentices becoming better than the master. In Chinese culture this concept is carried to extremes, through laborious repetition. The Chinese love to imitate; they have a super respect for the "master teacher," and typically learn through apprenticeship. I have been told that in visual arts the student reproduces the same painting of the master over and over, not daring for years to create a self-generated image. In dance I tried to engender a spark of creativity right from the beginning, promoting individuality, eliminating the fear of showing disrespect to me by being original.

Almost always the dancers I worked with were more than willing to please. Many times I was aware that what they were feeling and what they were saying were two different things. It was only my instincts that told me this; rarely did I have proof. Then one day during the final rehearsal of a duet I made for a man and a woman, *Two Cats: A Dialogue*, the costume designer came in with a hat for the man to wear. He had never rehearsed with the hat before, but, without hesitation, he did a run-through

Figure 8 Douglas Nielsen rehearsing dancers at the Guangdong Dance Academy

with it on. While he danced I could see he was wincing with pain. I tried to stop him but he wouldn't let me. Finally, when the dance ended, he took off the hat and blood trickled down his forehead. The hat was made with wire inside, a thing of beauty, but literally a crown of thorns. I was amazed and dumbfounded by the dancer's dedication. It came to me that very rarely did any of the dancers admit they were hurt or sick; they considered it a weakness to be hidden. By contrast, in America today more often than not dance students wear their discomforts like a badge. Injuries are quickly admitted to and given precedence to the work. I identified with the Chinese, and remembered never confessing to an ache or pain for fear of losing my part to some other dancer.

Working in Taiwan was quite different from mainland China. Whereas in China the dancers only had a background of ballet and traditional Chinese Dance, in Taiwan there is a modern dance tradition that has been rooted in the Martha Graham technique for many years. Most dancers are introduced to it at a very young age. However, even this did not really prepare them for my way of working. I don't teach dance by rote. I believe things learned that way are not necessarily understood, and are very difficult to apply. I use a conversational approach to dancing, and a vertical technique that is influenced by Merce Cunningham. It travels; it changes directions and facings, and it is not codified in a way that can be memorized. In Taiwan, as in China, the dancers could easily repeat any phrase I gave them. To make sure they really understood the principles behind a phrase, I changed the sequence every day—even though they had worked very hard at perfecting it exactly the way it was done the day before.

This method of variation is what I mean by "conversational dancing": perhaps saying the same thing from one day to the next, but not in the identical sequence. As I invent new phrases of movement, each related to the previous one but with its own identity, I inevitably see that what begins as frustrating becomes exciting for the students. This seemed especially important for the students I taught in Taiwan and China. If ever contemporary dance in the Orient is going to develop with its own identity, and not just be a Western transplant, the dancers there must learn to think for themselves, and not shy away from both the responsibility and freedom that accompanies it.

There were many contradictions in the culture of China as I saw it, revealed in ways not always expected. In *Gazing at Flowers on Horseback*, a dance I choreographed for nine pairs of men and women, there was a very pivotal moment in which the women lifted the men. During our first "open rehearsal," when journalists were invited to attend, this particular moment was greeted with dismay, and afterwards I was asked why I did it. I answered their question with a question: "In a country that believes in Mao Ze-dong's words, 'Women should hold up half the sky,' why shouldn't a woman hold up a man?" This logic was not wholly appreciated.

I performed twice while in China. I believe my work was well received, but it was difficult to judge. The Chinese don't clap a lot; someone pointed out that the

Figure 9 Douglas Nielsen rehearsing dancers at the Guangdong Dance Academy

audience was quiet, and that was a compliment. I went to another dance performance in Guangzhou where the audience was anything but quiet; they talked throughout the entire program, and even read newspapers during the show. Thankfully that didn't happen when I danced. One thing did happen that is apparently quite common in China; our performance dates were changed with very short notice, and no explanation. I can only guess that this was to accommodate "the leaders."

One last impression: I was encouraged to take a week off, fly to Beijing, and see the Great Wall, which I gladly did. When I returned to Guangzhou I found the academy next door had built its own wall blocking the windows of the modern dance studio where I taught. This new red brick wall was built practically overnight. There it stood, preventing the traditional dance students from watching my classes from the balconies of their building as they had been doing. I suddenly felt that China may not yet have learned about the negative effect a wall, big or small, can have on the people on both sides. I remembered reading a Chinese maxim that says "A flower blooming is not really blooming unless it is seen." I thought of the million flowers blooming in China behind a wall somewhere, and wondered if they might wilt before they are perceived.

Chapter Eight:
Chinese/Japanese Roots and Branches

An Interview with Ruby Shang

*Born in Tokyo, **Ruby Shang** began studying ballet at the age of five. She came to the United States to attend Brown University, where she received a B.A. in art history. Upon graduation Ms. Shang joined the Paul Taylor Dance Company, where she was a featured dancer from 1971-75.*

After serving for two seasons as co-director of the Dance Hawaii Company, she turned to presenting her own work and, in 1978, formed Ruby Shang and Company, Dancers, based in New York. The company has performed frequently in New York venues, and also abroad in Japan, France, and London. For the last decade Ms. Shang's work has focused on site-specific events conceived to celebrate people, places and occasions. Ms. Shang is on the faculty of The Juilliard School, and has taught in mainland China under the auspices of the American Dance Festival. Her numerous awards and honors include Choreographer Fellowships from the National Endowment for the Arts, a Fulbright-Hayes Cultural Award, Metropolitan Life Emerging Artist grants for creativity and innovation, and an AT & T Theater and Dance Project grant for originality.

Editors: In how many Pacific Rim countries have you taught?

Ruby Shang: Only China (Guangzhou), Japan, and briefly in Hong Kong.

E: For whom did you teach in Japan?

RS: I did three of the ADF summer sessions, and I was there intermittently on my own too, once on a grant from the Asian Cultural Council. Also, I grew up there, my family is there, so it's "going home" for me.

E: I thought you were Chinese.

RS: My father was Chinese, but my mother is Japanese and I grew up in Tokyo. I speak fluent Japanese. That's one of the reasons ADF wanted me there, to translate for Charles [Reinhart]. So I was there early on, and I did a lot on my own.

E: When you went under the auspices of the ACC, what did you propose to them?

RS: I wanted to do some site-specific work in public spaces. I did a piece in a long, narrow hallway at one of the Seibu department stores, and in Studio 200, also at Seibu. That must have been in 1984. I also returned to China then (I had been there for the first time in 1980) and traveled all over with my mother. Then, in 1988, I went to Guangzhou.

E: Having grown up in Japan, you must have started dancing there.

RS: I started studying ballet at age five.

E: And how old were you when you left Japan?

RS: I came to the States to go to college [at Brown University] when I was 18.

E: Your training in Japan was exclusively in ballet?

RS: Yes. I had never even seen any modern dance until my senior year in high school, when the Paul Taylor Company came through [1967-68].

E: I asked about your dance training in Japan to see if your early dance experience in the US represented "cross-cultural" training for you. It sounds as if it did not; your roots were strictly Western.

RS: Yes, I suppose my first real cross-cultural experience was with *Butoh*. When Charles and Stephanie Reinhart invited Dairakudakan to this country, they asked me to be their manager. That's when I got to know Akaji Maro. I just fell in love with him and his work. I did a piece with him and Bill T. Jones here in New York, which we later took to Japan and London. I wasn't crazy about the traditional Japanese dance forms; they seemed too formal to me. In *Butoh* I saw something that had an emotional resonance. It caught my imagination. I liked the physicality of it, the gravity, the groundedness.

E: You said you responded quickly to the modern dance you saw when you came here.

RS: Yes. I thought it was so much more interesting than the classical dance I was used to. It too was more grounded, more concerned with feelings and less with pure form. I remember knowing early on that I would never become a ballerina. It just felt too silly to be a bird, or a doll, or whatever. Modern dance made me feel that I could be a person and still be a part of an art form. In modern dance you don't have to pretend to be some other thing.

E: We might imagine that your reaction reflects the general appeal of modern for dancers in countries like Japan.

RS: Absolutely. There is very little access to the arts for the young person in Japan—other than the traditional Japanese art forms like the tea ceremony, which are *de rigeur* for Japanese children. Ballet and piano lessons might fall into that same package for the well brought up Japanese child, but that's about it.

E: It seems a bit strange that your Japanese acculturation included a Western art form, ballet, but perhaps that was because you showed no interest in Japanese dance forms.

RS: Also, because my father was Chinese we were already not traditional. I was a foreigner. I didn't really feel like a Japanese growing up; I even went to an American school.

E: Let's talk about your teaching experience in Japan first. Do you remember having done anything special to prepare yourself for that?

RS: I improvise a lot in my classes; I hardly ever prepare a class. I find that I can prepare a phrase or something like that, but then the level of the students turns out to be different than I expected. It doesn't work, so I give it up. I have a wide repertory of things that I can pick up and throw together. So I really don't remember preparing for the Japanese classes in any way that was different. What *did* happen was that I had to give material faster than I ever had before. They were so quick!

E: What you taught was technique?

RS: In the beginning, the early '80s, I always taught technique. Within the decade I gradually shifted to improvisation. I taught both intermediate and advanced classes for ADF, and they were much faster than my classes at either Juilliard or NYU. I would sometimes pack in a class and a half worth of material. At least on a surface performance level those students were so adept at interpreting the material! It was a different story when it came to improvisation and composition.

E: So that facility didn't necessarily carry over?

RS: Right. Theirs was a strictly technical facility, at lightening speed. When we got to improv and comp they were extremely inhibited. That was like pulling teeth.

E: Did you get the impression they were "inhibited" because this was something they hadn't done before, or was it some sort of cultural inhibition?

RS: I think it's both. There is definitely cultural inhibition, though it's getting better; the classes I taught toward the end of the '80s were much easier and more open than the earlier ones. I saw a great change over ten years. Considering the society and the culture, I thought they made great strides. I saw the students developing and opening up emotionally, psychologically. In the beginning it was like little Japanese dolls; it was very hard to get anything out of the students.

E: In an improvisation situation, where they worked together, were the students reticent to address one another?

RS: Yes. I think one of the most difficult things about improv for them was the releasing of weight. In the technique class I would say "Okay, you must do this fall this way," and they would learn it. However, that didn't mean they could release the weight throughout, across the board. So once we got to improv, where they really had to contact one another and give in and trust, it didn't work.

E: Is it the concept of the thing that they didn't understand? They could understand it if you showed it to them *in a particular movement*, but not the concept of weight shift as we commonly deal with it?

RS: Yes, and I think not to have a structure—just to feel one another's weight— was embarrassing to them. They felt not exactly humiliated, but just awkward and embarrassed because, having no precedent, they didn't know what to do. The culture is built on precedent; one generation does what the generation before it did. There are no ambiguities; improv was a whole class of ambiguities. They weren't equipped psychologically to deal with so many choices, to just explore a situation in which there is no right or wrong. That culture says there is only one way to do anything, so it was very hard for them.

E: What happened when they applied that to making their own phrases or dances?

RS: It tended to be derivative of things they had done in class.

E: Can we now compare these observations with what you found when you went to Guangzhou in '88? What did you teach there?

RS: I taught everything. We started with technique from about 8:00 to 10:30, and then went on to improv and composition. They loved to improvise, to just throw themselves around. They, too, had the problem with weight, not really being able to release because of their classical training. They are so held, but they are so advanced technically that they could really learn to fall. Later, I would help them rehearse their own work. They would do beautifully textured little things, based on the traditional forms, but completely modernized. They are inventive—the women, especially, I thought were just terrific—but they have trouble translating from improv to comp, and they are surprisingly undisciplined.

E: How do you explain this lack of discipline?

RS: Maybe it's because it is such a huge country with so many people. These dancers are really an elite; they're in the top one percent of the population in many respects. True, they only get the equivalent of US $60 a month, but they get to travel, they are given accommodations and taken care of. They're set for life. They really don't have to do anything except dance; that's all they have trained for since the age of 11 or so. I think that breeds a certain complacency. Even after they stop performing they will still choreograph or teach, or be part of a large song and dance ensemble, or something like that. I think there is more of a place for the artist in China than here.

E: They are taken care of for life, so they may not have to do your choreographic assignment!

RS: That's right, they don't have to. Nothing will happen to them. So what if I don't think they're working hard!

E: Whereas the Japanese would probably do it out of some...

RS: Well, they're so driven!

E: It would be an embarrassment to them not to do it.

RS: Yes, basically everything still comes from "the way of the sword"; *bushido* is so important there. So for a student not to complete an assignment is totally unbearable. They would "lose face"; in former days they would have to commit *hara kiri*. The Chinese just don't have the way of the samurai to live up to.

E: In terms of goals, what do you think the students in China and in Japan want to do with dance?

RS: Well, in Guangzhou I think they want to become a functioning modern dance company, and tour, and build their reputation. They are entering a lot of competitions, and that's part of their desire to become better known. Also, of course, they both need and want to raise some money.

E: Is there much *esprit de corps*?

RS: One thing about the Chinese is that they love to gossip; there's always a lot of back-biting going on. I noticed that a lot when I was in Guangzhou; not that they were necessarily talking about me behind my back, but they would talk about each other. There was constant finger pointing—Yang Mei-qi is this, and Mr. Mah (one of the other administrators) was that, and did you know they were fighting—that kind of thing. I thought "Oh my God, this is what I have always disliked about the Chinese, and you have to remind me!"

E: Beyond that, do the members of the Guangdong Company have a sense of the need to promote the company's well-being?

RS: Yes, I think that translates through their desire to go abroad. The one thing the Chinese are united in is the desire to get out of China. They are very intent on going other places, because they are so restricted in their lives. So I think their interest in the company stems from their desire to travel.

E: I remember Lucas Hoving telling us that there was a lot of competition among the boys.

RS: Yes, they're very competitive, and there are lots of cliques—this little faction won't talk to that one.

E: And they have to live so close together!

RS: Oh yes. I felt so badly about the fact that their dormitories had no heat, and they were taking cold showers, and washing their clothes in cold water. So I went to the Friendship Store and bought them electric heaters. That created the greatest controversy and furor, because the students were so thrilled— now they could warm up their hands and bodies, and dry their tights—and then the staff confiscated the heaters because the school didn't have enough wattage to run them.

E: When we were there they were taking class in their coats, sweaters, hats and gloves. It was really cold in those studios. Did you find it terribly uncomfortable living there?

Chapter Nine:
Faces in the Moon

Sarah Stackhouse

Sarah Stackhouse danced with the José Limón Dance Company for many years as a soloist and partner to Mr. Limón. In addition she has performed with the Alvin Ailey Dance Theater, the Louis Falco Company, The Workgroup of Daniel Nagrin, Annabelle Gamson Dance Solos, Inc., and has made guest appearances with the Viola Farber Company and Bill Cratty and Dancers. Ms. Stackhouse has taught at The Juilliard School, the American Dance Festival, and has given guest residencies in the United States, Europe, and Asia. Currently she is an Associate Professor of Dance at SUNY-Purchase, where she teaches technique, choreography and improvisation, reconstructs works of José Limón, and choreographs her own work. She was sent by the American Dance Festival to open its cooperative modern dance program with the Guangdong Dance Academy in the People's Republic of China, and has since returned to the Orient for residencies at the Hong Kong, Guangdong, and Beijing Academies of Dance.

"Three months? Charles, that's a long time!"

But I accepted Charles Reinhart's invitation to go to the Guangdong Dance Academy because the thrill of being the first American teacher to approach a new group of dancers just embarking on the study of modern dance was too great to resist. Imagine, teaching students not already full of preconceptions!

Then I began to consider the implications of my decision. Would I be involved in "cultural imperialism"? Probably not, as the invitation actually originated with Yang Mei-qi, director of the Guangdong Dance Academy. She had determined to create a modern dance program in China after having seen modern dance at ADF. Would I be doing "missionary work"? No. I think of art, dance in particular, as one of the few sane, healthy, intelligent, and ethical activities in which human beings can be involved. I have no dogmas or gods, no rights or wrongs, in dancing.

What to teach? I was told by well-meaning people with experience in China that "the Chinese students can do anything technically, but don't ask them to be twins, Zhang Li and Zhang Yi, apart. She told me all of the "English names" ("to make it easier for westerners"), but I wanted to try to manage their real names, so she drilled me on the proper sounds. It didn't seem so hard.

The festival celebration, for the modern dance students and all of those who were connected with the program, was very spare and simple. There were bare tables outside on the cement court, under the moon, with paper napkins for plates and Chinese sweets. I felt so much a part of that group and that place already. The anticipation was great. My emotions were high, and I realized the students' were too. This was the first time away from home for most of them. They told me the story of the festival. It involves a moon woman who comes to earth and falls in love, but then must leave her love and return to the moon. So, if you look at the moon and the person you miss does too, no matter where, you will see each other's face. For all of us, new to each other and far from our homes, that evening was the beginning of a powerful bond.

I loved the huge wood-floored studio, with wood-frame windows that opened to let in plenty of fresh air and light. I was overjoyed that there was no air conditioning or artificial light turned on all day long—none of that harshness of angle or slickness of atmosphere to which modern architecture consigns us. The studio was unassuming, with simple proportions that afforded the human body a comfortable setting. Even with the windows closed for the night, the floor was covered each morning with a layer of dust, which the students swept with little mops. Since I couldn't find a pushbroom in Guangzhou except in the hotels where they were not for sale, some of the students and I had fun inventing one by lashing several mops together with bamboo stays.

My first morning in Guangzhou I was up before the sun, awakened by the mosquitoes and the seemingly incessant hammering that went on in the construction of a series of new apartment buildings next door. I set out for a walk, hoping to discover the local exercise place. I walked along the mostly dirt road under the twisted trunks of shaggy barked eucalyptus-type trees, and was grateful to be on the outskirts of the city. It felt like a small town. The Academy is in a compound, partly walled off from the main roads. Within the walls there is also a sports academy and a "song and dance" company/school. There are a few alleys of mostly single-level patchwork dwellings. I was amazed at how each little dwelling had been expanded and arranged with "something out of nothing." Crowded conditions and scarcity of materials encourage mastery of invention and of little spaces. Would this show up somehow in the work of the dancers?

Just fifty yards past the gate of the compound I came to "The Monument" and surrounding park. This was it! Everyone was out at 5:20 a.m.: sword exercisers, pole exercisers, people running up and down the stairs, the inevitable stretchers, *Tai Chi*, badminton without a net, every imaginable kind of martial art and exercise, as well as lots of hanging around and talking. I tried not to stare, and everyone avoided staring at me, but I sensed they wanted to know about me as much as I wanted to know about them. If I was to be in China to teach something of my experience, I wanted to get something of theirs as well. I wanted to get to know some people outside of the dance subculture.

My teaching obligation at the Academy was four hours each day. We scheduled one and a half hours for technique class, a break, then improvisation and composition for two and a quarter hours. In the technique class I wanted to span the range from romantic to abstract non-referential movement. I wanted to avoid a build up of movement or style habit, and to let the students experience many ways of moving. I built phrases throughout the week's span and asked them to begin to experiment. For example, regarding time changes, we tried slower, faster and contrasting speeds within the phrase; we did the phrase in 2/4, 3/4, 5/8, then with another person, responding to his/her timing. We did similar exercises using spatial ideas or dynamic ideas, and then mixed them. Usually the concept of the technique class would be the subject of the improvisation as well, and would lead to a composition.

The first day I asked the students to bring their favorite Chinese poem to class; all Chinese school children have to memorize poems. In the composition I asked them to speak the poem as the only accompaniment. I wanted them to work with something familiar from their culture, that didn't have previous associations with dancing. I didn't give them any other parameters because I wanted to have a sense of what they would do intuitively with the idea. Zhang Yan, the youngest of the group, asked me simply if dancing had something to do with poetry. I told her to let me know her answer to that question after she had done her composition. Her answer was that the dance seemed like a silent movement poem, and that the poem had become more beautiful for her.

I was stunned with the results. Almost all of the pieces were handled in a non-literal way, and were slow. The students seemed to be working mostly with floating spaces and time, with abstract movement, with interesting detail. There was a sparseness of movement and thoroughness of motion. The slow and comparatively uneventful pieces allowed me to see each gesture fulfilled and defined in and around the space, and caused the body and the space to assume a beautiful proportion to one another. The pieces were quite serious, as though the students felt that is what "the modern dance" should be. I watched carefully for imitation of material from technique class, but saw none; nor did I see quotations from what I knew of Chinese Dance.

I did eventually encourage the students to use familiar movement material (dance or martial arts) or props. Jin Xing used *Tai Chi* material in a dance that expressed his pain and anger. With his formidable facility, he could have created a dance that was very physical and violent, but his choice and form made for a moving and compelling piece. Qiao Yang, a long-limbed and elegant dancer, used the long silk "water sleeves" that the Chinese throw and gather with stately dexterity in one of their traditional dances to make a beautiful piece about weeping. She discovered that it was hard to use the techniques and leave the context behind. I felt that some of the teachers of Chinese folk and classic dance who saw this work were put off by the

Figures 12-14   Three male solos, Guangdong Modern Dance Company

new context, although they never gave any direct comments. Jin Xing's *Tai Chi* teacher, on the other hand, seemed to like his piece very much and to be flattered.

I loved watching the other Academy classes, to see the marvelous range of physical training. Every studio had an oriental rug rolled up that would be put down for tumbling and acrobatics. In other classes I saw fan manipulation, handkerchief twirling, dizzying airplane spins, and the fascinating barre work that, as one teacher described it, was "Russian ballet legs and Chinese arms."

There didn't seem to be any sacred feeling about any of the traditional material when it was choreographed for performance. The performances I saw were clearly designed to be cute and winning, and usually fell into the area of kitsch. All that impressive flexibility and control, refined rhythmic sense and liveliness, that had been developed in careful training was scarcely put to use in dances of flirtation and coquetry. When I taught briefly at the Beijing Academy in 1989 I watched other classes in which I saw wonderful "real" folk dances that were exciting and full of stunning detail, but the pieces the Beijing Academy did at the Hong Kong International Festival of Dance Academies that year again belied the fine material of the classroom.

I was amazed at how well this training had prepared the students for modern dance. The bodies were quite well placed; the rhythm was lively. There was a good sense of spaciousness to their movement. The area that was least developed was weighted sense to give contrast to the lightness in their dancing. After working with me they began to achieve weighted quality in specific phrases, but it would take much more time for them to absorb that quality and sense it as a part of their intuitive material.

Early on in technique class I would ask the students to spread out. We American teachers take that class format for granted, and American students like lots of space around them. Not so my Chinese group. Even if I got them all nicely spread out to begin with, by the middle of the combination they would all have imploded on the middle of the room. Being rather claustrophobic myself, I was continually amazed, yet they seemed to feel much better close together. I think the movement they were used to doing, being less aggressive spatially, allowed them to work closer to one another. What I was asking them to do, however, was usually pretty rangy, and after a number of minor collisions they began to make the spatial adjustments on their own. Still, it was clear that there is a very different spatial sense in their everyday lives, and I came to enjoy the relaxed closeness with the students and others with whom I spent time.

I gave an assignment for improvisation one day that would lead to another piece: "In a solo, find movement that comes to you from anything in the room—e.g., geometrical patterns of the windows, shadows, floor boards, some clothing— whatever interests you and suggests energy, shape, or time pattern." Jin Xing began to come up with movement that was very amusing. I asked him what he was thinking of. After a moment of consideration he said he had been working from my sweatshirt, which was hanging over the barre. The movement that was coming out seemed funny to him; it reminded him of a puppy he had gotten but had to give away because people aren't allowed to keep dogs in the city. "That's great. It looks funny to me too! Go ahead and make a funny dance," I said. "But can modern dance be funny?" he asked me, incredulous. I wanted to let the dancers know that modern dance has no rules except the ones you establish for a particular piece—and then usually throw out. Modern dance needs to be re-invented day to day and can be whatever works and is truthful.

In China any composition to be performed in public must pass the censors. Wen Ge did a beautiful, very imaginative duet with his sister while I was there. A year later he revised this dance, adding another male figure, a fabric prop/set, and placing most of the duet on an oval platform in the middle of the stage. When I returned for a visit to Guangzhou during the rains and floods of Lucas Hoving's stay in 1990 I saw the piece in a new context: still a beautiful dance, it was more dramatically powerful, not as abstract, and it seemed to have a much more specific point of view. The two dancers rarely ventured from the oval platform, held there by a spatial tension that isolated them from the third figure. Wen Ge was sincere and emphatic when he said that this piece had no "meaning." He felt that it was abstract. It meant to me, however, an affirmation of the power and beauty of the intuitive and unspoken in dance. I felt he was expressing powerful feelings, of which he wasn't aware. This dance was censored from the works that would attend the Hong Kong International Festival of Dance Academies.

Jin Xing was thoroughly dedicated to his dancing. He had been allowed to come to Guangzhou by his former Army company only because he had refused to eat until they released him from his contract. He had a vigorous internal discipline and desire to succeed. The identical twins, Zhang Li and Zhang Yi, tall and elegant, were released from their Air Force dance company to study in Guangzhou for one year only. They were both beautiful dancers and very talented in their composition work. They could be found in the studio at any time, always together, writing up the day's class, working on their compositions, or studying their English language tapes, repeating the phrases in British accents. They loved to make jokes about the accent and the silly dialogue. They managed to talk their company into allowing them a second year at the Academy. When the demonstrations began in May, 1989, however, an Air Force plane from Beijing came to take them back.

Wen Ge had had six years of intense study of *Wu Shu*. He had shown his forms to me while I watched, drop-jawed at his breathtaking elevations and sharp attacks. His movements were remarkably integrated with space and had a physical logic and decisiveness that was as moving as any I have seen. Because he saw how interested I was in all of the Chinese martial arts forms, he made contact with some students at the sports college on the other side of town and asked them to demonstrate their work for me. We, Wen Ge, the twins, and I, made the hour long trip to the sports academy on bicycle, through the mad evening traffic. My cowboy-style New York City driving skills stood me in good stead. I thought I was keeping up with them; they told me later they were trying to keep up with me!

Arriving at the academy, we made our way around the good looking campus (the dance academy was clearly a poor stepchild by comparison) to the cavernous gym, where we met Wen Ge's friends. They were pleased that I had my video camera, and all performed with the usual rocket high energy and clarity of advanced martial artists. One of the boys had hurt his ankle the day before, but went along with full élan. Like the best of performers, he was infused with the urgency of the moment. One of the forms that they performed for us was punctuated with slaps and claps and reminded us of "A Time to Speak and a Time to be Silent," from José Limón's *There is a Time*, which I had taught them, so Wen Ge and Zhang Yi performed that while Zhang Li and I gave the clapping accompaniment. The sports students were as excited as we had been watching them, and the evening came full circle with enthusiastic talk about their work and training and ours. Our ride home was even more reckless with the joy of that sharing.

I particularly loved the bicycle excursions; it was terrifically exhilarating to be in that river of cyclers, all ringing their bells. Chen Yi-zhao, my translator, seemed to enjoy accompanying me, and was always game to go. We would be off during the lunch break, laughing and talking all the way. Those bikes are sturdy affairs, but often we had to stop to get one fixed at the market, just beyond "The Monument." The magic bike mechanic enjoyed our visits and was convinced that Chen Yi-zhao and I were sisters!

Going to the market was another favorite diversion. Although I was well supplied with delicious food by the lady who was in charge of my care and feeding, I went to the market often. I wanted to keep my apartment well stocked with fruit, peanuts, and anything else I could find to offer to the students when they came to visit me. They had the usual bottomless pits that all dancers are equipped with. Sometimes I went just for fun, alone, with students or with Chen Yi-zhao. One time a vendor from the country pulled Chen Yi-zhao over and asked her, "Who is this woman? She's always hanging around here. Are all of those kids hers?"

I wanted to begin to show the work of the students to an audience, to bring them up to performance level. I proposed a series of open classes to Mah Yo, the director of modern dance, and Yang Mei-qi; they were enthusiastic. Introducing modern dance to other local artists and the public would start to generate an informed audience, and hopefully win friends for, and influence acceptance of, the program. We had time to do four open classes spread over the three months of my residency. The first three would show some technique and the students' compositions, the last would feature a performance of sections of José Limón's *There is a Time*. I had already gotten in casual conversations with teachers in the Academy; not all were happy with the modern dance addition to their turf. "We're used to dances that have stories." "Why are the compositions so serious and slow?" "[The dancers] are on the floor a lot," etc. Partly as a response to these comments I taught the students some of *There is a Time*, based on Ecclesiastes, chapter three, "To every thing there is a season...." " the sections speak simply of the experiences common to all humans on this earth: "A time to be born, and a time to die; a time to plant and time to pluck up that which is planted..., " etc. The movement is not stylistically complicated or idiosyncratic. I felt it wouldn't impose an aesthetic on the students.

The officials from the Cultural Bureau, co-sponsors of the program, were invited, along with some local artists and musicians, local song and dance company teachers, and the students and teachers from the Academy. After the dancing we would have "discussion." The style of discourse was more on the order of a statement by each individual who wanted to talk, rather than interactive discussion. There were no questions the first time, although one of the painters felt that the students' sense of space wasn't well developed. There were very enthusiastic responses from the artists and musicians and writers; many seemed to want to be involved, which subsequently opened up some fruitful exchanges.

On one such exchange we were invited to visit the Art Academy where one of the artists taught. The students were very excited to visit his studio, and even more so to see an exhibit of painting and sculpture. At the painting exhibit, Yan Ying urgently pulled me over to a painting (a calligraphy, dynamic and alive with motion, at once very modern and very ancient) that she had been drawn to, and asked if I thought she could make a dance related to it. Yan Ying had been sent to the modern program by the ballet academy in Shanghai, probably because her body wasn't ideal for ballet. Her first days were full of home sickness and disappointment. Nonetheless, she put herself in the front row and began to dig into her new study with intelligence, discipline, and determination. Before long she was passionate about and thoroughly dedicated to modern dance.

At the same exhibit, the twins were asking questions and throwing around ideas faster than Chen Yi-zhao could interpret. All of the students wanted to return another time to improvise in the space with the paintings. It was interesting to me also how discerning they were in immediately spotting the insincere and the inept.

Wang Mei had a new dance, practically finished, in her head, stimulated by another painting. She was the oldest of the group at 29, and an exceptionally talented choreographer. She was a master of dynamic contrasts, with a spare, lean, clean look to her work because she dared to stay still at times. Hers was an almost painful devotion to dance; she suffered a love/hate relationship with the art form because she could see far ahead but was painfully aware of obstacles over which she had no control. She had a burning desire to learn more and more, and desperately wanted to come to the US, but had no resources.

I found most of the students to be very intelligent and curious, but during an outing with some Cultural Bureau personnel one of the "officials," a writer, asked Hu Qiong, a remarkably talented dancer, to recite a poem. When she couldn't, he embarrassed her painfully by implying that she was dull. She wasn't well educated because when students enter a dance academy at age 13 or 14 they study little other than dance and music. I suppose it is assumed that dancers only need to learn "the forms," and all other information is extraneous. Because their work is for the entertainment of "the military, the workers and the people," a prescription left over from the Cultural Revolution, the forms aren't expected to grow, nor are the students asked to participate as thinkers.

I was terribly hurt for Hu Qiong, and tried to explain that she had a rare gift: impeccable rhythm and musicality, and endless range of quality. Her intelligence in motion was stunning. The Bureau man had no interest in continuing this discussion, as a result of verbal elitism and more than a pinch of male chauvinism. This incident was still burning in my mind when, during a discussion after an open class, I put my free speech foot in my mouth by saying that the government was remiss in not offering a more thorough basic education to its dancers. An official from the Cultural Bureau attending the class turned to gray, cold stone, stood up, and perfunctorily terminated the discussion. (On the contrary, the Director of the Cultural Bureau, Tang Yu, since retired, was a wonderful man, thoroughly supportive of Yang Mei-qi and the program.)

The first group of Chinese modern dancers was exceptional in its number of very talented dancers and choreographers. Many have subsequently left. Zhang Yi and Zhang Li were taken back and Wang Mei chose to return to Beijing; Jin Xing and Wen Ge came to the US to study; Hu Qiong went to Australia; Jiao Jun had personal difficulties and returned to Beijing. I loved the students. Also I loved: Yang Mei-qi and Mah Yo, and their dedication to "modern dance"; the big plain studio; "my" apartment; the trees and red soil surrounding the Academy; my daily 6 a.m. *Tai Chi* lessons at "The Monument" nearby; the hair-raising bicycle rides into town with friend and interpreter Chen Yi-zhao; the heat and the cold; the midday break. I loved watching people open up another area of their lives.

If I hadn't had a family I would have found a way to stay. It was the experience of a lifetime for me, in teaching and in fun. I don't know what kind of teaching job I did; I never do. I didn't give them much in the way of specifics. Three months is a short time, and things get lost in translation, but I think we all touched each other deeply with the most honest and committed work we had in us. The tremendous hope and excitement of those first three months was a powerful moment in all of our lives; when we said good-bye the tears were flowing liberally. The students reminded me always to look at the full moon, so they could see my face and I would be sure to see theirs.

Part III:

Hong Kong

Chapter Ten:
Dance at the Hong Kong Academy for Performing Arts, and Some Thoughts on International Networking

Carl Wolz

After 19 years as Director of the Dance Program at the University of Hawaii, Carl Wolz became Dean of Dance at the Hong Kong Academy for Performing Arts in 1983. From that position he has exercised a major influence over cross-cultural exchange throughout Asia and the Pacific Rim. He has organized the annual International Festival of Dance Academies and Hong Kong International Dance Conference, and is founding President of the Asia Pacific Dance Alliance. In 1993 Mr. Wolz moves on to a university teaching appointment in Tokyo, Japan.

CULTURAL EXCHANGE

In discussing the exchanges that occur when two different cultures meet we can identify at least four types: cross-cultural, intercultural, intracultural, and multi-cultural. A brief definition of these terms as used in this paper follows, with full recognition that other uses and definitions are possible:

> Cross-cultural: when some distinct tradition crosses over more or less unchanged from one culture to another.
> Intercultural: when corresponding aspects of two cultures synthesize in a new form that is different from either original.
> Intracultural: when changes, exchanges, or developments happen within a given and recognized cultural group.
> Multi-cultural: when several distinct cultures live together in time and space within the context of a larger political or social unit.

Multi-cultural, which can include one or more of the other three culturalisms, is used in this paper as a general term for a mixed cultural context. It is a mosaic or patchwork

quilt of different groups, generally preserving their individual identities. In a multi-cultural society there is often a language problem; one culture is usually dominant, while the others assume a secondary role.

All of the above phenomena exist in Hong Kong, and at the Hong Kong Academy for Performing Arts. This analysis looks at the meeting of diverse cultures in an effort to explain the dynamics of an ever-changing and complex global society. It introduces both the positive and negative aspects of the many political, social and moral issues raised by cultural exchange.

A DICHOTOMY IN THE WORLD TODAY

There is a growing dichotomy in the world today: Nations are moving simultaneously toward (a) a global society with international styles in such areas as travel, education, and the arts, and (b) a greater awareness of ethnic differences. This latter situation produces two basic reactions: one is an increased sense of nationalism or ethnocentricity which can lead to hostilities among groups that are different, such as we see in what is left of Yugoslavia; the other reaction is a positive one leading to understanding of cultures that are different from our own. This state of mind is marked by a curiosity, an appreciation, and a respect for those who are different.

It is the role of education to prepare students for life by teaching them respect for other peoples and their cultural traditions. Cross-cultural learning broadens a person's world view. It takes a long time to change attitudes of hate and prejudice, and that is why it is important to educate the young with a multi-cultural perspective. It is not an easy task to balance one's self-esteem and ethnic identity with the assimilation of something different, new, perhaps strange. A sound education in a multi-cultural context should prepare students to understand and function within the dichotomy of an emerging world culture.

HONG KONG AND THE ACADEMY

Hong Kong is a city at the crossroads of Asia. Although it is clearly the most cosmopolitan city in the Chinese-speaking world, and a major commercial center, Hong Kong has long been thought of as a "cultural desert." Within the last ten years, however, through governmental and private efforts, that has begun to change; especially, there has been a tremendous growth of activity in the Performing Arts.

An interesting characteristic of Hong Kong that has contributed significantly to its cultural growth is the Chinese love of gambling—mostly Mah Jong and horse racing. The very successful Hong Kong Jockey Club contributes great sums from its profits to building projects that benefit the community. One of those projects, happily, was the Hong Kong Academy for Performing Arts (HKAPA). Those visitors who have been there know it is a world-class structure. This well-equipped and well-designed facility makes possible the pursuit of a rich cross-inter-intra-multi-cultural performing arts curriculum. In developing a School of Dance at HKAPA we began by asking such questions as: What already exists in the community? What are its additional needs? How can these best be realized?

GENERAL GOALS

In any location, the primary goal of a School of Dance is to train students to the highest possible standard as performers, choreographers, teachers, and sometimes as researchers. This mission always raises issues that are universal—i.e., apply to all cultural groups—and others that are specific to a particular locale, or population. These latter issues will be the focus of the first part of this paper; in the second part the implications of international networking in Dance will be discussed. Overall, the following questions will be addressed: What were the original goals of the School of Dance at HKAPA? How have they been realized? What has yet to be done?

THE ACADEMY DANCE CURRICULUM

In Hong Kong there are three professional dance companies: the Hong Kong Ballet, the Hong Kong Dance Company, and the City Contemporary Dance Company. Following a brief from the Hong Kong Government when the Academy was founded, the dance curriculum is based primarily on training professional dancers for those three companies. Therefore, at the "heart" of the curriculum there are three major areas of study: Classical Ballet, Chinese Dance both Classical and Folk, and Modern Dance.

Each student's Major Study is determined after vigorous entrance procedures. Students continue their Study throughout the entire course, but are also required to take classes in other majors as a Second Study; for example, a ballet major will also take classes in Chinese Dance and Modern Dance. The major in Classical Ballet is based on a syllabus developed by Academy teachers who represent a broad spectrum of international ballet, including English and Russian styles. RAD syllabus is also taught to prepare students who wish to take those examinations. The Chinese Dance major is based on the "Classical" Syllabus developed in China at the Beijing Dance Academy. It is a synthesis of Chinese Opera Movement and Classical Ballet. Chinese folk dances, selected from the minority groups of China, are also included. Chinese Dance is offered in two sections, one for women and one for men. The major in Modern Dance (or, as we frequently say in Hong Kong, Contemporary Dance) is based on several important American modern dance techniques, including Humphrey-Weidman, Limón, Graham, and Cunningham. The intention is to give the students a broad background in this genre.

Figure 19   Dancers of the Hong Kong Ballet in *Concerto Barocco*

In Hong Kong there exists a wide infrastructure of private schools teaching ballet and Chinese dance, so that students normally come to the Academy with good preparation in these genres. However, few contemporary dance classes were being offered in the community when the Academy opened. Also, in areas of British influence the term "modern dance" refers more to commercial dance, so many of the first applicants for the Modern major thought they were going to study jazz dance.

For the past few years the Academy School of Dance also has been offering a focus, though not a major, in "Musical Theatre Dance," which includes Jazz, Tap, Singing and Acting, plus classes in the other three majors. This program was designed to meet the needs of local producers who were beginning to present musicals and came to the Academy looking for dancers.

Two additional subjects that are standard in dance schools throughout the world are Dance Music and Dance History. At the Academy Music courses include theory, history and repertory; the History sequence includes a general introduction course, a survey course, a concentrated course for each of the three majors, and a final integrated course in Aesthetics and Criticism. In all subjects both Chinese and Western materials are covered and considered.

Two areas of study, new to Hong Kong and meant to integrate the knowledge learned in the Majors, are Movement Analysis (which includes Fundamentals, Laban Movement Analysis, and Labanotation) and Dance Composition/Choreography. These subjects were originally considered to be of no use by many local teachers, but ten years has shown their value and they are now an accepted part of the curriculum.

Labananalysis was chosen as the theoretical framework for the study of dance at the Academy because it has had the widest international acceptance as a movement analysis system. Moreover, this system already has a body of materials in every aspect of the dance field: notated repertory for performance; teaching manuals; documentation and research methods; and applications to many other fields such as Anthropology, therapy of several kinds, sports, and education. It was felt that the Laban system presented a comprehensive and broad tool for the study of many different types of dance in a multi-cultural context.

The integration of all majors in the composition classes has resulted in the development of a new Hong Kong style of creative dance, as many of the Academy dance alumni have continued their interest in choreography after graduation. They are producing some of the more interesting work in the community—for the professional companies, for a half-dozen new ensembles that have emerged since the first class graduated, and for the Hong Kong Schools Dance Festival, where Academy students have returned to their own secondary schools to choreograph works that are winning prizes.

It is important to create a syllabus that is flexible enough to accommodate international methods of composition and to foster creative work that evolves out of indigenous cultures, rather than only from imported foreign styles and concepts. A question the Academy staff discusses often is: "Is there a system of teaching composition that is truly not culturally biased?" As yet we have no definitive answer.

Another area of multi-cultural mix is repertory. Since the beginning, dance programs at the Academy have tended to be like variety shows, with pieces in the three major styles, plus related ones, included on the same evening. For the annual concert by the graduating class this format includes one or two pieces specifically for each of the three groups of majors, plus a large standard repertory work that is performed by students from all three Studies. These repertory works have always been very successful, and are done for two main reasons: to give the graduating class a sense of group identity, and to show that it is possible for dancers to achieve a high standard of performance in more than one style of dance. In 1988, for example, Hong Kong students from all three majors performing together in American choreographer José Limón's *Missa Brevis* produced a very clear example of multi-culturalism.

One major production each year has a unifying theme that includes many different forms of dance, either in a pure style or in an interculturally mixed one. Thus, the

Academy has presented productions such as *Fragrant Harbour*, a work about the past, present, and future of Hong Kong. These interculturally synthesized pieces are also becoming a "tradition" at the Academy.

OTHER FACTORS IN THE MULTI-CULTURAL MIX

Four other elements add to the multi-cultural mix at the Academy. They are the teachers, the students, the language of instruction, and the educational system.

Teachers at the Academy come from a number of different countries and are trained in a variety of dance traditions. Chinese Dance teachers over the years have all come from the Beijing Dance Academy. The negotiations to make that possible, begun in 1983, were complex; the experience itself, on both sides, has been frustrating, aggravating, exciting, and rewarding. The Academy's ballet teachers are mostly from Mainland China or Hong Kong, while the contemporary/modern dance teachers have come primarily from the United States, perhaps because of the background of the Dean of Dance. The first full-time teacher of Musical Theatre Dance is a Tunisian, raised in France, and trained by an American jazz choreographer in Paris. How cross-cultural can you get! In addition, many well-known master teachers from other countries pass through. Some come with dance companies that appear in one of the several local festivals. The Hong Kong Arts Festival is the largest of these, and it normally brings in dance companies from the US and Europe. The Asian Arts Festival presents Asian traditional and contemporary groups. The Regional (New Territories) Festival attracts companies from all over the world. Not only do these visits provide the Academy with contacts for guest teachers, they also provide opportunities for staff and students to see performances by companies from other parts of the world. This is a very important part of the education and growth of teachers and students.

What constitutes a good teacher in a cross-cultural setting? Who make better teachers, foreigners with wide experience, or locals who go abroad to study and return to share their new knowledge with people who speak the same language? There is no easy formula. Two basic and important criteria for successful teaching in a cross-cultural setting are dedication and sensitivity. A dedicated teacher is genuinely interested in the welfare and development of the student. This teacher instills a sense of discipline and love of the art in a caring and nourishing manner. A sensitive teacher is one who tries to understand cultural differences in people and to develop an approach to handling those differences.

The student body at the HKAPA in recent years reflects the multi-cultural nature of Hong Kong. At the Academy there have been, besides those from Hong Kong, students from China, Taiwan, Korea, Malaysia, Indonesia, and Vietnam. International students have a very positive effect on any institution; they contribute to the refinement of individual identities, and help to nurture a world view that appreciates our differences. International students do, however, present special problems,

Figure 20   The Hong Kong Dance Company performs *The Love Story of Dalai VI.*
Choreographers: Shu Qiao and Ying Eding

especially with regard to language. The language of instruction at the Academy has
been an issue of concern from the very beginning. Officially, English is the language
of instruction; practically, Cantonese has always been essential. With teachers from

Beijing and students from Taiwan, Mandarin is also widely used. The problem has increased recently with the influx of students from countries like Vietnam and Korea, who have minimal skills in English, and none in Chinese.

Another aspect of the multi-cultural mix that has led to a cross-cultural synthesis is the matter of educational systems. As a British colony, Hong Kong adopted the British system of education, with external examiners and "Honors" degrees. Recently, with the approval of an internationally accredited BFA Degree Course, an American style credit-unit system has been introduced at the Academy. This addition has led to an interesting hybrid, which seems to be thriving in the early stages.

CULTURAL FACTORS AFFECTING THE LEARNING PROCESS

In any social milieu there are always cultural factors that affect the learning process. Some such factors in Hong Kong and at the Academy are work ethic, the exam system, punctuality, space-awareness, energy, talking, pride, and taste. In dealing with these cultural factors in a dance-education context one must decide what to accept and what to try to retrain in order to be consistent with standards of discipline and etiquette in the international dance world.

The work ethic in Hong Kong is complex, and presents another kind of dichotomy. On one hand, the people of Hong Kong are among the most industrious in the world. They work long hours with few holidays, and are usually highly committed to their job. On the other hand, there is a local saying: "Get the greatest amount of profit (results) from the least amount of investment (work)." For some students this means doing just enough homework, or attending just enough classes, to get a passing grade. In the past few years, however, this attitude is found in fewer and fewer students. The dominant impression is that Hong Kong students work very hard.

With a passing grade in examinations students are able to get a "Certificate" or "Diploma" that officially proves they have accomplished something. Emphasis on the exam system both in China and in England compounds in Hong Kong to produce a focus on the final result rather than on the working process itself. Excellence *is* recognized within the exam system, but many students seem satisfied just to receive the final piece of paper.

For all of their hard work, many people in Hong Kong have a flexible sense of time. Punctuality is not considered a virtue. This affects the operation of the Academy both in class and at performances. Frequent tardiness for class has led to an elaborate system of assessment, and continuous advising in groups and with individuals stressing the need to be punctual, particularly for technique classes. Hong Kong audiences prefer to arrive for a performance at the exact time indicated on the ticket. As a result, many people cannot be seated without delaying curtain time, so we routinely plan a point in the program to stop, turn up the house lights, and seat late comers. A "slipping clock" is common in many parts of Asia, and there are culturally accepted ways of dealing with it in most countries. However, it is one of the traits that the faculty in Hong Kong have tried to retrain.

Awareness of space is another factor in Hong Kong culture that affects the study of dance. Perhaps because Hong Kong is so densely populated, with many Chinese living in small, crowded apartments, there is a lack of awareness of individual space. Everywhere belongs to everyone; people are always bumping into each other, especially getting on and off elevators and subways. This carries over in the early years of study to a lack of clear awareness of the spatial position of others in the studio and on stage.

Perhaps because they live in such a crowded, busy city, the people of Hong Kong are full of vitality, always trying to accomplish many things in a single day. Wherever even a small group of people gathers there is always a lively, animated, sometimes noisy atmosphere. This also applies to students, and teachers must be sensitive to the group dynamic and not try to maintain quiet when it is not necessary. One can see this at performances as well. It is quite common for groups to talk during dance or music events, and students do the same in lectures.

The opposite side of this group energy is an individual reticence. It is difficult to get students to ask questions in class, or to answer when asked a question by the teacher. This is attributable to both lack of language skills, and the educational format of the Hong Kong schools, which stresses rote learning rather than discussion. Teachers often say of the Hong Kong students that they talk when they should be listening and only listen when you want them to talk.

Much has been written about the concept of "face" in Asia, which is really an aspect of pride. One way this manifests itself with students at the Academy is in covering up rather than admitting to poor language skills. Our teachers find they must be very careful in asking "Is that clear?" or "Do you understand?" Some students will say "yes" when in fact they have not understood a word.

The final and most difficult factor is the issue of taste, as this is the area in which there is most discussion and least agreement. Questions of national aesthetics and criteria for making assessments are not the focus of this paper; "taste" is mentioned here in the context of cross-cultural training. Teachers at the Academy have had to be aware that the idea of good taste is definitely not universal. Historically, Chinese art has been mostly ornate, with many decorative elements. This applies to theatre traditions as well; the Chinese have a long history of dance dramas in which the style of expression seems overdone and histrionic to Western eyes. Until recently there has been no pure or abstract dance in China. Hence, teachers in this cross-cultural setting need to exercise caution that they are not reacting from a Western bias. In creative work they must be clear that the students may use materials from their own cultural background in exploring and developing new dance compositions. Many of our early students felt they had to create something that looked like "Western Modern Dance." That problem has been addressed, and composition teachers now include specific units in their courses on this topic. In discussing the work of outside Chinese choreographers it is important again to understand the background of the work and not judge it by imported criteria. This is also a matter of diplomacy. At the Academy there have been several instances of strained public relations when teachers have been critical of local choreographers and these opinions found their way back to the artists concerned. One always has to weigh freedom of opinion with discretion and positive community relations in which local dance artists must also "save face."

EXCHANGE IN THE CHINESE SPEAKING WORLD

A clear example of intra-cultural exchange is dance development in the Chinese-speaking world: China, Hong Kong and Taiwan. History and geography have made of this region a complex pattern of many different sub-cultures, yet in all areas there is still an over-riding Chinese identity through the written language. It is interesting to note in passing how the sub-cultures each have evolved organically a different multi-cultural dance world based on the personalities, the needs, and the politics of the given area. It is also interesting to note that there is a great deal of exchange among dance personalities, not only in contemporary dance but in ballet and traditional Chinese Dance as well. The International SinoDance Association (ISDA) has been established to facilitate such exchange among dance artists of Chinese background from all over the world. A full study of these exchanges and developments will have to wait for a future volume.

RELATIONS WITH LOCAL COMPANIES AND SCHOOLS

The relationship between the Academy School of Dance and the professional companies in Hong Kong has had a positive growth over the years. Many of our graduates have danced, and are dancing, with all these companies. Their artistic directors are invited to sit on a Community Advisory Board for the School of Dance, as well as serving on panels for entrance auditions and boards for final examinations. Meetings are being held at present to build even stronger ties between the companies and the Academy. With regard to its mission of training dancers for Hong Kong (and beyond), the Academy is well on its way to achieving its goals.

Envisioned in the original plan for the Academy was a vocational secondary school to prepare students to enter at the college level. A primary school program was also planned. For various reasons, mostly financial, this support system was scaled back to a part-time activity on Saturdays and weekdays after school. This Junior Program as it is known locally is quite successful; enrollment (except for boys) is high, demonstrating interest in dance in the community. However, it does not in any way fulfill the original goal of preparing and training students for college-level work.

The education of doctors or lawyers is not short-changed because there is not enough time; they are normally not ready for their profession until they are much older than most graduates. But dancers cannot wait; physical skills must be nurtured at an early age. Creative movement in the primary grades and structured dance training at the secondary level would allow students to progress throughout their formative years.

At the Academy too much time is spent doing basic work, at the expense of a more liberal, intellectual education. Dancers have a reputation for being uneducated because they spend all their time in the studio. Gelsey Kirkland's book, *Dancing On My Grave*, is a sad indictment of the training regimen which causes some dancers, who are extraordinary aesthetic athletes, to be emotionally starved and alienated by the structure in which they find themselves doing their life's work. Surely educators can do better. It is important to train, besides the body, the mind, the emotions, and the spirit. Dance is the total integration of these four aspects of the human being, but do we really educate them all in our schools? At the Academy, because of the time constraints imposed by the problem described here, we have been able to do an excellent job with the body, less with the mind, very little with the emotions, and virtually nothing for the spirit.

Part of the problem with the Junior Program lies with the private dance schools and the public schools in Hong Kong. The private dance schools understandably want to keep their students, especially the more talented ones, to themselves. Hence, attempts to establish scholarship classes at the Academy for the top students from all schools have not met with much success. The public schools actually are very active in that there are hundreds of extra-curricular dance clubs in both primary and secondary schools throughout Hong Kong and the New Territories. Indeed, each January there is a Schools Dance Festival that consistently reveals a good variety and quality of dance activity in the public schools. Because of heavy homework loads and the examination system, however, there are long periods of the year when students must give up their dance classes or at least spend reduced time in them.

The greatest obstacle to the study of dance in Hong Kong is a cultural factor. The majority of Chinese parents do not see dance as an acceptable career choice, and in many cases put pressure on their children to go to a university and study for a profession, or go to work for a company that offers prospects of promotion. There are many students at the Academy who are studying dance against their parents' wishes, which puts a heavy strain on them emotionally and sometimes financially. Perhaps this will improve as it becomes more widely known that Academy graduates actually *do* get employed.

For the future an important goal is to provide more performing and choreographing opportunities for advanced students through the Academy Dance Ensemble. This new endeavor will be part of an Outreach Program which takes small groups into public schools and community centers in order to build and educate an audience for dance, and to identify young talent, getting them more involved so that they can eventually make an informed decision whether or not to pursue a career path in dance. It is also an exercise in recruitment for the Academy.

tend to roll-in, or pronate. Eagerness to display 180 degrees of outward rotation exaggerates this problem. There are also injuries to the knees and backs, but with less frequency. When injury does occur, dance students from Mainland China tend to fall back on the traditional Chinese concept that water should not come close to the site of injury. The belief is that if the injured area is exposed to water or ice, such problems as arthritis will eventually result. They often use heated herbs and massage for injuries ranging from sprains through tears to breaks. The majority of the Hong Kong students will use ice on injuries.

One intriguing remedy practiced by several of the HKAPA students involves the cooking of body parts of a chicken (for instance) which correspond to the injured part of the dancer. Thus, a dish is made of chicken feet for injuries to the foot. One student reported having asked her mother to prepare a soup made from chicken heads, as the student felt she needed to improve her ability to memorize dance combinations. This particular case is probably exceptional, yet the message for foreign teachers is clear: one should be aware that what might seem mere superstition to a Westerner can be serious business in Hong Kong. Concepts of good and bad fortune, charms, and lucky money are sometimes tongue-in-cheek, but usually contain underlying significance.

Dance teachers are necessarily mindful of the possible careers for which their students might qualify. In Hong Kong itself there are three professional dance companies—one ballet, one modern, and one Chinese Dance. Aside from those

Figure 24   The Hong Kong Dance Company performs
The Love Story of Dalai VI. Choreographers: Shu Qiao and Ying Eding

options there is commercial work in video, television, and dancing "back-up" for Hong Kong's many "canto-pop" stars. The government provides very little support for smaller or experimental dance companies, which further curtails the career options in Hong Kong. Of course, one might go abroad to continue one's studies and work, as a small percentage of HKAPA graduates do. In teaching at HKAPA I have therefore tried to balance company-preparation work with other survival skills. I teach students how to move efficiently, work without excessive tension, and prevent injuries through intelligent motor skills. I emphasize musicality, phrasing, textural concerns, and performance skills. Basically, rather than teaching a style I try to help the students arrive at resolutions to broader issues that they can apply to their choice of styles.

Finland, by enormous contrast to Hong Kong and the US, provides abundant financial subsidy for its dance artists. Many more grants are available. One choreographer I met had a fifteen year life-support grant from the government! In Helsinki alone there are two state-theater dance companies and numerous small companies. There is substantial dance activity, ranging from classical to experimental to musical theater. As a dance teacher there it was heartening for me to realize that the majority of my students would have ample opportunity to perform professionally, although the recent international recession, which hit Finland hard, may have changed some of the funding practices in effect when I was there in 1990-91.

Two other countries I have taught in recently are Estonia and Indonesia (Java and Bali). In direct contrast to Finland and Hong Kong these two countries are struggling economically, and there are few opportunities for dancers to make a living wage. While teaching in Estonia I realized that the concepts of spatial projection, upper space, and presence in space were practically political statements. The dancers in class faced abysmal conditions for studying dance. One couple traveled two days by train just to see what modern dance might be.

Indonesia has a tremendously rich artistic heritage. The dancers I taught were students at ASTI (the National Dance Academy of Indonesia, in Yogyakarta, Denpasar and Jakarta), Jakarta Institute of Arts (Institut Kesenian Jakarta), Indonesian Arts Institute, Yogyakarta (Institut Seni Indonesia), and Advanced School of Arts, Denpasar, Bali (Sekolah Tinggi Seni Indonesia). They all worked with highly refined dance skills. I was completely humbled by their abilities, and wondered what importance American modern dance training could possibly have for them. Their dance traditions are exquisite: Why add this foreign ingredient? My only, rather tentative, answer is that dancers are curious beings, whose rebellious natures help them to push boundaries and navigate uncharted waters. As I taught about the concept of the "center of weight" I saw that my students used several "centers of weight" in their various Indonesian dance forms. I felt like a monotheistic preacher in a land given to animistic pantheism. In fact, I had much to learn from them.

I started with the typical Western dance class format of showing a movement sequence and then expecting the dancers to repeat it. It quickly became apparent that this was unusual for them, and that the class flowed more smoothly if I kept dancing with them, changing exercises without stopping or breaking rhythm. There was no talk, just movement. The classes ended with enormous whoops and cheers. We felt that a real communion had occurred. Who taught whom? The whirl of energy between teacher and students was similar to that which occurs between performer and audience—the transcendence that keeps dancers hooked, and propels us deeper into the mysteries, hardships, and truths of our art.

Many Asian dance techniques require specific weight placement that must be altered to accommodate the air work called for in Western dance styles. While the use of a supinated foot and the carrying of weight on the outside edges of the feet is desirable in some Asian techniques, it could prove disastrous in *grand allegro* (high jumping) or even *petit allegro* (quick jumping) phrases. Alwin Nikolais has been known to comment, as he does in the film *Nik and Murray,* by Christian Blackwood, that Indonesian dance forms are clearly connected to the earth; that the dancers do not wish to disassociate themselves from the power of gravity. They are not compelled to perform repeated high jumps, much less put on a pair of pointe shoes. Nikolais further speculates that the desire to defy gravity may have the religious connotations of aspiring toward heaven (up) and avoiding hell (down)— all basically Western concepts.

The dance students I taught in Indonesia, and those I deal with now in Hong Kong, have relatively little difficulty in learning movement sequences that use odd meters—7s or 9s, for example—and mixed meters. They are able to feel these rhythms and use them in movement through space. The Helsinki dancers, by contrast, had a very hard time with this type of dance pattern. Perhaps this difference can be explained in part by exposure to the various types of indigenous music and folk or ethnic dances of each region. In any case, the Asian dancers and accompanists that I have worked with do better with odd meters than did my Finnish students.

I am now in my second year of full-time teaching in Hong Kong. The only thing I know for certain is that this is an extremely complex culture, one vastly different from my own, and that it will be a very long time before I am completely acculturated, if ever. Perhaps this is an inappropriate goal. Once last year as I walked down the street to the Academy for Performing Arts I remember feeling somehow comfortable, adjusted, almost at home. It was then that I noticed a restaurant advertisement boasting of "Fish Head in Sour Gravy." So much for that feeling of being at home! Indeed, every time I get near the feeling of being adjusted another reminder greets me. Thank goodness for such signs; they keep the expatriate on track. I am a foreigner here, with an opportunity to teach and to become enriched by experience in the cultural matrix that is Hong Kong. In the training of dancers here, as anywhere really, one must work with the materials at hand, molding them toward some practical set of goals. At HKAPA we are trying to bolster the growing dance scene in Hong Kong and Asia by fostering the creativity of Asian dancers.

Chapter Twelve:
The Emerging Contemporary Dance Companies of Hong Kong and China

An Interview with Willy Tsao

Born and raised in Hong Kong, Willy Tsao received his college education in the United States, after which he returned home and obtained his Master's Degree in Business Administration at the University of Hong Kong. Mr. Tsao established the City Contemporary Dance Company in 1979, and has directed and choreographed for the company ever since.

In May, 1988, Mr. Tsao was invited to teach modern dance at the Beijing Dance Academy, and in the same year he received the Dancer of the Year Award from the Hong Kong Artists Guild. In 1990 he was selected as one of the Ten Outstanding Young Persons in Hong Kong.

Mr. Tsao has been associated with the Guangdong Modern Dance Company in Guangzhou, China, since September of 1987, when he became advisor and teacher for the company. In 1991 he was invited to be its first Artistic Director.

Editors: You have, of course, been a fixture in the Hong Kong dance scene for some time, and we know you have been working with the Guangdong Dance Company, but apparently you have recently formed some connections in Beijing as well.

Willy Tsao: Yes. Three years ago I went to choreograph a piece for the ballet students at the Beijing Dance Academy, and the director of the Youth Dance Company saw it in performance and came to ask me to be an advisor to the company, to bring in some modern dance. That was the first contact. Then, two years ago I choreographed a piece for them, and that's how it started.

E: How often do you go there?

WT: They want me to be there once a year. So far I have been going for just a week or two at a time, but I have all of my material ready to go when I get there, so we just start setting a dance and it moves quickly.

E: What is the level of that company?

WT: They are actually a collection of the best college graduates each year, and those who enter the college are only the best of the high school graduates, so they are very good indeed—bright-minded and physically very capable. The purpose of the company is to experiment with new works.

E: How many members does the company have?

WT: The last time I was there there were 14, but several others were "on loan" to other companies.

E: So the membership changes often.

WT: It's not a permanent company; they take the most promising graduates with the understanding that they will stay no more than two years. The company is an affiliate of the Academy, which pays the dancers' salaries. They are still considered to be students; that is, the State has not yet assumed responsibility for them. They are still living in the student dormitories. Eventually they have to go, and then they are recruited by other companies, and get their own housing, etc. It's a great arrangement for the Academy: they get the best dancers, make use of them, and then they go away, so there are no aging dancers sitting around and grumbling.

E: When you are there, do you teach them?

Figure 25   City Contemporary Dance Company
in Willy Tsao's *Wanderings in the Cosmos* (1989)

WT: Yes. Every morning I give class at 9:00, and then we rehearse until evening. Because they are still students, they have the whole day available.

E: Do they have other outside people coming in as you do?

WT: Not that I know of, though at one time Ben Stevenson came to teach at the Academy, and mounted a piece for the ballet students. But they don't specifically invite guests.

E: And what kind of training does the Academy provide?

WT: They have three sections: Ballet, Chinese Classical Dance, and Chinese Folk Dance. The group I work with consists mainly of classical and folk dance students. Last year they had only about 12 ballet graduates, who were immediately grabbed up by companies. In fact, the Academy got sued by some of the local companies that didn't get any of the dancers.

E: Do they pay you when you go?

WT: I have to pay my own airfare, but when I get there they pay me well in the local money. I don't spend much because they provide room and board, and I don't really have time to spend money. It's quite good by local standards— about the equivalent of $35 US/week, or more than most people make in a month.

E: So you are the primary modern dance influence on those dancers.

WT: I can't really say that, because in China they have Wu Xiao-bang. He studied in Japan in the early '30s, and was heavily influenced by Hanya Holm and Mary Wigman, because Germany and Japan were very close. He came back to China before the War and started a new dance movement, using dance to make political statements and reflect local life. He was really the pioneer in Chinese modern dance; he's still alive at almost 90 now.

E: He survived the revolution?

WT: He wasn't allowed to perform his works after the 1950s-during the Cultural Revolution. In the early '50s he set up his own group called "Flying Horse" ("Pegasus"). His influence is still very strongly felt. In China there is always a very small minority that is trying to do something creative; they are considered his disciples. Before 1979 those people were constantly criticized for not following the proper line, but now there are people like Tsui Chow, the director of the Hong Kong Dance Company, from Shanghai, who are quite successful and are considered his followers. There is also Wang Lian-cheng, a teacher at the Beijing Academy, who studied with Murray Louis and Alwin Nikolais in the early '70s. He went to New York and then returned to Beijing. He wasn't allowed to teach at the Academy, so he taught in the remote provinces. He conducted workshops using Nikolais' method, and made some very impressive videotapes which I have seen. He's in his 60s, and has eyesight problems, but I think he is really the one who spread the modern influence. Finally, starting in about 1986, he was allowed to do short workshops at the Academy; actually, I was invited there to augment his

Figure 26   Willy Tsao's *Bird Song* (1990), performed
by the City Contemporary Dance Company

work. From time to time I still receive letters from remote areas where he has obviously been, saying, "we are so bored with this doctrinaire dance discipline. We want something of our own that will express our needs." Now a whole generation is coming along, like Po Gin-ping, who is not a dancer but a researcher and contributor for the *Dance Magazine of China*, and Wang Mei, who worked with the Guangdong group for two years before returning to Beijing, where she now leads the modern dance contingent. She's really a one-woman effort, doing short-term workshops and trying to form a section, but there's a lot of infighting. Still, I think she is highly respected by now.

E: You see, we are very naive about the history of Chinese dance. I thought before Yang Mei-qi there was no Western influence in Chinese dance other than Russian ballet.

WT: There was always some, but it was never systematic.

E: You span the worlds of Hong Kong dance and Mainland China dance. Are there other people who are in that position?

WT: When the Guangdong group started there were several people who contributed there, like Wong (King) Lan-lan, and Chiang Ching. But because they were so far away [in the US] it was difficult for them to have much impact. Because I was so much closer—just two and one-half hours away by train—it was easier for me. In fact, last week I found myself spending one day there, one day here!

E: How do you think of the Guangdong Company in the overall context of dance in Mainland China?

WT: The dancers obviously are the most versatile around; they can do classical dance and ballet in addition to modern dance, and they are open in a way that is rare in China.

E: Is that because of how they were selected?

WT: No, it's more the way they have been trained since they got to Guangzhou. I think it's the environment, the atmosphere. We have some new dancers who have just arrived, and they have caught up very quickly. I always think modern dance training only opens you up to a certain extent—it needs to be in the mind. If you do Graham technique you may become a Graham dancer, but not necessarily a modern dancer. For me being a modern dancer means being *open*; it's never just a style of movement. So those new kids coming in had a brief transitional period—a period of wondering "what's going on?"—but then they molded into the group, because they are good dancers. Before, they were told "You have to do things this way," but then they came to this new environment and they said "Of course we can do this." Once the mind was released, the body adapted. I think the Chinese dancers tend to be particularly adaptable because they are exposed to a variety of styles early in their training.

E: How were these new dancers selected?

Figure 27   City Contemporary Dance Company members in
Nine Songs (1991), choreographed by Helen Lai

WT: Actually, they just came by themselves. They dropped by, and we said "Come take class with us." They saw the potential and worked very hard, and it just happened. Others have come and their minds aren't really on the dance; perhaps they just want to be in Guangzhou. After a few days they drop out, because it's hard work.

E: We understand there is no intention to bring in a new group or class at Guangzhou.

WT: Right. That original group will be the nucleus of the company, though we continue to take in new people. We are always grooming new blood from all over China. In fact, this year we are planning another tour to recruit new people. There will never be another four-year training program, because we think it is better now to build on the foundation we have created.

E: Is there any plan to bring in more Western teachers?

WT: Yes. Of course it depends on the funding available, essentially, whether the Asian Cultural Council continues to support the scheme.

E: What is the American Dance Festival's role?

WT: They are responsible for assigning the teachers, but the money is from the ACC. Also, Dance Theater Workshop has become involved. They sent two artists, Art Bauman and his wife, to do a two-week workshop. So there are still these organizations and friends that are interested.

E: But the ACC has been the principal funding source?

WT: Yes, and they also provided scholarships for the Chinese dancers to go to New York, but many of them didn't come back, so they stopped that.

E: When you go to Guangzhou, who pays you?

WT: I am essentially paid "in kind," and, as a matter of fact, my company, CCDC [City Contemporary Dance Company, of Hong Kong], also contributes all the costumes, the floor, publicity, technical assistance, etc. Because, you see, for the first five years they only had one administrator besides Yang Mei-qi, Mr. Ling, the headmaster, to take care of everything. More recently Mr. Chew has come out of retirement to help, and the government has now allotted them 38 "spaces," meaning they will support that number of people, providing their housing and salary. Of those spaces they consider that 20 will be dancers, and the rest support staff. So the company is finally on firm footing. But, because they are now officially a company, the government will, of course, pay more attention to what they do.

E: Would you expect the government officials who oversee a company like this to be well qualified?

Figure 28   Willy Tsao in rehearsal at the Guangdong Dance Academy

WT: Some of them are quite knowledgeable in the theater tradition, but whether they are open enough to accept new things is another matter. Of course they have a lot of considerations beyond the artistic; they have to decide whether the work goes along with the national objectives. When they see anything that isn't light and happy, they might have a problem. At the company's recent inaugural concert, for example, we did all works by the company members. They all turned out to be quite heavy—no humor, no fun. After the concert the officials who were there were very distant, very cold.

E: Did that "heavy" quality in the student pieces surprise you?

WT: No, but it did surprise a lot of people. For instance, there was an Australian dancer there, and afterward he said "You must not copy the West. Oh, I wish you had more humor in your work." I replied "Maybe what you are seeing is the real thing in Chinese modern dance; what they produce when they follow their instincts."

E: Modern dance, when it started in the US, was anything but funny. I mean Martha Graham, or Mary Wigman for that matter, was hardly known for her sense of humor!

WT: That's right, and these kids are really at that stage. It's easy for a Westerner now to come in and say "I expect a little humor," but if you understand their lives, their struggles—I really respect the choices they are making, even if they are a bit heavy. There are two or three dancers in the group who are potentially good choreographers.

E: If the Guangdong Company is seen to be a great success, would there be a possibility of other companies being formed?

WT: I hope so, but at present it doesn't seem likely, as we are still very much in the experimental stage. There is plenty of interest in other places, but I don't think those provincial governments are bold enough yet to get anything done. There has been quite a bit of Western dance in China by now, and most of it is well accepted, especially the modern ballet. Yet, to the Chinese eye much of the modern dance is too dark, too depressed. They tend to be very concerned with content, and they want to see work that says positive things.

E: Where does such dance criticism appear?

WT: First, there are the comments of the dance audience. In Beijing alone there are 36 companies, all supported by the government, each representing perhaps 200 professional dancers from age 17 through 50 or so. They were all trained in the Dance Academy when they were young, so for their entire lives they have thought and moved in the same constricted ways. There are about 6,000 dancers, all with basically the same mind set. That is the dance audience you face when you go to Beijing.

E: What I really meant by my question is who, if anyone, *writes* about dance?

WT: There is a lot of research going on, and then there are the government officials such as those who came to the Guangzhou inaugural. They make the initial

Figure 29   Beijing Dance Academy students performing
By the Bank of River Mongtung. Choreographer: Ling Chu

judgments about what can be performed. Then the dance researchers write about those works. The researchers, I think, know more about dance. Of course the things they review have already been screened and approved, so they generally write favorable reviews. One negative comment will entirely destroy a work.

E: Their articles appear in the newspapers?

WT: No, in journals. The newspaper reviews are just *pro forma* favorable comments—how the audience "reacted warmly," that kind of thing. If there is any debate, it takes place in the journals, usually at quite a high level.

E: And how has the Guangdong Company been received by these Beijing researchers?

WT: They have only performed once in Beijing, in 1990, when they presented two concerts. The first was my work, all very light; it was well liked. "Strong movement with a positive message, although it has little to do with China. It is mostly about Western pop music and lifestyle. Still, it reflects something of what Guangzhou is becoming." In fact, the company is bringing that program to Xinjiang in the Northwest silk-road area, because those people have asked for it. The second night was student choreography, more controversial on the government level, so they specifically arranged a discussion period for the following night. All the scholars came, and were very supportive: "Ah, we must ask the Cultural Department to protect this group," they said. I think they were properly proud of this company.

E: Let's talk more personally about *you*, as an example of what cross-cultural dance training can produce.

WT: First, strangely enough, I never consider the dance I am doing to be "Western." I remember my first encounter with modern dance was in Hong Kong. I don't even recall the name of the group (it was from America), but I was sitting in the audience and the movement impressed me so much I thought "I must join them on stage." It was so expressive; it was like speaking in my own voice. We had classical ballet and Chinese Dance and Cantonese opera in Hong Kong, but none of it ever attracted me much, because in all of those forms the dancers were playing roles. It was beautiful, but not related to me. Then, I saw those modern dancers on stage. They were Westerners, but to me they were primarily human beings. And that has come to be my concept of modern dance: The dancers are never American or Chinese or whatever; they are just human beings. I always think of modern dance as making the universal statement—as speaking a language that is equally available to everyone. When I study it, I can take it in easily; I don't have to imagine myself as a Western prince or an Eastern hero or anything of that sort. I can just be myself, Willy Tsao. I have my emotion, and that says it all. The fall and recovery, that's my nature. I control this technique so I can be free. When I formed my company in Hong Kong, people said "Why don't you do something Eastern; why do you copy Western dance?" I replied, "Oh, is it Western?" When I try to do something Eastern, it becomes a *style*— nothing that I can really relate to. Sometimes I feel that I have to dig into the drawer to find something that will satisfy people's desire for "Eastern" dance, but that's really ridiculous. It's totally against my nature and my belief and my concept of dance. While forming a company and getting established I have witnessed many changes in the society of Hong Kong and of China. No doubt my work reflects something of that. However, I am never just trying to show something traditionally Chinese; it's always my interpretation. Although I may be portraying an ancient Chinese hero, it's always my version of the hero. In a sense, it's always myself. So people don't say "Oh, he's Chinese," although I may think of myself as acting out a part of Chinese history. Nowadays I think we, my fellow artists in Hong Kong and I, are much more comfortable with the identity issue. We don't think any more in terms of East meets West, especially since the Basic Law went into effect.

E: The Basic Law?

WT: Yes, that was the British-Sino agreement signed in 1987 that gave us our own system of Hong Kong law.

E: It's a whole system of jurisprudence?

WT: Yes, we have our own jurisdiction, and our Final Court established in Hong Kong. Basically it preserves the British rule, but we don't serve the Queen.

After that Hong Kong artists felt an initial compulsion to address specific Hong Kong issues, like 1997, but then things kind of settled.

E: Because the Basic Law agreement guaranteed you the ability to practice your art after 1997?

WT: Yes, though people continue to have lots of questions even about the Basic Law. For example, under British rule there was the I.C.A.C.—Independent Committee Against Corruption. We still aren't sure how that kind of guarantee of freedom of expression will be handled under the new system. Yet, we are obviously now much more free to define our own identity. In Taiwan, the Cloud Gate Company represents things Taiwanese, and in China Beijing represents China, but in Hong Kong there is a lot of variety now. We all respect one another, and want to "do our own thing." Precisely because we don't consider ourselves a nation, we don't carry the burden of proving ourselves as any one thing in particular. I think we have more confidence in the quality of our works. The fashion designers, for example, are saying "We are aiming for an international style." The painters, who used to feel they had to use Chinese ink as an expression of the Hong Kong style, are now saying "Why not use oil or airbrush?" Among ourselves we no longer ask "What is the Hong Kong style?" We just say "produce good works."

E: And how are the new artists, especially in dance, being trained?

WT: Of course the Academy for Performing Arts (APA) is very important, as it trains a lot of dancers in three "streams"—ballet, modern dance and Chinese Dance. There are so many dancers coming out that CCDC and the other professional companies can't take them all; it's almost like New York! They have to make their own performance opportunities, form their own companies or whatever. It's becoming busier, the competition is keener. The drawback is that it is difficult to attract dancers into the professional world, because Hong Kong's young people are quite practical. They want to have security, so many consider it better to go for an M.B.A. and dance in their spare time.

E: One hopes that the graduates of APA will want to become members of the world dance community, rather than being limited to Hong Kong.

WT: It's really vice versa, because we (the professional companies) don't think of ourselves as limited to Hong Kong dancers.

E: What percentage of the dancers in CCDC are from Hong Kong?

WT: We have about half local, and the rest are from all over the world. It's very mixed.

E: And the other companies?

WT: Of course the Hong Kong Company is mainly Chinese, about half local and half from the Mainland. The Hong Kong Ballet is very international, with relatively few locals. I think they have 26 dancers now, with only five or six from APA.

Figures 30-31   City Contemporary Dance Company in
Willy Tsao's *The Long March* (1990)

Figures 32-33 City Contemporary Dance Company in
Willy Tsao's *The Long March* (1990)

E: Isn't there some kind of agreement with the government that that company has to take APA graduates?

WT: Yes, they take them in, but they also turn them over quickly. I don't know why. That's the way it is in ballet, whereas the Chinese companies are very stable. Hong Kong is probably the best place in the world for a Chinese dancer to be. It is a relatively good place for modern dancers as well. That's because we are still small, rather like a family.

E: How many are in your company?

WT: Sixteen: eight boys and eight girls.

E: How long do your dancers usually stay with you?

WT: The foreign dancers not too long. I don't think it is wise for them to stay more than two or three years. We have local dancers who have been with us for eight or more years

E: Has the dance community of Hong Kong any interaction with Taiwan?

WT: Yes. CCDC is very close to Cloud Gate. I'm very good friends with Lin Hwai-min, the founding director of Cloud Gate. He always comes to APA to be one of their examiners. He invited us to Taiwan and we invited them back, and as a matter of fact I arranged for him to go to Guangzhou last month to do a lecture. He did a wonderful presentation on Isadora Duncan. They loved him, and I think he enjoyed it.

Figure 34 *Invisible Cities* (1992), choreographed by Helen Lai for the City Contemporary Dance Company

E: How would you compare CCDC with Cloud Gate?

WT: I think Cloud Gate dancers are very strong, very high energy, and they have a recognizable style.

E: That's from Lin Hwai-min?

WT: Oh definitely! They're all little Lins on stage. Even the girls develop that kind of rough-edged, macho style. At CCDC the background is more varied, and I intend to keep it that way. I want our dancers to be more adaptable. I require them to take class each morning as a group, but I want them to retain their individual qualities. Also, I encourage them to do their own choreography. Cloud Gate's work is always held to the highest quality, whereas I am a little more relaxed.

E: Cloud Gate is a complete corporation. They do all their own technical work, publicity, etc. They are heavily managed. Is that also true of CCDC?

WT: Yes, we do everything in-house.

E: You maintain a staff of how many?

WT: 40; 24 in staff, plus the dance personnel.

E: You must be quite busy, with commitments not only to your company, but also to Guangdong.

WT: Yes, but by now I have good experienced help at CCDC, and I find it exciting to be involved in something that is still quite new. I hope to

Figure 35 Members of the City Contemporary Dance Company in
Willy Tsao's *Journey to the West* (1990)

have another year or two with Guangdong, and then they won't need me any more.

E: What kinds of things do you see for the future? What do you think Hong Kong needs?

WT: Actually, I have a secret wish for post-1997. Right now it's hard to push CCDC internationally because people think "What, Hong Kong...?" whereas when they hear Guangdong, they think "Oh yes, China!" Maybe after 1997 CCDC will benefit from the same recognition, as one of the premier companies from a major world power. I personally get lots of requests. Malaysia recently asked me to set up a modern dance company there, for instance. Maybe I will go there, or even to Mainland China, where there are lots of cities that could support a company. Maybe that's the direction my career is to take, as initiator of new companies in a part of the world that is crying out for them.

Chapter Thirteen:
Day Trip

Tom Brown

Tom Brown holds an M.F.A. in Dance from Sarah Lawrence College, and is certified as a Labanotation Reconstructor, Notator and Teacher by the Dance Notation Bureau in New York City. Since 1985 he has served on the faculty of the Hong Kong Academy for Performing Arts, where he is currently Head of Modern Dance. He taught previously at SUNY -Purchase, Oberlin College, and Snowbird Summer Institute. As a performer he co-founded, directed, and performed with Dance Junction (1979-85), and danced with the Daniel Lewis Company. As a choreographer he has consistently produced several new pieces each year since 1977, including recent works set to traditional and contemporary Chinese music. His reconstructions from Labanotation span a wide range of modern dance, with emphasis on the works of Doris Humphrey. Mr. Brown is a member of the International Movement Notation Alliance (President, 1984-86), the International Council of Kinetography Laban, the Dance Notation Bureau, and the Congress on Research in Dance.

I

It is 9:00 Monday morning and I am meeting my Advanced Diploma Two Modern Dance Technique class at the Hong Kong Academy for Performing Arts. These students are in their fourth year. Like dancers anywhere in the world they have swathed themselves in odds and ends of clothing worn as much for the comfort and reassurance of something familiar while beginning their daily journey of discovery as to ward off the slight chill in the air of the studio. They cluster in groups of two or three, with an occasional solitary figure at the barre, stretching, massaging sore muscles, chatting about the events of the weekend or plans for the coming week. I greet them with "Jo san," Cantonese for "good morning." A few murmur "good morning" or "Jo san"; some just smile shyly.

I say hello to my pianist, this morning Nelson Hui, a Chinese-American from Hawaii. He is a very gifted musician who uses piano, drums and flutes to transform my exercises into dances. On other days I might have any one of the other four or five Modern Dance accompanists. Two of these are my former dance students, Julia Mok and Amy Yung, who decided to work as freelance dancers/choreographers rather than join the only professional modern company in Hong Kong (City Contemporary Dance Company) or continue their education abroad, which are the main choices for modern dance students after they complete their studies at the Academy. All of the accompanists at the Academy are good, but these three are especially so. Nelson in particular makes the technique class an event that I anticipate with enthusiasm. Early this term I demonstrated a *petit allegro* combination with a shaking motif and asked Nelson for some rock and roll. He played and sang *Good Golly Miss Molly* with so much "juice" that it has inspired me to choreograph a suite of dances this spring to Little Richard's music.

After my salutation to the class and to Nelson I take roll call. One or two students always seem to slip in at the last minute. Although Hong Kong is small, some students need to give themselves one and a half to two hours to get to school during the morning rush hour. The wealthier and more enterprising ones occasionally get together and rent a room or small apartment in Wanchai, the neighborhood where the Academy is located. Wanchai is famous because of its association with Suzy Wong and the H.M.S. Tamar, the British Naval base that acts as a landing site for the world's sailors when their ships anchor in the harbor on R&R or re-provisioning stops. When the Academy first opened it was one of the few "straight" enterprises in this erstwhile tenderloin district. Today it's the other way around; the nightclubs are in a definite and declining minority. New buildings have gone up all around the Academy, including Asia's tallest, a 70 plus story reinterpretation of the Empire State. Together with the buildings, prices have soared, and fewer and fewer students are able to solve their commuting problems by renting rooms close to the Academy.

Today's class consists of fifteen students. Twelve have registered for the course. Of the others, two are graduates—one dancing for the Hong Kong Ballet, the other teaching occasional classes in private studios—and the third is a professional dancer spending a few months in Hong Kong who has asked to join the class for maintenance purposes. The students have distributed themselves in four lines around the 35 by 45 foot studio. They seem to have a tacit agreement about this arrangement; it changes daily, and I have not been able to figure out how the rotation works. Perhaps it is only random, but occasionally a temperate discussion erupts between two of them and they exchange places, the other students contributing comments from the sidelines.

I begin class with a long *plié* combination, *demi* and *grand*, with breath-initiated torso bends and gentle swings in the upper body. I change the combination daily, emphasizing curving one day, tilting the next. Sometimes I'll have the movement led by the head, other times by the sternum, or through expulsion or intake of the breath. Alternation of syncopated and regular timing may dominate the daily *plié* exercise,

Figure 36-37 Hong Kong Academy for Performing Arts dance students in *With My Red Fires*. Choreographer: Doris Humphrey; Director: Tom Brown

Figure 38-39   Hong Kong Academy for Performing Arts dance students in *With My Red Fires*.
Choreographer: Doris Humphrey; Director: Tom Brown

as may twisting and off-vertical emphasis. I demonstrate the exercise once, in one position, on one side, then do it in time once, and then we're off.

One of the long walls of the studio consists of windows that look out to the harbor; the opposite wall is mirrored. For these first exercises I start the class facing toward the harbor, and after about half an hour we turn to the mirrors. My teaching style derives from many sources. The content is eclectic. It has elements of Limón, with whom I was fortunate to study at the Philadelphia Musical Academy for a year and a half, dancing in a repertory company under his directorship. There are also Wigman influences in my work: I studied at Temple University with Helmut Fricke-Gottschild and danced in his Zero Moving Company, as well as in its predecessor, Group Motion. Peter Saul's brand of Cunningham technique emerges in one or two facets of the class, as does Eric Hawkins' work. There are ideas gleaned from reconstructing Doris Humphrey's choreography, and others that found their way into my vocabulary during fifteen years as a performer with choreographers as diverse as Anna Sokolow, Rudy Perez and Daniel Lewis. In my teaching style and class management, however, I borrow the most from Peter Saul. Like Peter, my facing the class away from the mirror in these opening exercises is a strategy to get the students away from fixating on their image in the mirror and into focusing on their bodies in real space. For the most part the plan succeeds, but it has its occasional drawbacks.

Some mornings the air is so clear, the sky so luminous, the cloud formations so magical as seen through our giant windows, that I can't help stopping the class to look. The students giggle, but look and enjoy. Sparrows nest in the superstructure of blue tubular steel that cascades from the Academy's roof to the ground below like a giant tinker-toy. Sometimes their morning play is in perfect synchrony with our movements. Eagles swoop down from their thousand foot high reconnaissance and hang outside the windows at our level, catching our eye as we return to the vertical from a deep full-body swing. A foreign aircraft carrier will depart from the H.M.S. Tamar with scores of dress-white attired sailors aligned in a file around its perimeter. A Gurkha rescue team on maneuvers will drop a man from a hovering helicopter along a cable for a couple hundred feet to the roof of a building, where he will neatly unfasten his harness and hold the line taut for the next guy coming down. From our vantage point the wire is hard to discern, the helicopter sometimes out of view; we are caught unawares, and see only men defying gravity, floating down a magical column of space. Sometimes the events outside our window provide me with fortuitous images; I can use them to evince a quality in the movement we are doing. "Remember the breathlessness you felt when you thought the man was falling from the sky" (one student cried out the first time we saw the Gurkhas in their exercises). "That's the way you should feel as you suspend at the top of the great falls." At other times our observations from the studio windows remain poetically beautiful images that we store in reserve. I justify these occasional interruptions by saying that the eyes are part of the body on which our morning ritual focuses, the mind in its ability to perceive beauty, magic, and wonder is also a part, and the space outside our studio window is part of the real space in which we dance.

The class proceeds, but unlike Peter I do not eschew generous amounts of touching to get my ideas across to the students. My Cantonese is abominable and I'm never sure of their English, so gentle touching, prodding, kneading, pushing and pulling frequently stand in for verbalizing. In these opening exercises I work on the students' alignment, breathing, muscle tension and relaxation. The changes that take place during their four years at the Academy never cease to amaze me. Most come to us with little training, almost all with no modern dance training. By the time they leave they are throwing themselves around as if they own the space they dance in, sure of themselves, of the steps they take, knowing that their bodies will not fail them. They achieve this transformation through an indefatigable, tenacious energy. Their capacity for work is prodigious and inspiring.

In my morning class they continue to work at overcoming bad habits. Not forcing turn out is always a big issue; unfortunately, much of the teaching at the Hong Kong Academy, as at many of the world's academies, still encourages it. Core support strengthening seems an everlasting concern, and although there's not enough flab in the whole room to compete with the schmaltz from one chicken, frequently the wrong muscles are overdeveloped. The men are thin, wiry, muscular, straight up and down. On first inspection their muscles seem to be hard, taut, unyielding. The women are, for the most part, only slightly more curvaceous. Both achieve a remarkable degree of flexibility in the hip joint (most as a result of strenuous hands-on stretching). The proportions of a Southern Chinese person's body are somewhat different from the classical European model that is familiar to most Westerners. The lengths of the whole leg and the lower leg are a bit shorter, frequently making the torso seem longer. I list my height as five feet eight inches on forms requiring that information. Only a handful of the two hundred plus students I have taught at the Academy are taller than I am.

One of the problems Westerners perceive when teaching at the Academy derives from the Hong Kong students' thin frames on average-height bodies. Western dancers use their body's mass to emphasize strength when hurtling through space. Their long limbs underscore indulgence in time when they unfurl their leg or reach their arm. The sensuousness of curved bodies enveloping one another, or an imaginary partner, or force in space, helps to draw American audiences into a kinesthetic rapport with American dancers. Initial reactions from guest teachers at the Academy frequently include citing a lack of qualitative differentiation in the Hong Kong students' dancing. As with all students, teaching them quality, one of the prime ingredients of artistry, is a central issue, one that I address in all my classes at the Academy. Different bodies will emphasize different concerns. It is part of an ongoing process; Hong Kong dancers and choreographers are discovering a style, a voice, a vocabulary of the body and of nuance, with which they can address issues of importance to them. (To be fair, not

Figure 40   José Limón's *Missa Brevis,* performed by students of the
Hong Kong Academy for Performing Arts

all visitors note qualitative deficiency in Academy dancers. I remember Daniel
Lewis' reaction when he first saw Antoinette Mak's performance of the *Crucifixus*
solo from José Limón's *Missa Brevis*. "My God," he said. "I know a few

professional dancers in New York who would love to be able to perform that solo with as much eloquence as this student does.")

Currently the students have technique classes Monday through Saturday. The faculty constantly debates the relative merits of one- or two-day weekends. Those for a two-day weekend cite the need for more recuperative time in the students' heavy schedules (most students at the Academy have 24 hour-and-a-quarter or hour-and-a-half classes a week. These include both studio work and academic courses). Those faculty members in favor of the six-day week argue that our students' entering technical level is weaker than elsewhere, and that after two days of holiday it takes considerably more effort to pull them back into their work. This morning the students let their bodies sing. Their Sunday of rest has restored them and they have returned to class with fresh enthusiasm. I make my rounds during the *pliés*, the *port de bras*, the hinges and swings. I may stand in front of someone and breathe with them, or remind one student of his ribs, another of her pelvis. I rub one student's tense neck, rein in someone else's overly turned-out feet.

My first classes in Hong Kong often seemed to confuse the students. They would stop in the middle of an exercise and look around, lost, as if suddenly awakened from a bad dream, not knowing where they were. Sometimes they would persevere through an exercise at the expense of mowing down their classmates. I would stand on the sidelines, helplessly gesticulating or stunned into silence. Out in the streets of Hong Kong, on the other hand, I would be the one out of place. I was forever bumping into people or ending up squeezed against a wall or down in the gutter, while the rest of the crowd seemed to move along unhindered, albeit in what I interpreted as a haphazard fashion. Besides negotiating the twists and turns of traffic differently from my fellow pedestrians, I frequently found myself impatient with their pace. They seemed to go about their walking much more slowly than I was used to doing in New York. The Hong Kong person's sense of space was definitely different from mine, and this seemed to have implications for how fast they moved in crowded places. In the studio I like to give movement that slices through space with quick and abrupt changes of direction, covering big distances with fast locomotive phrases. Sometimes I'll give an "A" and a "B" phrase in canon, causing the dancers to move past and around each other, consciously setting up near misses. For the neophyte Hong Kong dancers these were new and difficult tasks, ones that seemed not to be reinforced by their daily non-dancing habits.

In the *petit allegro* I observed another phenomenon that was different from my experience in American dance classes, and related, I think, to the Hong Kong environment. I would usually divide the class into smaller groups to perform the combination, each group consisting of six to eight students. I would space the students in the studio so that each had enough room to do the movement comfortably without worrying that they might collide. By the middle of the combination the whole group would be clustered together in one part of the room, as if attracted by a magnetic force. I would subdivide the two groups again, and *voilà*, like water rushing to a drain, the students would reduce the enormous studio to an area no bigger than the average New York City bathroom.

I remember going to dinner at Carl Wolz's apartment when I first interviewed for the job in Hong Kong. After dinner we had coffee on his terrace. Spread before me was the spectacle of the densest city in the world. Buildings packed together so tightly that I could imagine being able to see the dinner plates of the apartment occupants across the road. Not only did the buildings seem closer than in New York, but there were more people on narrower sidewalks abutting even narrower, car-choked streets. On my annual trips back to New York City I have noticed an increased awareness of the city's streets. I have begun to see New York's avenues, especially in non-rush hours, as vast empty spaces, full of potential hidden danger and threat. Of course I have friends in New York who have lived there while I have lived here who share this foreboding.

An incident this summer reinforced my belief that my perception of space has changed. I took a boat trip in Hawaii with a Chinese friend from Hong Kong. We were queuing on the dock, waiting to board the boat. As our turn came to step onto the gangplank the ship's crewman who was helping people board looked at me and said, "Stop crowding there. Don't push." Well, I was offended. I wasn't pushing. I was vacationing and completely relaxed. I wasn't in a rush. Reflecting later I realized that I had closed the gap between the person in front and me; I had made the space between us narrower as people do in Hong Kong, as my Chinese friend behind me did. I had become accustomed to using less space. People use less space in Hong Kong because there is less space available and more people to use it.

Despite these apparent cultural differences Hong Kong students are quick to gain an appreciation for the alternate choices that I use in my work. My Advanced Diploma Two students eat up the space with big-stepping movement. They perform a quick series of four or five direction changes and step out with certainty into yet another new direction. They have learned in their four years of study to modulate their dancing with a full palette of emotional colors. They are always eager to learn more, and compel me through their enthusiasm to continue to create for them. We finish the class at 10:30. To me it always seems as if only a few moments have passed since I said "Jo san." We have a fifteen minute break before our next class begins.

II

Like the rest of the faculty I teach twelve classes a week. It is a heavy schedule that demands efficiency and great concentration. Sometimes during production preparation, when rehearsals are added to the schedule, we feel overworked. At those times, however, we are so geared up to getting our ideas on the stage, so much into the work that we have spent our lives developing, that we barely notice the extra hours. We are fortunate to have a support mechanism, the School of Technical Arts, whose faculty and students help mount each dance as if it were being shown at Covent Garden or the New York State Theater. Also, the dance faculty works very well together, possibly because of its multi-national, multi-cultural origins. Our differences sometimes seem so great that only by learning to respect the differences have we been able to accommodate them. Maybe our rapport derives in part from the fact that ours is a new faculty in a new institution.

My next class on this Monday morning is Modern Dance History. It is designed for Advanced Diploma One and Degree Year One (third year) students. In their first year the students have a semester-long course entitled "Introduction to Dance" that explores dance's niche in world culture, as well as various models for examining non-verbal communication. Their second history course, a survey of world dance that is taken by all majors in Ballet, Modern Dance, Musical Theater and Chinese Dance, is two semesters long. In their third year the students in each "stream" go their own way, taking a two-semester history course focusing on their major field of study. The History mode is completed in the fourth year when everyone takes a one-semester Aesthetics and Criticism course. All of the courses meet once a week, and are complemented by Cultural History and History of Music classes.

I teach in English, although this course has been taught by Cantonese speaking teachers. The school has an English proficiency entrance requirement, and the students study English throughout their time at the Academy. Many of the Southeast

Figure 41   *Triptych,* by Takako Asakawa, performed by students
of the Hong Kong Academy for Performing Arts

Asian students are able to speak Putonghua (Mandarin), which is also taught at the Academy, and learn Guangdonghua (Cantonese) both in especially arranged classes and during their daily encounters with their Hong Kong classmates. The English levels of the students vary. Because of this, and the intricacies of language needed to discuss the leading choreographic artists of the twentieth century, I give time for translation. The more adept English speakers translate for those who are deficient in English skills. Many of the students also bring hand-held translation computers to class. Translation in today's class is into Cantonese, Mandarin and Korean. The Academy attracts students from all over Asia, and occasionally from the United States and Europe as well.

Because of the early colonials' inability to pronounce Chinese names it is customary for Hong Kong students to choose English names. In today's class the "English" names run the gamut from the ordinary, like Shirley, Margaret, and Anthony, to the more exotic, like Koala, Gory, and Sean. One of our graduates chose the name Satan. He won a scholarship to study during the summer at the American Dance Festival in Durham. When he enrolled for classes the Registrar there asked him to use another name. He became Damien.

This morning's class is our second about Martha Graham. The students have read Deborah Jowitt's chapter on Graham in *Time and the Dancing Image*, a chapter in Ernestine Stodelle's *Deep Song*, and looked at the Graham *Notebooks*, as well as a number of videotapes of her choreography. Today we will discuss two different films of performances of *Appalachian Spring*, the 1958 one with Graham as the young bride and the 1977 version with Yuriko Kimura in that role. My aim is to identify the different interpretations of this role and to talk about how these differences affect our appreciation of the choreography. On the surface my proposal seems straightforward, but there are difficulties that emerge as we begin our discussion.

In the United States my job would be to keep the discussion on track—to avoid allowing tangential material to creep in, and to move from one point to the next without getting stuck on small details. In Hong Kong my greatest difficulty is getting the students talking, and keeping the discussion going. I will ask a question in class and be met with complete silence, even if the question is "What did you have for breakfast?" I rephrase the question. Still no one answers. I go to my roll book, call a name, and ask the question again. The student stammers, blushes, holds her hand to her mouth, looks down at the floor, and still does not answer. I begin to wonder if my fly is undone, or if I have broached a subject that is taboo, or have simply taken leave of my senses. There have been seasoned teachers who, when confronted with a classroom of downcast faces and blank stares in response to a simple question, have stormed out of the room, sure that a conspiracy against them was afoot.

After lengthy discussions with secondary school teachers and students who have gone through Hong Kong's education system I have discovered a few of the underlying causes of the students' classroom demeanor. Primary and secondary education in Hong Kong, up to and including Secondary Form Five, is generally based on lectures delivered from compendious notes. The classroom subject matter is prescribed by the Board of Education in extensive subject syllabi. The minimum size of a class is 40 students. Because of the scope of the material that the teacher needs to cover in each class session there is little time for questions. The students are constantly tested on their level of understanding. Their main strategy for success on these tests is memorization of the teacher's notes. The tests culminate in the Hong Kong Certificate of Education Examinations (HKCEE), which are held at the completion of Form Five [equivalent to the junior year of high school in the United States]. Continuation to "A Levels" preparation (Form Six and Seven), or equivalent programs (such as the Academy's Diploma program), and subsequent continuation to college level education, depends on attaining five HKCEE passes. Compounding the effects of this tradition is the premium placed on reticence as a positive behavioral trait for women and reservedness as the proper attitude for men in Chinese culture. There is also the proscription against losing "face." Mistakes cause loss of "face." Even when the student thinks she has the right idea or has made an interesting observation she hesitates to verbalize it until she is certain that the formulation of her idea is "correct"—i.e., that it conforms to the models provided her by those in the endless notes given by her teachers. Multiply all of this by the fact that the students must translate their ideas into English, a second language, and the magnitude of the problem is clear.

This morning, to get the ball rolling, I make the first few observations myself. I point out that Yuriko seems to slither in one movement, and then ask them to describe Graham's performance of the same movement. I allow one student to make her observation in Chinese, then ask another to translate it. This removes the stigma of misformulation from the observer and misinformation from the translator, who can't be held accountable because she is performing a job for which she is untrained. After a while the students take over. They are working among themselves, relaying observations, opinions, and arguments to each other and to me. They question apparent contradictions between performances. They cite information gleaned from their reading. They also get off the track, revel in gossip, and generally duplicate experiences I have had with their American counterparts.

These students have had the benefit of seeing, meeting with, and learning from many of the leading modern dance artists of our time. Hong Kong is "the gateway to Asia," and is frequently one of the stops on Asian tours of dance companies from around the world. Regular faculty and guest residencies at the Academy have included Lucas Hoving, Daniel Lewis, Sarah Stackhouse, Marcia Siegel, Mel Wong, Rosalind Newman, Takako Asakawa, Larry White, Lin Hwai-Min, Chiang Ching, Connie Kreemer, Tom Borek, Ruth Solomon and Daniel Maloney. Master class teachers have included the directors or company members of almost every dance company that has passed through Hong Kong since the Academy opened. From the first to the fifth year of its history the Academy hosted an annual festival, during which its students performed for and acted as hosts to students from the world's leading dance academies. International conferences of dance scholars and artists were held in conjunction with these festivals, enabling the students to attend presentations of the most current scholarship in dance's many fields of interest.

At the end of our class this morning the students present topics for their semester research paper. These include: The White Oak Project; Doris Humphrey's use of breath in *Water Study*; Pina Bausch's Tanz Theater; The Judson Church and Steve Paxton; an examination of Merce Cunningham's *Points in Space*; a study of Yvonne Rainer's *Trio A*; and a study of Maurice Bejart. I have allowed the class to run over, impinging on the students' lunch hour. Now I let them run to the canteen, pack up my books, films and papers, and head for my office. My break is considerably longer than the students', as I don't teach again until 2:45, the second period after lunch. I will use the time to finish preparation for my afternoon composition and repertory classes.

III

Students participate in repertory throughout their studies at the Academy. The material and the number of classes devoted to repertory varies according to a student's level. The content of a class may consist of Standard Repertory, where teachers use their performance experience to teach dances drawn from memory, videotape, film, and notes (Labanotation scores are another important source; three of the Modern Dance faculty are Labanotation literate), or, at higher levels, regular and guest faculty create new dances in the repertory classes. In the Modern Dance stream we have also been fortunate to have members of City Contemporary Dance Company teach works from the company's repertory.

The students perform the dance phrases, sections, and complete works learned in repertory classes in a variety of informal settings. They also present repertory class material in concerts open to the general public at any of the Academy's three theaters, at other Hong Kong venues, and on international tours. The works shown in these concerts are produced with costume, set, sound, and lighting designs contributed by staff and students from the School of Technical Arts. Costume and set construction is done in the Academy's workshops. The technical crew is augmented by staff and students of Stage Management. Musical accompaniment is often provided by staff and students of the School of Music.

In my repertory class this afternoon there are both third and fourth year students, and one postgraduate fellow. I am choreographing a duet and teaching it to three casts. One of the men is from Malaysia and the second is a graduate of Beijing's Central Academy. He was awarded a scholarship to study modern dance at the Hong Kong Academy and is on leave from China's Army Dance Company. The third man is a graduate of the Dance Department of the Seoul Institute of the Arts, and danced as a member of Park Il-kyu's company. All three women are from Hong Kong. Two were recipients of scholarships to study at the American Dance Festival in Durham this past summer.

I am using Lou Harrison's *Garden of the Sun* as music for the duet. The students giggled and started improvising chinoiserie when I first played it for them. Most of these students took part in a project earlier this semester in which other members of the dance faculty and I choreographed a series of dances for a production that we took to Canada as part of a Hong Kong festival there. (By the time they leave the Academy most of our students have participated in at least one international tour.) In one of those dances I used traditional music from the Yue people, and developed my ideas from Chinese Dance motifs. Thus the fun poked at me (and the recognition of Lou Harrison's sources).

I have given the students a motivational idea for the opening chords and ask them to come up with their own movement. Their task is to use the ideas of folding and unfolding in three partnered phrases. Two of the couples are working feverishly, and have devised material that seems to belie my sense of their culture's premium on reticence and reservedness. The man from Korea, Sean, and Scarlet Wong, whom previously I had considered one of the primmest women in class, have created a lift in which he holds her with her pubis at his face level. She has stretched her legs horizontally behind her and arched her upper body so that her face is almost parallel to the ceiling. They have trouble coming out of the lift into the next folding, so we work on that for a while. The man from Beijing, Zhao Ming, and Rachel Yip, one of the scholarship awardees, have made three different sets of foldings and unfoldings, and we go about trying to select from among them. The man from Malaysia, Keat Lim, and Vanessa Cheung, the other scholarship recipient, are having trouble coming up with the first unfolding. They are the least experienced of the six dancers. Keat and Vanessa are approximately the same height, and Keat has already confided in me that he is afraid he won't be able to lift Vanessa with the same effortlessness that the other men lift their partners. One of my goals for the duet is to give the students the opportunity to experience partnering work, so I have designed quite a few lifts for the dance. I have assured Keat that I use counterbalance for much of my *pas de deux* work, and that I will teach Vanessa and him the cooperation that is needed to accomplish the lifts. He seems unconvinced, but throws himself into the work with energy.

My habit when creating a new work is to sketch my ideas in raw form during early rehearsals and return later to develop them. I frequently work in a similar way when teaching existent material. The students in lower levels take some time adjusting to this way of working; they tend to hold on to the first thing I give them, ignoring later emendations. It takes a while to convince the students that the rehearsal process is as much about exploring the possibilities of an idea as it is about stating the idea. I have worked with my three couples this afternoon enough that we understand one another perfectly. As each couple shows the material I have choreographed so far, I make slight changes that they adopt immediately. Sometimes all three couples will change to accommodate the new material; at other times I make changes based on the needs and abilities of the individual dancers.

The repertory class is over. We have recently cut the length of afternoon classes to an hour and fifteen minutes each (from an hour and a half), so that the students' day goes from 9 AM to 5:30 PM. I would like to have the additional 15 minutes to work on my piece, but it is time to move on.

IV

My last class of the day is also my favorite, Diploma Two Composition. This is the students' first composition course; they will continue to study composition through-out their stay at the Academy. Students are now able to major in Composition, Performance, Dance Direction (which includes a strong notation component) or Education within their chosen stream (Ballet, Modern Dance, or Chinese Dance). We plan to continue these concentrations in Master's level work, and add the fields of Dance Ethnography and Community Dance. When Roz Newman was here she and I frequently combined and co-taught our composition classes. That worked so well that I have continued the practice with Roz's replacement, Betsy Fisher. We aim to teach the students compositional theories and allow them the opportunity to develop work based on those theories. It is also our intention to develop their ability to observe each other's work and verbalize those observations. The latter aim is supported by the work the students do in their Laban Movement Analysis, Labanotation and Dance History modules. We draw parallels between the theory and practice of composition and material they are covering in Technique and Repertory classes. It is in the composition class that all of the students' experiences can be brought together and used to build a unified understanding of the art form.

In devising ways for the students to look at dance and talk about what they see I have relied upon techniques developed by Marcia Siegel, Claire Porter, and Martha Davis. Marcia has taught week-long seminars at the Academy on two occasions, once for dance critics, Academy faculty and interested students, and the second time for our composition teachers and invited students. In both instances she based discussions about dances on the idea of "Lexicon," a way to discern the essential elements of a dance work that leads to interpretation. The methods she espoused have proven invaluable to me in getting the students to see what is going on in a dance and talk about it.

In this afternoon's class we will look at and critique first showings of a study we started in the last session. Betsy and I gave the students an assignment to make a dance about a journey. We told them that the journey should embark and should conclude; in between we asked them to include an encounter. This is a solo study, and we have given the additional instruction that all locomotion should be led by the center of gravity. We allowed that the journey could go through an interior landscape. In our last class we improvised travelling through space led by the center of gravity, we took various pathways through innumerable imaginary landscapes, and we explored the ideas of beginning and ending. In today's showings and their critiques we see the occasional rearrangement of classroom vocabulary, and hear, now and then, stories remarkably similar to *Genesis*. However, we also see movement that springs from the idiosyncratic need of its creator, and descriptions of movement that dwell not in the imagination of the observer but are based on actual events.

The end of class brings to a conclusion my daily journey. There are no evening rehearsals tonight. I'll go home, eat, sleep, and prepare for tomorrow's journey. It has been a satisfying day. This day trip that has run on for eight years seems to have been well spent.

Part IV:

Indonesia

Chapter Fourteen:
Tradition and Change in Bali

I Wayan Dibia

I Wayan Dibia was born in Singapadu village of Gianyar (Bali) to a family of well-known artists for traditional Balinese theatrical forms. He has trained in classical Balinese music and dance with various masters from his island. He studied at the Conservatorium of Indonesian Traditional Performing Arts (KOKAR), and received his B.A. at STSI Denpasar, where he served as the Institute's Assistant Director. He studied dance in New York, and received his M.A. and Ph.D. from UCLA under the sponsorship of the Asian Cultural Council and the Fulbright-Hays Scholar Program respectively. He is now a faculty member at STSI Denpasar. Mr. Dibia has won the highest acclaim as one of Indonesia's finest dancers, choreographers and scholars specializing in Balinese performing arts. His original works have been seen throughout Indonesia, and he has performed in Asia, West Germany, the United States, and Australia.

My involvement with cross-cultural dance has been life-long and multifaceted. I learned modern dance in my home region, Bali, from American dancers. I have been trained in Javanese dance as well as Balinese. One might not immediately think of that as "cross-cultural training," but those forms are actually the products of quite different cultures. I went to West Germany in 1976 and to the US in 1980, where I taught and conducted workshops in Balinese dance. During my residency in Los Angeles I often performed Javanese dance at the California Institute of the Arts. Over the last five years I have enjoyed a very fruitful collaboration with Keith Terry in the United States.

Let me try to put my career in something like chronological order. I started out studying Balinese dance from my parents. My father was a well-known dancer in *Topeng*, the masked dance drama, and *Arja*, the Balinese operatic form. My mother was also an *Arja* dancer. Hence, dance has always been a part of my life. In Bali it is common for someone who has grown up within a family of artists to continue in that occupation. This is because our community sometimes requires that we take on that obligation. Since my family has always been regarded as the leader of performing arts by the local villagers, whenever there is need from the community for arts performances, like temple festivals or other village celebrations, the villagers will ask someone in my family to prepare whatever art form might be suitable. I have a social obligation to my community to carry out that duty.

I believe that in Western societies as children grow up many of them reject their parents' line of work, in order to be independent. For me that was never an issue; assuming those responsibilities that my parents had traditionally borne was something respectful, and I am very proud of the duties I am now carrying. I have had some bitter experiences when the local people have put down some of my works because they didn't live up to expectations, but generally I feel that my works and those of my family have been appreciated. The fact that my present duty was passed on to me from my grandfather and my parents gives it very special meaning to me and my life. Again, my situation is quite different from that of most Western artists, who start from nothing—with no "credits"—and have to build from there. I started off in a tradition and therefore had respect from the beginning. In cultures like mine, where art is part of religion and of social life, the artist enjoys a privileged position.

Let me go back to my earliest experience. When I was 9 years old my father taught me a warrior dance called *Baris,* but at that time I thought that I wouldn't be a dancer. I thought that because my skin was so dark I wouldn't look good in that dance. I learned the dance anyway, but at the same time I tried to switch to playing gamelan, and until the third year of high school (at KOKAR, Indonesian Conservatory of Performing Arts) I concentrated mostly on that. Then, one of the main dancers of the *Ramayana* dance drama in my school became ill, and he chose me to replace him. That was a great challenge, but as I knew the music very well I could see the structure of the dance through the music. After only three hours of very intensive training I performed the role of Hanuman. The head of the school was pleased with my performance, and asked me to leave the gamelan and concentrate on dance.

In 1962 I went to ASTI Indonesian Dance Academy in Denpasar, and there began to learn dance forms other than Balinese. When I graduated from the Academy in 1973 I went to ASTI Yogyakarta, in Central Java, for my *Seniman Seni Tari* (or Indonesian M.A.) degree. For two years I learned Javanese dance music and dance there. To perform my role (Hanuman) in the *Ramayama* I utilized a lot of the Javanese movement that I liked and found suitable for enriching the movement vocabulary of this character. Thereafter, I have tended to use some Javanese dance movement in all of my choreography.

After I got my SST degree I returned to ASTI Denpasar, at which I had been employed since 1974. Then, in 1980, I was invited to participate in a project in New York City called "Workshop in Southeast Asian Theatre." The project was sponsored by La Mama, and the director was Julie Taymor. From then on I had direct exposure to modern dance, because I was given a small grant to observe dance activities around New York City. I went to modern dance concerts, to ballet,

Figure 42 I Wayan Dibia performing with members of the
Indonesian State College of the Arts (STSI), Bali, Indonesia

and to other art forms. Then I was given a six-month grant by the Asian Cultural
Council to take classes, so I studied at the Graham Studio, the Cunningham School,
and with Nikolais, as well as attending some jazz classes.

All of this I found very interesting; it really opened my mind about how to make
elements of Balinese dance alive in the modern world. Before, I felt there was a
sort of stagnation of the tradition, for almost no new works were being introduced.
From modern dance I learned the value of the individual approach—of different
points of view. Out of that experience I have choreographed at least 75 works, most
of which have been well accepted by the local people. I had just one bad experience
before I went to New York. That was when I choreographed a piece utilizing
postures of modern dance I saw in copies of *Dance Magazine* sent to me by a
friend. Perhaps I went beyond the limits of my culture. Some people became
offended watching that work.

It has been said that the Balinese are quite fanatical in preserving their traditions,
but I believe they are not conservative. They are quite eager to see new works. One
can even, for example, make variations in a classical piece like the *Ramayana*, as
long as the story is still there and the spirit and phrasing of the movement is still
Balinese. Our motivation in Bali has always been to create something new to be
added to the vocabulary of the traditional Balinese art forms. But that can be done
only by someone who has been trained in the traditional forms. Without that there
would be no freedom for the artist. He might want to extend, or add, or transform

have the same motivation because, again, the challenge we have from our society is to create something new that enriches the tradition, or helps it to survive. I would like to create what I call "modern Balinese dance." By this I mean using the techniques of Western modern dance to elaborate on the forms of traditional Balinese dance.

In the larger context, concerning dance in Indonesia, I have already indicated that there are two major things happening. On the one hand there is Bali, which moves forward very slowly, with a strong focus on preserving its traditions; on the other hand, Jakarta strides into the future with a much more cosmopolitan perspective. There is a big conflict in terms of motivation at both the national and the regional level. At the national level we are to create new dance which gives visual expression to the variety of Indonesian art. In Bali our concern is to maintain the Balinese identity of our works. For me, as long as we maintain an awareness of the regional within the national we should be able to work out a synthesis. Also, the thing that makes us optimistic is that our traditional art exists within a religious context. Our artistic activities are always oriented toward, or guided by, the religious activities; so as long as the one is preserved the other will be as well. My most recent modern Balinese dance, for example, entitled *Aum*, is based on the trinity of Balinese Hinduism. I explore the relationships between Vishnu, Brahma and Shiva, and how the qualities of the Preserver, the Destroyer, and the Creator can be transformed into a new dance form. This may sound idealistic, but I think I will achieve that, because I have been trained in that tradition for long years, through the blood of my parents and grandparents.

Chapter Fifteen

The View from Jakarta

An Interview with Farida Feisol and Sal Murgiyanto

Sal Murgiyanto holds an S.S.T. (M.F.A.) Degree from ASTI (National Dance Academy of Indonesia, Yogyakarta), a Master's in Dance from the University of Colorado, Boulder, and a Doctorate in Performance Studies from New York University. Mr. Murgiyanto is a distinguished performer of classical Javanese dance, a choreographer, teacher, dance writer and critic. He has published more than 100 articles, and also wrote "Dance of Indonesia" for the Festival of Indonesia 1990-91 in the US. In 1984 he taught Javanese dance at UCLA's Asian Performing Arts Summer Institute and in 1987 at Cornell University's summer program. He has received grants from Fulbright-Hays, the Ford Foundation, and the Asian Cultural Council. Mr. Murgiyanto is currently a Deputy Rector of the Jakarta Institute of Arts, a consultant to the Executive Director of the Jakarta Arts Center "Taman Ismail Marzuki," and Chairman of the Society for Indonesian Performing Arts.

As a child Farida Feisol studied ballet from Dutch teachers in Jakarta, Indonesia, and she continued her training in Moscow during the 1960s. Later she added modern dance from Martha Graham and Merce Cunningham in New York City to her armamentarium. Back in Jakarta, Ms. Feisol established her own ballet school and Co-chaired the Jakarta Arts Council. She is currently a member of the Jakarta Arts Foundation, Director of the Jakarta Theater (Gedung Kesenian Jakarta), and Founder-Director of the Sumber Cipta Ballet School.

Farida Feisol: Historically speaking, Western influence in dance came to Indonesia first by way of the Dutch. That was before the Indonesian Revolution at the beginning of this century, and the influence was specifically ballet as brought in by Dutch teachers. The remnants of that original influence were still active in the early '50s; in fact, I was one of the last accepted in Jakarta. Or people just bring their new work here first because they feel it will be rejected in their region, and that might make it impossible for them to show it here.

E: In addition to choreography, what else do the students study at the Institute?

SM: All the traditional dances: Javanese, Balinese, Sumatran, Malay, etc. Of course, not everyone can study all of them; they choose from what is available.

E: Where do the teachers come from?

SM: For the most part, the Javanese come from Java, the Sumatran from Sumatra, etc. Also, when students develop a special interest in one tradition or another we often let them go to that region to study with local teachers.

E: And when they choose to study, for example, the dances of Java, what they study is essentially the dances themselves—the repertoire, so to speak. I mean there are no technique classes *per se.*

SM: Well, it's not technique as you study it in the West. They start out, for example, learning walking steps, and then they go on to phrases.

E: How long do the students study at the school?

SM: Four years for a Bachelor's degree, and now we are planning a Master's, which will be a two-year program.

E: When the students leave your school, where do you expect them to go?

SM: That's a very difficult question.

FF: We don't have any professional companies, so they have to take various jobs. At my school, I arrange for some of them to teach, and we try to get them into whatever commercial jobs come available—dancing at a discotheque or whatever—just in order to survive. That's true not only of the modern dancers, but the traditional dancers as well.

SM: Many of the dancers are recruited by the schools, to be instructors, but soon the supply will be much greater than the demand. Teaching in the schools is all right in the regions, because you can live there on the small salaries, but not in Jakarta.

E: Do any of them go to the United States?

SM: Some, but it's not like Japan or Korea or Taiwan, where there is financial support; the Indonesian students all have to try for grants, which are very limited. Actually, I think our dancers and choreographers have the same quality as the people from those other countries, but their options are more limited because of the lack of funds.

Part V:

Japan

Chapter Sixteen:
Promoting Dance in Japan

Mayumi Nagatoshi

Mayumi Nagatoshi studied modern dance at the University of Redlands in California and at the American Dance Festival. In 1986 she founded AN CREATIVE, INC., the first Japanese organization to provide managerial and other services for dance performers. Through it and Nagatoshi Productions, created in 1989, she promotes domestic and international dance performances involving Japanese artists. Since 1987 Ms. Nagatoshi has produced the International Summer School of Dance held annually in Tokyo, and she also organizes tours of Japanese students to attend the ADF summer festival in Durham, North Carolina.

In the summer of 1982 I went to the American Dance Festival as a scholarship student on the recommendation of my dance teachers at the University of Redlands in Southern California, where I had been studying for two years. That happened to be the year Mr. Miyabi Ichikawa showed up with several Japanese dance companies in tow. There was only one interpreter, Ruby Shang, for the whole group, they sometimes needed help, so I would leave my own classes and pitch in. That is how I got to know, and be known by, official ADF.

Some time later, when I got back to Japan, I heard that plans were being made for ADF-Tokyo. That surprised me, so I called to find out about it, and the person who answered my call was Mr.Ichikawa. He told me that Kei Takei, Betty Jones, and several other familiar faces would be there. Of course I wanted to see them again because I had had such a wonderful experience at ADF-Durham.

By the time I learned of ADF-Tokyo the classes were all filled, so I couldn't enroll, but I went to say hello to all the people I knew. Mr. Ichikawa told me then about how the program had come about. It seems that when they were together in Durham Charles Reinhart mentioned to Mr. Ichikawa that he was looking for some organization to sponsor ADF in Tokyo, and Charles always tells me that he can remember the very moment when Mr. Ichikawa said "I can do that!" So Mr. Ichikawa personally became the sponsor of ADF-Tokyo. He asked various friends to help him, and they all worked very hard, and that first year was a great success.

students. The situation is further complicated by the fact that the Japanese people are very shy; they don't easily show their emotions in public. In my own case, because I had been studying dance since the age of five and was captain of the dance club for which I was already choreographing pieces, I was a very big challenge to the teacher, so we didn't get along well.

By the time I went to the States I had been so "turned off" by the experience I have described that I thought I was finished with dance. I told my parents I wanted to go to the US to study business—to be a secretary or something like that (I lied!). I had some idea about going to California, to see Disneyland and Hollywood, so I looked at catalogues of schools in that area. By that time it was already popular for Japanese students to go to college in the States, and I felt I wanted to avoid them as much as possible; also, I preferred a small school. So I just happened upon Redlands, and it had the kind of English course I needed to improve my use of the language; that is why I applied. When I got there I realized that there was a Dance major, and I was looking for ways to increase my American friendships (as an International Student it was all too easy to associate mainly with non-English speakers), so it made sense for me to use my dance experience that way. It was a very small program, there were only two faculty and eight majors, but we were given a great variety of information about the dance field. I loved it; it was very comfortable for me. And of course I loved dance; the only reason I had thought to leave it was because of circumstances, not the art itself.

After two years at Redlands I went to ADF, and from there on to New York, where I took more classes. Then I tried going back to Redlands, but within two weeks I knew that was no longer what I wanted to do. The East Coast experience had shown me that I was much more attracted to the professional dance world, so I returned to New York. There I took classes at all the big studios, but I began to realize that just performing was not enough for me. Also, it became very clear to me that dance in the US and dance in Japan were very different things; not that one was better than the other, but they were just different. I thought that there must be other dancers in Japan who, like myself, were ready to become "dance drop-outs," and that they needed to get a different idea of dance, as I had.

At the same time that I was getting involved with ADF-Tokyo I was in touch with a friend who had a music production company called An Creative. He not only gave me advice, but also a corner of his office and some financial backing to get started. Through him I made many contacts, and he taught me a great deal about contracts and the other legalities of production. I became a temporary member of the An Creative staff, in exchange for which I was to teach English to my friend, his family, and the other An Creative staff people.

Soon, my friend's business took a turn for the worse. He was a composer by profession, and really just wanted to be on his own. During the time we worked together my business was starting to go, and he was essentially trying to get out of his. I was using the name An Creative, and people had begun to associate me with that, so eventually he and I just arranged to change places: I took the company, and he kept some office space.

At first I had no concrete idea what I wanted to do with An Creative, though I knew from the beginning that it should be an agency for promoting the dance community of Japan. I was fortunate enough to stumble into some things, like the meeting with Mr. Ichikawa, and my momentum carried me forward. I kept researching and researching, and gradually other like-minded people gathered 'round. Now An Creative is involved in numerous activities. One is producing dance performances; another is taking 20-30 Japanese students to ADF-Durham each of the last six years. We also do dance workshops and conferences; that is the kind of thing we really want to do, but it is not financially very rewarding. Also, individual artists hire us to represent them, to do their publicity, produce their concerts, ticketing, etc. Just a year ago we started promoting several Japanese dance artists on an international basis. These are small companies, but very talented, and they have been doing a wonderful job. Finally, corporations that are involved with arts festivals hire us to do their programming, or to advise them in the selection of artists to be sponsored for various purposes. In recent years the big Japanese corporations have become quite supportive of the arts; they need to show the people of Japan, and indeed the rest of the world, that they can do more than just make money—that they have larger interests in the lives of the people. They are actually creating foundations to promote the arts, and building facilities in which the arts can be practiced and shown. This provides wonderful opportunities for artists, but there is no tradition here for making use of them; Japanese artists for the most part do not know how to promote themselves. Through An Creative we want to encourage them to learn to stand up for themselves, but until they do we have to provide those services for them.

An Creative is a unique company as far as the Japanese dance community is concerned, though there are some individuals who do the same kind of work. These are all very busy people, but when we see one another there is always an open exchange of information. Each has her specialty. Beyond Japan, my primary area of interest has been the US, the result of the fact that I speak some English, and went to school there, and made many contacts. Still, my international interests are not limited to the States. Recently I have been doing a lot of business with Europe, Africa, and especially the other Asian countries.

One of our major projects involving the States is the International Summer School of Dance. An Creative developed this two-week summer training program, with the assistance of Mr. Ichikawa and Sumie Yonei, one of Tokyo's leading modern dance choreographers, essentially to fill the void left by our failure to maintain ADF-Tokyo on a regular basis. Each summer we bring to Tokyo a high-level faculty from the US and Europe, carefully selected to address what we take to be the current needs of dancers in Japan. The Japanese dancers usually just want technique classes, because that is what they know; they aren't accustomed to studying improvisation, or composition, or dance therapy, for example. So we have to have lots of technique classes, but we also want to introduce the students to the kinds of classes that they can't find regularly here. We want more variety, to show them what is going on in the rest of the world. We want them to know that there is more to dancing than getting your legs up. Graham technique is still very popular in Japan, but we try to find good teachers of other techniques as well, and we have as much variety in classes as we can. We are even thinking of doing music- and acting-for-dancers classes. It is hard to get much accomplished in such areas in our two-week season, but maybe we can pique some new interests.

The main reason I want to do more such cultural exchange, especially in dance education, is to encourage Japanese artists to be influenced *mentally* by Western artists. We need some of their toughness, their independence, their willingness to take chances and be different. We need more impetus to keep moving forward. Often I hear Japanese students who have been with the same teacher for a long time complaining about the teacher, and I always say that is wrong; if you don't think you can get any more from that teacher, then it is time for you to graduate! They don't know what they would do without the teacher, so all they can do is complain.

Even if performances by dancers from overseas are successful here—they regularly draw larger audiences than the local companies—until the Japanese artists get established nothing really will have changed. Although some Westerners say that the Japanese lack originality, there are really many creative people here, and they need outlets for their work. A few big artists like Saburo Teshigawara, Sankai Juku, or Kazuo Ono have been very successful in obtaining sponsorship because of their professionalism and confidence in what they have to offer. That is what I want from Japanese artists generally—that they believe in themselves more strongly. As a promoter I need that kind of help. For the Japanese audience "dance culture" still means quite exclusively something that is brought here from the outside. Only when Japanese artists take responsibility for their own careers and teach their audience that dance is also a part of Japanese culture will we have made progress.

Not only do the Western companies draw larger audiences; we can't even get enough publicity for our Japanese dancers because the dance publications are only attracted to foreign artists. For example, we have a *Dance Magazine* in Japan, which is quite comparable in format to its American counterpart, but it mostly picks up news of foreign companies. That is what its readership wants to know about; if it published news of Japanese companies its readers wouldn't be interested. This may not be only the problem of the communications industry; Japanese artists have not been well promoted, and both sides are at fault.

For me personally, as a producer, I often find it easier to work with dance artists from other countries because they seem to have more professionalism than most Japanese artists. Also, the Japanese government and corporations that might provide support for contemporary artists don't trust them, don't think they are good enough. This is true not only of dance; Western movies and music, for example, are also generally thought to be more advanced, and are therefore more popular. This may seem strange, as Japanese society was for such a long time essentially closed off to the rest of the world; one might think the Japanese people have always been quite nationalistic. However, through the Meiji Period, up to the beginning of the First World War, they became very international. They made a very positive integration of Japanese and foreign elements. But the war closed up the country again. After we lost World War II we had to accept the help of the United States to rebuild our country. That created a generation gap between those who lived through the war and those who grew up with a more international perspective. The younger generation wanted more and more Western influence; also, perhaps, there was some rejection of the experience of their parents' generation.

So now the problem is to convince the Japanese people again—especially, from my point of view, the artists—that they can stand on their own feet. They have to understand that they are good enough to take ideas from wherever they find them and develop them in their own unique way. The Japanese way of seeing and doing is bound to be different from all others; not "better" or "worse," but different. That is the main point about all matters of cross-culturalism. Each culture has a heritage that is more or less uniquely its own. Then it comes in contact with another culture, and they begin to exchange ideas. The problem, of course, is for each of them to maintain what is best in their own culture while taking on what the other has to offer. It is a very delicate balance; no one involved in cross-cultural exchange honestly wants to impose his "thing" on what the other person brings to the exchange. It is always a question of affecting a merger; not "What I have is better than what you have," but "What each of us has is *different,* so let's put things together and see what happens."

That is exactly what I have been trying to do. I want the people I work with here, the various elements of the Japanese dance community, to understand that I fully respect what they do, but I am interested in doing something a little different. I think it, too, is important, and I want their support.

Chapter Seventeen:
Dance Education in Japan

Michie Hayashi

> *Michie Hayashi has been on the faculty of Osaka University of Health and Sports Sciences since 1973, where she teaches modern dance technique and choreography, dance history, and various methodology and theory courses at both the undergraduate and graduate levels. She is also a regular faculty member of the Summer School of the Teachers Society of Dance Research in Osaka. Ms. Hayashi has both authored and translated into Japanese books and articles dealing with dance in education, as an art form, and as recreational activity.*

INTRODUCTION

Dance education in Japan has traditionally had a unique relationship to the culture as a whole. After the sixth century many kinds of dance came into Japan from China and Korea. The Japanese government fostered professional dance instruction in shrines and music-and-dance institutions, and promoted it to the populous at large. Those dances that were imported from foreign countries were gradually incorporated into such traditional Japanese styles of dance as *Bugaku, Noh,* and *Kabuki.* However, these traditional dance styles (and the Japanese folk dances that were transmitted from ancient times) were not taught in the public schools.

After the isolationist policy of the Edo Era (1603-1868), the Meiji government essentially imported an educational system based on European models. At the same time Western dance culture was being introduced to the dance world of Japan. The Western dance styles were very different from the Japanese, which had developed from a communal linkage of life style with religion. In general it can be said that the beauty of Japanese dance resides in "stillness"—in posing of the human figure— whereas Western dance values the dynamics of movement. In terms of the emerging Japanese system of education, therefore, Western dance was seen as most in harmony with physical education. A special dance style, isolated from traditional Japanese dance and known as "school dance," or "physical education dance," or "creative dance," was developed in the schools.

The goals of physical education have been influenced by political and social conditions, fluctuating with changes in governmental policy. For example, during the Second World War dance was utilized as an instrument for increasing the physical prowess of the Japanese people, and emphasizing a collectiveness and unity of spirit. As a result, the originality, creativity and beauty that are the most important elements of art were suppressed. I believe, therefore, that it was a mistake to incorporate dance into physical education. Human beings have an innate desire to express their inner mind, and dance is a formalized method of human expression, utilizing movement. Hence, it should be taught as an art form.

SOME RECENT HISTORY

In Japan, public school education is controlled by the Ministry of Education; especially at the elementary, junior and senior high school levels policy is established by the Ministry. Dance, which was identified as physical body movements, was placed in physical education as a result of policy statements issued during the Meiji Period. Before the Second World War the pioneers of Japanese physical education studied the modern methods of physical education and dance that were just then being born in Europe, especially in Germany. Later, many dance leaders went to Europe to study the theories and activities of Rudolf Laban and Mary Wigman, who established the philosophy and practical methodology of modern dance. They introduced the new techniques to school teachers all over Japan through short courses sponsored by the Ministry of Education. It seems that the European dance culture took education in Japan by storm.

After the Second World War this approach to dance education came under close scrutiny, and several problems were discovered. Primarily, it was found that the students' creativity, or expressivity through dance, was not being fostered. Hence, in 1947 new teaching guidelines were established by the Ministry of Education. This policy introduced "Creative Dance" to the physical education curriculum, with the explicit purpose of encouraging creativity in each student. Thus the concept of dance education was enlarged from being just dancing to include creating works or expressing oneself. This revealed a major change in educational values, with a new emphasis on spontaneity and active involvement. Since then the policy has been revised each decade, with special attention to matching educational conditions with social values.

It is instructive to compare the guidelines of 1977 with those for 1990. In 1977, in the lower grades of elementary school, dance was treated as imitative movement; that is, the children were to imitate animals, vehicles, toys, etc., in movement terms. In the upper grades dance was treated as expressive movement, and the teaching stressed free expression: The children were encouraged to choose a theme from among the things around them and explore it through movement. Dance was a coeducational activity in the elementary schools, but in junior and senior high school it was limited to female students. Male students were taught *Budo*, the traditional Japanese martial arts; thus the study and appreciation of dance was closed to them. For the most part the female Japanese students tended to hate studying Creative Dance, because they were forced into making works whether or not they had the ability or desire to do so. Also, at that age students are often embarrassed to express feelings through their bodies in front of other people.

Nowadays in Japan, without distinction as to age or sex, dance is becoming popular in daily life. Young people dance in discotheques; older people dance in social dance schools. In many towns schools devoted to the study of jazz, aerobic, modern, and social dance have been opened. Hence, we have had to reconsider the meaning and value of dance in daily life: How do we teach dance to students in order to make dance education in school useful in their future lives? Dance education and dancing don't end in school, but continue and harmonize with the physical and mental life of each person.

For about fourteen years the main focus of dance education was on expression and creativity, and it is impossible (and unnecessary) to deny that the teachers gave their students genuine pleasure through rhythmical movement. The new guidelines in 1990, however, emphasized the importance of dance in daily life, and the need to acknowledge students' interest in such things as music with a fast tempo and strong beat. The main differences in content of the present policy from the previous one are that dance has become elective and coeducational. By the former guidelines dance was a compulsory subject for female students only; male students couldn't take a dance class even if they wanted to. Although dance has a tendency to be more popular among female students, especially in recent times many male students have become incredibly interested in dancing. This is evidence that dance is not only for female students but for both sexes, and that it is important for everyone to experience the aesthetic feelings made possible by rhythmic movement of the body.

The teaching contents have changed. Until recently only Western creative and folk dances were taught in dance class. Now Japanese folk dance, jazz, and aerobic dance have been added. This broadening of perspective is an acknowledgment of the fact that although dance culture in Japan has been strongly influenced by Western forms since the Meiji Era, it is also necessary to recognize the Eastern dance that our ancestors created.

DANCE CURRICULUM IN THE UNIVERSITIES

In Japanese universities dance is taught through physical education programs. There are virtually no dance departments that train dance specialists, dancers, or choreographers; nor, of course, do the universities train Japanese traditional dancers. Only one national university, Ochanomizu University, has a dance education major, while a few private universities have dance courses in their Theater Arts or Fine Arts departments. Dance has generally been taught as "sport," like any of the others needed by physical education teachers. Therefore, the content of dance courses stresses theory and technique for teaching dance to children and other students. Recently, however, the number of children in Japan has decreased, so fewer teachers are needed in the schools. This has caused the universities—especially those of Education—to adjust their educational systems and curricula to accord more closely with student interests and the needs of society.

My own (private) college has been educating students to become school teachers since its founding about twenty years ago. Four years ago the curriculum was reformed. The Dance Major was incorporated into the Sports Coaching Course, and new classes were added: Dance History and Theory, emphasizing ballet and modern dance; Dance Aesthetics; Ideokinesis; Teaching Methods (including creative movement for students); Modern Dance (technique and choreography); Ballet; Jazz and Aerobic Dance, as well as Physical Training. We are going to train students to be not only teachers of physical education, but also dancers and dance teachers.

TRADITIONAL DANCE IN SCHOOL EDUCATION

The traditional Japanese dances were made by the people of different districts or small regions, according to their own aesthetic values and customs of movement, which have a long history. We can say that these dances are very much a part of our precious Japanese heritage. There are many such dances, and they have traditionally been taught to the younger generation in small district or private schools. Japanese traditional dance forms are very different from Western dance. In general, the characteristic features of Japanese dance are upper body movements, especially hand gestures. It has few leg and foot movements, like the jumping and leaping that appear in Western dance. Nor is there any lifting.

As I mentioned previously, the Japanese government established a new educational system after the isolationistic policy of the Edo Era, modeling it on the European system. The Japanese traditional dances were not included in the system. There were several reasons for that. One reason is that the Japanese people, awakening after long sleep to the realities of the modern world, were very surprised to see how far the European countries, in particular England, had progressed into industrialization. They became determined almost over night to introduce the new industrial technologies to their society, very much at the expense of established cultural values. Thus such traditional forms as dance, and the educational methods used to perpetuate them, virtually disappeared from the training of the younger generation.

In the case of dance this transformation was exacerbated by the fact that the aesthetics of the traditional Japanese forms could not be easily assimilated—as Western dance could—into the curriculum and teaching methodologies of physical education. Japanese dance is based on stillness, whereas Western dance values dynamic movement. Furthermore, in Japan dance has traditionally been taught from man to man, or master to apprentice. This was the special method fostered to develop professional performers, and it would be very difficult to teach many students at the same time. In the modern schools, on the other hand, it is not the objective to train professional dancers, but to teach dance as a liberal art and to educate students to appreciate the arts.

Recently Japanese education has experienced a new surge of concern for preserving our cultural heritage. Some Japanese traditional dancers are seriously thinking about how to introduce traditional dance into the school system. We are searching for methods that might allow us effectively to teach many students simultaneously. In a very hopeful sense we seem to be reaffirming our responsibility for passing on our knowledge to the next generation.

Chapter Eighteen:
On the History of Western Dance in Japan

An Interview with Miyabi Ichikawa

> *Miyabi Ichikawa holds Bachelor of Law, Master of Arts, and Doctoral degrees from Waseda University, Tokyo. He has served in each of the following positions for many years: Lecturer, Waseda University; Lecturer in the Graduate Division, Ochanomizu Women's University; Vice President of the Society of Dance Research in Japan; Co-investigator in Asian-African Language Laboratory of Tokyo Gaigo University; and President, American Dance Festival-Tokyo. He has also produced/directed a number of festivals and programs in Japan, including the International Summer School of Dance. As critic he contributes to Asahi Shimbun and the Japanese periodicals Dance Now and Dance Magazine. He is the author of numerous articles and eight dance books, including most recently Homage to V. Nijinsky (1990).*

Miyabi Ichikawa: Cross-cultural exchange involving Japan was quite limited until just before or after World War II. Our country was closed (except for Nagasaki) until about 100 years ago, when we opened the door to foreigners. Then, of course, we closed and opened it again because of the war.

E: Would you describe the history of cultural exchange specifically in dance?

MI: After the Russian Revolution many people escaped to Japan through Siberia and China, especially Shanghai. For example, Nadejida Pavlova and Eliana Pavlova, two sisters, came here and started teaching in Tokyo and Kamakura. That was at about the time of the great earthquake in Japan—1922. The great Anna Pavlova also made her only visit to Japan then, and performed not only in Tokyo, Osaka, and Nagasaki, but in many local towns as well.

E: And the Japanese people were interested in that?

MI: Yes, especially her *Dying Swan*. During that tour the great *Kabuki* actor Onoe Kikugorou V gave a performance for Pavlova; that was one of the early cultural exchanges. Before that Mr. Rossi of the Alhambra Theater in London came here to teach ballet and opera at the Imperial Theater (Teigeki). He was here for five years.

After the war many foreign companies came, especially from America, including Martha Graham, Merce Cunningham, and Paul Taylor. The Graham style of dance was particularly popular. From Europe Serge Lepin, ballet master of the Paris Opera, brought his ballet company.

E: Before that big influx of foreigners how was dance being taught in Japan?

MI: During the war we were prohibited from using any foreign languages. Also, no tights or short skirts (tutus) were allowed. So we were very limited in what we could do with ballet. Before the war we did, of course, have a close relationship with Germany, so we had a strong influence from German expressionism. Many Japanese dancers went to Dresden and Berlin to study at the Wigman school. Then they came back to teach here.

E: So at the end of the war there was at least some instruction in modern dance and ballet going on. What about traditional Japanese dance?

MI: Well, Japanese traditional dance is the same as *Kabuki* dance. In the 1920s female dancers appeared and began to choreograph. They helped to bring about some great changes in the style, especially the development of what was called *Shinbuyo*—"New Dance." Two people were very popular then: Ms. Fujikage and Ms. Gojo. They came from the Geisha world. Ms. Fujikage actually went to Paris, where she made a dance on the theme of revolution using "La Marseillaise" for music. Ms. Gojo made abstract dances based on the *Kabuki* dance idiom—that is, she used the vocabulary, but not the narrative line.

E: Did they have disciples who continued their work?

MI: Yes, but until very recently *Kabuki* has been closed—a very tight "family." Now the Shochiku Company has proposed to make instruction in *Kabuki* movement available to everyone. It will recruit students once a year, and the graduates will be engaged almost as in "family" theater.

E: Is there a tradition of movement that has developed in the colleges of physical education here?

MI: Yes. It came into this country around the turn of the century from Germany and Denmark.

E: Do you think of that kind of movement as influencing dance in Japan?

MI: I think it is a kind of dance, but the purpose is different. One is exercise and the other is art.

E: In Kobe last weekend at the All-Japan Dance Festival we saw many groups representing extracurricular dance clubs from high schools and colleges—all very beautiful, very exciting. We noticed, though, that all the dances were quite similar, with everybody dancing together, in big ensemble movement. It was not just exercise, but true dance choreography with lots of falls and recovery, yet there was no individual movement at all. As many of these groups were from schools of physical education, we wondered if this was related to the tradition they were learning in the schools.

MI: No. As you implied, these are extracurricular clubs. This does, however, raise an important point for understanding Japanese culture. Japanese people like to do things together. Ordinary is good; extraordinary is not good. This is true even in the arts. That is why we have the Ballet Association and the Contemporary Dance Association—to promote harmony, which is very important in Japan.

E: You said American companies started coming here in the '50s, and Graham had the greatest impact. Why do you think Graham was particularly appealing to the Japanese?

MI: First, I think it was important that several Japanese women went to join the Graham company. Also, the Japanese people like emotional drama, and they found that in Graham (although by now the Japanese dancers are attracted at least as much to other modern dance styles too).

E: Let's talk a little now about ADF-Tokyo, and the International Summer School of Dance. We understand that *you* personally were responsible for bringing ADF here.

MI: Charles Reinhart got a lot of money from the US-Japan Friendship Commission in Washington for cultural exchange between the two countries. I don't know who recommended me to him, but Charles wrote to say that he and his wife Stephanie wanted to come here to see which Japanese companies might be invited to perform at ADF. He was more interested in *Butoh* than in contemporary companies. I helped him select one *Butoh* company and two or three contemporary companies. That was ten years ago. Charles and I started working closely together in 1986. We brought many American teachers here, and also we produced concerts by Laura Dean, the Bill T. Jones/Arnie Zane Company, and Pooh Kaye/Eccentric Motion.

E: That was all on the original grant Charles had gotten?

MI: Yes. Then, unfortunately, the American economy went down, so he asked me if we could get financial assistance in Japan.

E: And you arranged that?

MI: Yes, but it was very difficult. In 1987 and '88 we continued to bring American teachers, but not to do the productions. Mr. Reinhart did not like using the ADF name if what we produced did not include performances, so I changed the name to International Summer School of Dance. Two years from now, in 1994, we expect to try again with ADF-Tokyo.

E: We have been told that it was very risky to try to do a summer school like ADF in Japan because Japanese dance students are accustomed to studying with just one teacher. It was possible, given the ADF concept of studying simultaneously with several teachers, that nobody would come. Is this true?

MI: Yes, that is true. Also, of course, dance instruction is a business, and the Japanese teachers might not have been willing to allow their students to study with the foreign teachers. Fortunately, they agreed to it. That is why I succeeded.

E: Why did they agree?

MI: I think because the teachers we brought in were foreigners, who would be here for just two weeks. Then they would go away.

E: What are the goals of the International Summer School of Dance?

MI: It is always necessary for students to learn about new trends in the world. They have to absorb many things. We always try to provide a variety of good teachers who represent a broad perspective on what is happening in the dance field. The students tell me that the opportunity to study with different teachers shows them a good deal about themselves. They learn what they are capable of.

E: You helped with the Japan Asia Dance Event (JADE) that was held here in 1993. What were the goals of that conference?

MI: Carl Wolz created this event and held it for many years in Hong Kong. When he decided to leave Hong Kong, he thought it best to hold it in other Asian cities, including Tokyo. This conference is connected with the World Dance Alliance, so we judged it important to have it here. The problem was money. All of the other Asian people think Japan has lots of money, but it is difficult to find support here for the arts.

E: How do you think dance in Japan is influencing dance in the rest of the world?

MI: I would point out that there are two concurrent "streams of influence" at work, one to accept, the other to reject. The rest of Asia is composed of strongly traditional societies, so they are creating new dance based on their traditions. However, Japanese dancers reject tradition, as in *Butoh*. Have you seen *Butoh* dance?

E: Yes.

MI: *Butoh* is influencing some nouvelle dance in France. Interestingly, the Underground Dance Theater in St. Petersburg has also gotten some *Butoh* influence. I saw their performance in Hanover, Germany, with about ten young Russian men with shaved heads and white powder, just like in *Butoh*.

E: I think *Butoh* is very interesting to Americans too. It is certainly having some influence on the new choreographers in the United States. Is *Butoh* popular in Japan?

MI: It is hard to tell. Professor Miki Wakamatsu presented statistics at the International Dance Conference in Taipei which indicate that *Butoh* represents a very small percentage of the dance activity in Japan, but I think he may have made a mistake. The statistics he adopted were taken from the Japanese performing artist associations, but *Butoh* dancers don't belong to those organizations. So they may not be accurately represented in those statistics.

E: Would you discuss what happened to modern dance in Japan from approximately 1954 to 1984. The American companies started coming, but were people teaching here or just performing?

MI: Mostly performing, though sometimes the American Cultural Center in Tokyo invited American teachers to hold workshops. For example, Anna Sokolow was here. Kei Takei took her workshop at that time, and Anna Sokolow was very impressed with her. She recommended Kei Takei to the Fulbright Committee, and that is how Takei got to the United States. Unfortunately, the American Cultural Center no longer exists.

E: So your summer school is now the only organized effort to bring Western teachers here?

MI: For modern dance, yes, though there are other programs in ballet. There was a big ballet workshop in Sapporo in July, 1992, with teachers from many European countries.

E: So during those years in question modern dance in Japan was taught almost exclusively by Japanese dancers who went elsewhere to study and brought back what they learned.

MI: Yes. Yuriko Kimura, for example, is teaching now in Nara, and Akiko Kanda has a studio in Tokyo. You see, we don't have institutions specifically for dance, and the Ministry of Education has prohibited hiring foreigners to teach in Japan, so there aren't any openings for outsiders in the public schools. Carl Wolz, for example, has been thinking for some time to come here, but no institution can accept him. [In September, 1993, Mr. Wolz joined the faculty of the Japan Women's College of Physical Education in Tokyo.]

E: Because he is a foreigner?

MI: Yes, only for that reason. Still, little by little, things are changing. Now jazz and aerobic dance are very popular in Japan, and some Western teachers are staying on to teach that in private studios. Many of the private studios here actually look like dance departments in American universities in that they have the same kind of diverse faculty.

E: And these studios attract lots of students? I know in Taiwan, for instance, there is a problem in that parents don't want to pay for their children to study dance because dance has not been very well thought of, and there is little opportunity to pursue it as a career.

MI: Japanese parents like to pay for their children's education, in any field. Also, we have a long tradition of studying the arts. Young women especially are expected to do that.

E: How do you see the future of dance in Japan?

MI: Recently Japanese foundations have begun to support dance activities. The government also shows signs of becoming more supportive. So maybe the dancers will become more active in seeking grants and producing their work. I think the future looks bright.

Chapter Nineteen:
Ballet Training and the Studio Scene in Tokyo

Yasuki Sasa

An internationally known teacher and choreographer, Yasuki Sasa's early training and work was with Masahide Komaki, one of the ballet pioneers in Japan. At the invitation of Antony Tudor Mr. Sasa studied for two years in New York at the Metropolitan Opera Ballet School and at the Juilliard School. He was on the staff of the University of Hawaii for 15 years, and is now a freelance artist working out of Tokyo. In addition to many engagements in Japan, Mr. Sasa has taught at the Hong Kong Academy for Performing Arts, the Beijing Dance Academy and for the Universal Ballet in Seoul, Korea. He has set his own choreography on numerous dance groups, and is well known for his staging of the ballet classics.

I started ballet training at 16, and at 18 I became a member of the Komaki Ballet Company. I stayed with them for nine years. Then I moved to the United States, where I studied at the Metropolitan Opera Ballet School and at Juilliard with Antony Tudor (only with Tudor, because although he said it would be all right for me to study with other teachers, I could tell he preferred me not to, and I respected his feelings). For almost two years I went every Monday, Wednesday and Friday to the Metropolitan Opera House, and Tuesday and Thursday to Juilliard.

I didn't perform in New York, but in 1966 I came back to Japan with Tudor and performed in a concert of his works. That was with a new company called Star Dancers. It was just being formed at that time, and is today one of the best companies in Tokyo. I danced *Lilac Garden, Undertow, Dark Elegies*, and *Little Improvisations*.

After that I taught at the University of Hawaii for the next 15 years, until 1984, when I went to the Hong Kong Academy for Performing Arts. I stayed there for one year and then returned to Japan. When I came back it was difficult to find a teaching position. I had been away so long that a whole generation did not know me. Little by little, though, I began to find work, with the Matsuyama Ballet and Noriko Kobayashi Company. It turned out actually to my advantage that I had been away so long as to be considered a "foreigner"; I could teach the "big stars," whereas the Japanese teachers were too modest to do that.

Gradually my work has become better known here. Now we have the Japan Ballet Association, and they have invited me to choreograph, or stage works, or give combinations for the competitions. There are four or five other associations as well, for folk dance, modern dance, critics, scholars, etc., and all of those associations together form what is called the All-Japan Dance Alliance. The power of these organizations seems to be increasing all the time, and they are involved in many activities. The Ballet Association, for example, gives a performance every year, and sponsors the Japan competition every other year and the Asia-Pacific competition every third year. These competitions are very popular in Japan (and throughout Asia), although the really fine, established dancers do not enter. The competitions are really for students in two divisions: "Juniors" from age 14-18, and "seniors" from 19-25. They are similar to what one sees in the United States in Jackson, Mississippi.

There are many ballet companies in Tokyo, including seven major ones: Tokyo Ballet, Asami Maki, Matsuyama Ballet (which is about 50 years old), Momoko Tani, Noriko Kobayashi Ballet Theater, and Star Dancers. Few if any of these companies make money; they pay their dancers very little, and only for performance. So a dancer may rehearse for three months without pay, and then be paid perhaps $85 for each performance. The companies provide costumes, but the dancers pay for their own shoes. They also have to sell tickets. Many of the dancers in these companies have their own studios, so when they perform they sell tickets to their students. Tickets here are very expensive too; for the Tokyo Ballet, for example, a ticket might cost $80. One other thing: male dancers are often hired for the school recitals, for which they might be paid $2,000 per performance. They can get rich on that!

The main source of support for professional ballet dancers is teaching in the private studios. Best of all is to have your own studio, but as that is very expensive most of us have to work for the owners. There is an abundance of studios throughout Tokyo; many are small or makeshift, housed in kindergartens, or the basements of buildings, or wherever there is space. All of these studios give recitals at least once a year. That is really where they make money. Each student might pay from $300-$1,000 to perform, with from 50 to 200 students in a recital. That is just the performance fee; they must also make their own costumes. The teacher uses this "performance fee" to cover rental on the hall, lights, etc., so it doesn't matter much whether they have an audience or not. These recitals are usually free (this is different, of course, from professional company performances). So we have lots of school recitals.

Almost all ballet teachers in Japan are Japanese. Some foreigners come for short stays, to do workshops for a few weeks, but no one can afford to keep them long-term. It is too expensive. Many years ago there were some Russians here, but that was possible only because the Russian government paid to send and maintain them. Now there is no government support anywhere for that kind of thing. The short-term visits are helpful of course, but really the work of training Japanese ballet dancers is being done by Japanese teachers, and I must say they are doing quite well. I believe we have an advantage in this, because Oriental bodies and Western bodies are entirely different. When Oriental dancers go to the United States or to Europe the training they get does not take this difference into account; they are considered good or bad by the same standards as are used to evaluate Western dancers.

For myself, I know that different training is needed for different body types, and in dealing with Japanese students I find out from my own body what is needed. I know that if I just train in the Western way it doesn't work, so I make some small adjustments—maybe ten or twenty percent! Then it works. The main problem is that most Oriental bodies have little natural turnout. If the training starts very early, it may be overcome, but even then it will take much longer than with Western bodies. For many students here it is a lost cause. We teach them because that provides income, but we know they will not really be dancers. The teacher must have an eye good enough to know what is possible. Much depends on the individual. Sometimes with lots of discipline and hard work we make progress.

Most of the training in Japan now is good; I would say we are on a par with the United States. Some Japanese teachers are even better, because they work hard. Concerning choreography, on the other hand, we need a lot of help from the West. We have no training for choreographers here, and what we produce is not good. So Japanese companies perform the classical Western repertory almost exclusively. Also, the sense of hierarchy is very strong in these companies. Only the Artistic Director is allowed to choreograph; talent is never promoted from within the ranks. When a company wants to try something new they have to bring in a Western choreographer.

I am not sure there is any way to make composition classes available to the dancers here; we certainly have no mechanism for doing that at present. Some students might be interested with a very respected teacher. If a famous choreographer came here and offered a choreographic workshop it would attract interest, since name recognition is very important in Japan. This is a really unfortunate situation: We have so many good teachers and so many good dancers; if we had the money I am sure we could develop our own choreographers. Not that money can make choreographers, but if there were money to support the effort more people would try, giving us more from which to choose.

Chapter Twenty:
Ballet in Japan:
Where Does It Go From Here?

James Sutton

James Sutton received his ballet training from Maggie Black, Gabriela Taub-Darvash, Zena Rommett and Robert Joffrey. He has performed with a number of ballet companies including his own James Sutton and Dancers, and with the Kathryn Posin Dance Company. His most extensive teaching experience is with the Metropolitan Opera Company and the American Dance Festival, for which he has taught several years in Japan. Mr. Sutton is a prolific choreographer, and he has recently become a contributing writer for **Ballet Review.**

Few of us are fortunate enough to feel passionate about our chosen profession. When this passion is also a passport to other cultures the resulting exchange of perspectives offers rare, unanticipated pleasures. As the American Dance Festival, where I have taught ballet since 1985, has become increasingly international, I have taught dancers from all corners of our "global village." From Asia, Africa, Europe, Australia, and Oceania, and across the Americas have come students, each unique, and from each I have learned more about the world I inhabit, the art form I love, and both the specialness and commonality of dancing in every culture.

In particular, through travels in Japan, and performing and teaching there, I have both shared my world and gained insights into that modern samurai society. This voyage of discovery has not, however, been without its confusions and limitations. To attempt to know the Japanese people in any depth is to drop a pebble into a bottomless pond. The surface ripples are obvious in all directions, but beneath is the imperceptible, endless fall.

The "global village" concept notwithstanding, each culture has its unique approach to the acquiring and passing along of information, an outgrowth of the social and interpersonal traditions of that culture. Learning and teaching must exist within a social context. As one relates to family, friends, and associates, the seeds are planted for the acquisition of knowledge. No culture has so rigid a sense of the

197

order of human action, I suspect, as that of Japan, where each aspect of a person's life is governed by formal rules of behavior. Life itself is an art form.

As a foreigner, a *gaijin* (anyone not Japanese), I have often felt a paradox in people's response to me, a strange mixture of canonization and contempt. Intrigued by my difference, my spontaneity, yet appalled by my lack of civilization in the Japanese sense, they have inevitably made of me a source of great curiosity. The mediating circumstance is that my position as teacher has eclipsed my oddness as *gaijin*, and in the classroom I have always been treated with deference and respect.

In the United States the first priority in teaching involves simply getting the students' attention. Classroom focus is, more often than not, internal and peer-oriented. The teacher is an unwanted intruder who must earn the class' focus. Even in the rarefied atmosphere of dance instruction, where one would presume the students to have an avid interest in the subject matter, attention span and concentration are not to be taken for granted. This is, most emphatically, not the case in Japan. The status of teacher is an honored one, above question, beyond doubt. Optimism and enthusiasm are not out of style in Japan. Japanese students compete in eagerness and interest just as American students do in apathy and sullenness. Focus is absolute, and the teacher faces an earnestness and zeal so free from question and irony as to smack of totalitarianism. The student may be impassive, but never indifferent. It is common to find students working before class, perfecting combinations from the day before.

The highly codified and technical framework of ballet, its emphasis on perfection of form, and its mentor-disciple means of transmission all make of it a natural for the Japanese artist. However, these may well be the very aspects of the discipline that most often override the potential for the development of a singularly Japanese voice in ballet. Form is only the most obvious aspect of ballet, a vehicle that must be fueled with emotional substance to propel it beyond technical display into visceral experience.

Ballet has its roots in renaissance Europe, far distant in time and space from present-day Japan. First popularized in Japan in this century, it has evolved into a highly technical and explosive form in their hands. The soaring leaps and multiple pirouettes of ballet at its most virtuosic are seen as the pinnacle of training, and indeed Japanese dancers are at the cutting edge of athleticism in ballet. Gold medals at international competitions are frequently awarded to Japanese contestants, and are regarded as a badge of national honor. Yet, this emphasis on competitions and technique may in fact have kept the art of ballet from flourishing into a choreographic whole in Japan. At a recent concert in Tokyo of prize winners, most still in their teens, the technical display was indeed dazzling, but what of the substance of these traditional *pas de deux,* seen only in excerpts? By contrast, invested with the rich magnificent spirit of Japan, the wooden figures of *Bunraku* are more resonant with humanity than these living dancers. The synthesis of athleticism and artistry is incomplete.

Historically, as the ballet "diaspora" has moved around the world, its pattern has consistently been first to duplicate the imported technique (in Japan largely the Soviet Russian style), then to reflect the social demands of the new culture. The development of a national style of ballet is completely dependent on the development of a national repertory. As Marius Petipa (a Frenchman) defined the Russian style, and George Balanchine (a Russian) defined the American style, it remains for a choreographer in Japan to refract the Japanese spirit through the prism of ballet technique.

A nearby example of this process of cultural assimilation is Mainland China. There, the same bravura Russian style has developed into a spectacular form of dance-drama extolling the virtues of communism: a propagandist poster come to life. In a country where women were forced to bind their feet and walk in tiny steps well into the twentieth century, the role of the striding ballerina is of particular cultural significance (despite the dubious exchange of the bound foot for the pointe shoe). Unique to Chinese ballet, some of the steps have been re-named, with poetic Chinese terms replacing the French terminology sacrosanct around the world. In China (and in Japan), unlike Western nations, there is no social dance tradition; young couples have not historically danced together as an aspect of courtship. Hence, the romantic subtext of the traditional *pas de deux* is removed. Brothers and sisters are portrayed through *pas de deux* more readily than lovers. At a somewhat more advanced stage than in Japan, an altogether new perspective on ballet performance is emerging.

The current emphasis on Olympian technical achievement in ballet has also created a gulf between ballet dancers and dancers of other disciplines in Japan. While this is largely true in the West as well, I have seldom encountered so many hard-working, talented dancers who were so discouraged by their struggle with ballet. Though I am neither anatomist nor anthropologist, I have found, generally speaking, most Japanese dancers to have "easy" muscles, strong spinal structure, and almost uniformly flexible feet—assets for dancing in general and ballet in particular. Unfortunately, an early overemphasis on turning out and an obsession with perfection seems often to have blinded them to ballet's usefulness as an Esperanto, or universal language, of dancing: a private dialogue with the body to supplement performance in any idiom, rather than solely a performance technique.

The training of dancers in Japan is, as in the United States, a haphazard affair. Ballet, in a culture so rich in ancient artistic traditions, is a decided newcomer. Financial and popular support are fragmented and inconsistent. Companies must compete fiercely for the diminutive pool of resources. Though there are many fine teachers in Japan, they commonly groom their prize pupils as extensions of themselves and jealously guard their progress and exposure. Devotion to the teacher must be absolute. A student's wish to sample other styles of training offered in the Tokyo area, for example, is regarded as an affront to his teacher—a dishonorable act. This unwillingness to share resources (not particularly different from the situation in the United States) is counterproductive to building a national tradition.

Somewhat emblematic of where ballet companies in Tokyo have been is Star Dancers Ballet, its name a telling reference to the Japanese infatuation with overachievement. On my last visit I sampled rehearsals of this lovely company, directed by Ruriko Tachikawa and Bonjin Atsugi, in preparation for an all-American evening of choreography. Melissa Hayden, former ballerina of the New York City Ballet, was staging two Balanchine works, stressing the movement impulse and physicality in the ballets: "It's the technique of the choreography…. Your leg belongs to your waist…. Tell them to stop making pictures." She constantly pushed them away from the replication of steps, into the dynamic realm of pure dance energy. Director Bonjin Atsugi, himself a well-known choreographer, spent many years away from Japan, and worked extensively in modern dance. Now directing this ballet company in Tokyo, he is in a special position to influence the direction of dance in Japan at large—toward, one assumes, the synthesis of ballet and modern dance that is at the core of contemporary dance around the world.

The current tyrannical grip of competitive ballet technique will surely give way to fresh approaches to expression; indeed, it *must* if ballet in Japan is to evolve beyond its current form. The struggle between individual vision and cultural consensus in the arts is by no means uniquely Japanese; the spontaneity and novelty of art in the United States are born as surely out of our cultural chaos as the serenity and focus of Japanese art are rooted in their cultural stasis. With the guidance of people like Mr. Atsugi, who have the breadth of perspective East-West and across genres to see the art form in all of its complexity, ballet in Japan may be in the process of turning its next important corner.

Chapter Twenty-One

Tokyo, New York, Tokyo

Kei Takei

> *Kei Takei is a native of Tokyo, Japan, where she spent her childhood and served a traditional apprenticeship with the creative dance master Kenji Hinoki. While at his school she began to choreograph seriously. In 1967, on the recommendation of Anna Sokolow, Ms. Takei went to New York City on a Fulbright Scholarship to study at the Juilliard School. She also studied at The Martha Graham School, The Merce Cunningham Studio, American Ballet Theater School, with Anna Halprin, and with Alwin Nikolais. Two years later Ms. Takei began the creation of what has become an epic work entitled LIGHT, which at present consists of 30 parts. She has subsequently received innumerable grants and commissions to develop this work with her own company, Moving Earth, and set parts of it on student and professional companies throughout the world.*

I was quite a sensitive child. I still remember the first time I felt anything very strongly. It was when I was about four years old. I looked at the ground and saw a bean seed growing. I remember that I was very moved by it. Now I analyze the things by which I am very much moved, and I see that they are all connected with time and movement, with changing visual space, like a bean seed growing. Those elements are still in my choreography. Throughout my youth and high school years that sense of wonder never changed. I would always see things, and be surprised and moved by their beauty. I didn't know, though, how I could express my deep feeling so that I would be satisfied with it.

I had many different kinds of training—from different dance teachers, from being a member of theater groups, and from seeing performances. I knew that I was looking for something, that I needed to meet someone, some Master. One day I went to a solo performance by Kenji Hinoki. Then I knew that this was the "someone" I was looking for. The next day (it was in February) I held a white flower in my hand and went to his studio. There I met his wife, Fujima Kiyoe, the master performer and teacher of Japanese Classical Dance *(Nihon Buyo)*. From

Figure 43   Kei Takei performing *The Daikon Field Solo* from *LIGHT, part 16*, 1982-83.
Photo: Johan Elbers

that day onward, Kenji Hinoki and Fujima Kiyoe were the guides of my dance life, the people I could totally trust artistically.

Also at that time I was greatly influenced by the Americans who came here: Merce Cunningham, José Limón, Paul Taylor and many others. They not only performed but also gave workshops, which were quite popular with the young Japanese choreographers. I especially remember a workshop with Lucas Hoving and his wife, Lavina. The dance I was exposed to by the American dancers was different from what I had known in Japan. I felt you could talk about the American modern dance but not the Japanese. American modern dance has very clear themes, movement, structure, expression. Japanese modern dance at that time was of many different kinds—some gymnastic, some emotional (non-structured), some "modern dancerly."

Then one day Anna Sokolow came, and she was a great inspiration to me. I showed her a piece of my choreography, although I knew she didn't like much of the Japanese choreography she saw. She said to me, "you are very honest." Later she helped me obtain a grant to attend the Juilliard School, where she was teaching; that is how I got to the United States.

When I learned that I would be going to the States the first thing I started thinking about was how I would work with those different bodies, faces, hair, etc. It struck me very forcefully that I would have to deal with those differences—in part because I was in my early 20s but had never been outside Japan.

In New York I stayed at the International House. I went to the man in charge there and said, in my limited English, with great naiveté: "I want to give a dance concert. Please give me use of the auditorium." He said "OK," and I put on a very informal concert, all by myself. It had been suggested to me that I send invitations to certain people. I sent just one, to Maurice Edwards, director of the Cubiculo Theater. He came, and he liked my performance, so he started producing my work at his theater. That is how I got started.

Of course I was studying at Juilliard at that time, which I found really difficult. I didn't have any idea then about American modern dance technique; they must have thought me a terrible student. Additionally, I spoke very little English. Although I received low marks in most of my courses, I got "A's" in composition. The only thing that kept me in school was Lucas Hoving's composition class. Also, for the first time in my life I enjoyed ballet classes, with Alfredo Corvino. He didn't think I was terrible; he gave me confidence. I tried very hard to learn the modern techniques that were taught at Juilliard, and I went to all the concerts, but I found that American modern dance was very different from what I was looking for.

Miyabi Ichikawa was in New York at that time, and he introduced me to the avant garde scene there. Through him I found some very interesting things. I met Meredith Monk and Trisha Brown—the people who were performing in lofts then. It was a very beautiful time. I felt really inspired, and I realized that I couldn't go back to Japan because things were just beginning to open up for me.

I remember very clearly one day walking in Riverside Park, feeling depressed and confused, not knowing quite why I was there. I was walking in dry leaves, and the theme of those leaves—death, the passage of time—crystallized at that moment into Part 1 of *LIGHT* [Ms. Takei's *magnum opus*]. I saw that everything I had thought previously about my choreography became "detached" from me; it wasn't me. Now I was taking a first step in the right direction. Often I had a dream about my own death. I saw myself lying in a white box, rocking back and forth, surrounded by dead leaves. Those are the elements of *LIGHT, Part 1*. So I became confident that I knew where to start, and how to start, and *LIGHT, Part 1* was born. When I performed it for the first time in New York some of the important reviewers, like Deborah Jowitt and Marcia Siegel, were very supportive.

At that same time I taught my first classes at Dance Theater Workshop. That was terrible! I had no idea what to teach, and everyone was very confused. Still, I felt it was important to keep doing it, and a part of my adjustment to being in the United States was that I was able to become a teacher. American teachers are very clear; they like to talk about what they are doing. Japanese teachers don't talk, they just do; that is the traditional Japanese way. There is no analyzing; the students just have to look, see, and do. Little by little I learned that I had to structure my classes carefully, and speak clearly, and analyze. I still didn't consciously bring ideas with me to teach, but I knew they were there, and in class my inspiration would lead me to them.

When I came back to Japan in 1991 I felt as if my body didn't want to move anymore; my body needed to "sit down"; it needed to stay in one place. For a long time I had noticed that I was moving around too much: walk, dance, travel; move, move, move. I had been pushing myself to move as far as humanly possible. It was like a competition to see how much I could do—a race with myself to the end of my limits. I was crazy, like a wild horse. The only way this wild horse could be stopped was to bring it back to Japan, to put it into the earth, and to sit down.

Then I finally did sit down—in December, 1991. It was a cold winter day, but the sun was really beautiful. It reminded me of the time I sat down on the dry leaves in New York's Riverside Park shortly after I first arrived in the United States. I was once again at a starting point.

Again I threw away the dance that I had been doing for a long time. This time, though, I stayed sitting there, rejecting, for seven months. Whereas during my US sitting I found my new direction right away—*LIGHT, Part 1*—this time I was questioning if there was still something left in me that needed to dance, to create, to be expressed. If I stood up I would dance. If I continued sitting, I would find another way of expressing my creativity—maybe some handwork. Then, suddenly, I resumed dancing.

I went to teach at the 1992 International Summer School of Dance in Tokyo. The first day I went to the classroom without an idea of what I was going to teach, only the strong feeling that would usually lead me to where I could find a beautiful idea on which to improvise. Usually, inspiration would start to grow inside me. My body would become alive with excitement. That day, however, nothing happened. I was shocked. I used my mind and experience to get through the class, but that hour and a half was a long and difficult time for me. I wondered if dance had left me, had gone somewhere. That night I thought about it, and I discovered what was wrong. I had tried to jump back to my same old me—to the way I had been doing things before. I should have known that I was just standing up after seven months of sitting.

The next day I started to improvise from where I was that day at that moment, and then my love, and my need, and my creativity came back to me, like a spring of water. I knew that I had started my new direction.

It was important for me not to go back and forth between Japan and the US after going off to attend Juilliard. I didn't come back to Japan for ten years. In that way I became free of attachments to family and citizenship, of identifying with any particular group. In the anonymity of New York I could be a citizen of no one place, a part of no family, not a Japanese choreographer, not an American choreographer, just a human. Not until 1978 did I return to Japan. That year I brought my group of 12 dancers and three staff for a two-week tour of Japan. Then I returned to New York City and continued to tour all over the States, Europe, and many other countries before returning to Japan in December of 1991.

I find Japan much changed, although some things are still the same. For example, there is still a very strong Modern Dance Association, which sponsors expensive productions in the big theaters, with lots of well-trained dancers. That work is very impressive, though it is not like mine. To me it is like going into a department store and seeing all the high-priced clothes; those things are nice to look at, but I don't want to put them on.

Now I find that in addition to the members of the Modern Dance Association there are also lots of "free" dancers around. They are not tied to just one teacher. They are creating their own work, and they are finding new ways to get it produced. I think this is an important and promising development. For the first time in Japan I feel there are people here I would like to work with as a group. It's like when I got to the States and saw people to whom I could say "Would you like to dance with me?" Because of the new feeling of freedom here I think that is now possible in Japan as well. Whether I will stay here remains to be seen. I now know that dance is international, so I can do it anywhere. There are many things in my personal life that may keep me in Japan for a while, but I think it is wrong to get stuck in one place. I will try as much as possible to remain international. My approach to dance, and especially to teaching, lends itself to that. What I give to students is a very basic approach to movement. In the States I studied many different techniques, but I didn't put any one of them on myself. What I developed through those ideas was a basic technique for relaxing and concentrating on the movement. My repertory pieces are based on the same principle. Because it is so basic my work is totally international. People from anywhere can do it, though those who have had a lot of ballet or jazz training look different, because of their technique. For that reason I prefer to work with dancers who are interested in physical expression—improvisation and composition—rather than those whose whole emphasis is on technique.

Figure 44 Kei Takei with Laz Brezer in *Pine Cone Field*

I think body training is very important: knowing one's own body, how to use it, how to move. This could be called "technique," but it should not be carried on a dancer's outside as a visible, technical form or style. What I call technique is like a food: eat it, digest it, and it becomes part of your body, so you can use it when you need it. Only what is valuable stays inside. The unnecessary part should be allowed to pass through, eliminated. So each person is different in what part is kept and what part is let go.

Most of the dancers here in Japan are primarily interested in "technique," but increasingly I find good people who also have the other interest. For the first time my improvisation classes at the International Summer School of Dance are full. I always say that the Japanese are the best improvisors in the world. Their whole life, you see, is one of improvisation; without it they could not live. How to connect with other people, how to serve, how to walk, how to follow other peoples' ideas, how to relate to a very confined space; these are all things that require constant improvisation of the Japanese people.

Many Westerners seem to think that because the Japanese are compelled to react to all these demands and limitations they have, as much as possible, reduced their lives to a given form. We do have forms, but we feel if all you did was follow the forms you would be dead! Because there are so many limitations in life you must constantly improvise to maintain your freedom—to keep your spirit alive. The Japanese are always dealing with the relationships of time and space—the important elements of improvisation. When we go to somebody's house, for example, there are the issues of when to bow, when to give the present, when to sit down, when to have a drink.... There are rules, just as in an improvisation. They serve the same function in both cases—to establish a structure within which we move. Whenever I give an improvisation to Japanese dancers it is always a success because they understand immediately the "give and take" of the situation. If there are ten people they will all give their ideas and without any problems make a dance. In the States ten people would never be able to put together a dance. There would just be a lot of talk. To get anything done I would have to divide them into smaller groups. This has to do with the American emphasis on remaining an individual, but in Japan you can't just be you, pushing your own ideas. You need to know the structure. This is true even of Japanese businessmen. Their lives are very structured, and success is measured by the ability to improvise within the structure.

Improvisation is really about exploring *you*, but always through the structure. The structure is always there. That is what allows you to interact with others. Improvisation is what we all do throughout our lives.

Even in solo improvisation there is always a structure; for example, the air you are in, the space, the relationship and give and take between you and yourself. Improvisation is not you having a good time and going crazy. In improvisation you always have your own creative eye looking at what's happening—talking, connecting, judging, leading. I think sometimes people confuse improvisation with forgetting oneself and getting crazy and having a good time like dancing at a party. This is not what I consider creative improvisation.

As improvisation has to do with getting in touch with and expressing emotions, you have to help students gain the confidence to do it. This is not only true of Asian students; American students have this problem too. They get closed off from their emotions by their education; they are so anxious to learn that knowledge covers over their emotional life. The Japanese "closure" is different; it results from too much structure or too little experience. The Japanese are repressed because of the need to be part of the group. Too many people are afraid to explore how they really feel as individuals. I think this is changing, but it takes time.

Chapter Twenty-Two:

Some Scholarly Reflections on Dance in Japan

An Interview with Miki Wakamatsu

> *Miki Wakamatsu has been a fixture in the dance world of Japan and beyond for many years. He helped form Six Avant Garde Artists with T. Hijikata (dancer), T. Mayuzumi (musician), M. Moroi (musician), K. Kanamori (stage designer) and others, danced and choreographed for television, and created his own dance company which won many prizes from the National Cultural Department. He is a Professor at the University of Tsukuba, and the author of four books on dance.*

Miki Wakamatsu: I grew up in Paris because my father, who was an abstract painter, had gone there to study and work. My first ballet teacher was Nola Kis, from the Bolshoi. Back in Japan I continued to study ballet through college, though by graduation time I had begun to choreograph some modern pieces. There were very few modern dancers in Japan then, and they were in two styles, German and American (almost all Graham). This was because before the war people went to study with Mary Wigman and Max Turpis in Germany, and with Graham in the United States. After the war some Graham dancers came here, to Tokyo, to teach at the American Cultural Center, which had started in about 1946, and closed sometime between 1965 and 1970. Also, the Martha Graham Company performed in Japan in 1952 or '53. It was very popular. At about the same time the Bolshoi Ballet was here, and a few years later the New York City Ballet. The Bolshoi was very successful, but the New York company was not at all. In those days the Bolshoi was very fine—sixteen *pirouettes,* triple *tour en l' air,* huge technique!

Editors: Following the Russian Revolution, through the '20s, didn't many Russian ballet people come here by way of Shanghai?

MW: Yes. We say there were "3 Pavlovas" in Japan: the famous Anna was here on tour, and then there were two sisters who came to teach, mostly at the Matsuyama Ballet.

E: So European ballet was well established here before the war. Then, during the war, I assume no foreigners came in.

Part VI:

Korea

Chapter Twenty-Thress:
Bringing Modern Dance to Korea

Yook Wan-soon

*Yook Wan-soon is a dancer, choreographer, writer, Ph. D. in dance, and Professor of Modern Dance at Ewha Women's University in Seoul, South Korea. She was the first person to introduce American modern dance to Korea, in 1963. Since then she has founded five modern dance organizations, including the Modern Dance Association of Korea and the Modern Dance Promotion of Korea. Ms. Yook has written five books and translated eight dance-related books. She also publishes a dance magazine, **Dance and Image.***

To date she has created more than 150 original works, including Jesus Christ Superstar, *which has had nearly 200 performances in Korea and abroad. She not only leads the way in developing modern dance in Korea, but also takes enthusiastic responsibility for cultural interchange between South Korea and foreign countries. Among other things, she organizes an international dance festival each year.*

I made my first trip to the Unitied States in 1961, with a teaching fellowship at the University of Illinois, Champaign-Urbana, and in the summer of 1962 I went to ADF. I had already completed my graduate work in Korea and was teaching at Kyung Hee University, but I went because I thought I could further my studies in the United States.

Although I was there only a short time it was one of the most valuable periods of my life, because I was able to meet so many famous teachers. Even before I went to ADF I did a one-month intensive course at the Graham studio in New York, where I studied with Miss Graham herself, Yuriko, Mary Hinkson, Ethel Winter, and David Wood. I was so happy to study with all of those people. Then, in 1963, when I came back to Korea, the Limón Company was here, so I got to meet all of them, including Ruth Currier and Betty Jones. That was the first time Koreans were really able to see modern dance.

Before I went to the States I had studied ballet, Korean dance, and what we called "Modern Dance"—that is, walking and jumping and hopping, which was at the same level as exercise for the high school students. Also, my teacher at the University taught some Dalcroze material. When I came back I taught what I had learned in the States, primarily at Kyung Hee University for the first year and then at Ewha Women's University. I also taught on a part-time basis at Seoul National University and Han Yang University; after school I organized a dance group called "Orchesis," for dancers throughout the Seoul area. I used the Orchesis group for all of my performances. Then I got too busy, and Ewha suggested that I teach only there, so I dropped my other affiliations. As I began to produce students, however, they went to teach at the other universities. Now, 95% of the modern dance teachers in Korea are my former students.

I encourage my students to work very hard to promote modern dance. Also, in 1980 we formed the Modern Dance Association of Korea, which has really taken the lead in organizing the dance community. We have especially influenced people in ballet and Korean dance to do more creative work within their traditional forms. By now even the young dancers who specialize in the other forms prefer modern dance, but I always tell them "Do your own thing. Don't just copy. You have to find and develop your own way of creating." I like the idea of using our Korean emotions as a foundation for creating a dance form. Any Korean movement can be our "soul." Even though I was trained by American teachers I am a *Korean* modern dancer, and I train my students to think that same way.

The dance my students and I do has a different sensibility from Western modern dance, though that difference is difficult to describe in words. If you see our work you will recognize the difference. For example, Korean dancers have a unique way of using their arms. Also, the music makes a big difference; if I use Korean music the soul and emotion of the movement will be different than if I use Western music. Of course the content of the dance is very important too. Korean dance tends to be more inward-looking, more introspective.

When I first started showing my work here people did not know Ruth St. Denis, or Doris Humphrey, or Limón, or Graham; if they knew anyone it was Isadora Duncan. But very quickly after I began popularizing modern dance and educating people about it they started saying "Your dance looks like Graham's." I responded firmly "No, this is my work." I had to educate the Korean audience as well as my students.

In 1975 the President of the National Dance Association for that year, Evelyn Lockman, invited my group to perform at the American Alliance for Health, Physical Education, Recreation and Dance Convention in Atlantic City, New Jersey. We followed that performance with a one-month tour to New York City, Washington, Chicago, Nashville, Los Angeles, and San Francisco. The first section of our program was traditional dance, and the second was Korean modern dance. I also took my students to study for a week at the Graham studio, and that was the first time Miss Graham met my students. She took care of them so well!

During the 1970s it was very difficult for Koreans to get visas to travel abroad; also, of course, it was quite expensive. In the '80s, however, things began to change

Figure 45 *Jesus Christ Superstar*, choreographed by Yook Wan-soon

for the better. So when the International Council for Health, Physical Education and Recreation (ICHPER) invited us to perform at their conference in Vancouver in 1987 we went, and then we did a week at ADF's Baldwin Theater in Durham, followed by an appearance in New York, where Dr. Patricia Rowe invited us to show our Korean modern dance at New York University. I met Barbara Metzler at that time, and my students took her composition class. Also, I let my students spread out on that trip, to study at different studios, so they could get a variety of experiences. I always encouraged them to study different things from those that I taught, to broaden their perspective.

In '88 I couldn't organize a trip to the States because I was choreographing for the Olympic Games in Seoul, but the next year I sent 53 students to ADF. That was a turning point in the history of dance in Korea. When those students got back they were so enthusiastic that I decided to bring ADF here. 1990 was their first year here, and now we are in our third year.

Nonetheless, many students still want to study there, and that's very important too. I want them to know what is available in New York, and to see as many performances as possible. So starting next year we are going to do ADF-Seoul every other year. One especially interesting development: Last year I convinced Charles Reinhart, Director of ADF, to create a scholarship for one Korean student, since traveling to the States remains so expensive that many of our students just can't do it. This year we were able to have two scholarships. The Korean parents are very conservative; they won't send their children unless there is someone to oversee them, so several other teachers and I are going to share that responsibility over the six weeks of ADF's program. This has the added benefit of giving the teachers some experience.

I am very pleased with what I see of the way modern dance is being taught in Korea today. Dance teachers in Korea are divided into two groups. One group runs and teaches in its own studios; the other teaches at universities. In general, this latter group is highly regarded in Korea; a dance professor at a university is not only responsible for dance education, but also does creative activities and socio-cultural work. His or her professional sphere is much larger than that of the studio teacher, who only creates dances and prepares for performances. In a word, the university professor is now better received in Korean society, though this wasn't always so. When I was a student at Ewha Women's University we didn't have any dance department; I studied dance as a means of physical education. Consequently, those of us who studied dance at the university weren't considered dancers. The dance studios at that time were prosperous, and growing rapidly. People thought of studio students as "real dancers." When I came back from the States I felt an anger at these circumstances, and resolved to reverse the situation. Dance education in the universities should be validated, I thought; a good dancer can and should be made through systematic and scientific education. With that determination in mind I worked hard at Ewha to nurture good modern dancers. What we see today is a result of my resolution; the universities understood the necessity of accepting dance into the regular curriculum, and took the initiative in developing the dance world of Korea. Unfortunately, the studios suffered a corresponding loss of status.

What does the future hold? Will we be able to maintain our involvement in international dance exchange? Due to the economic development of Korea, and in light of our growing prominence in international affairs, there is every reason to expect increased involvement. Indeed, if I may speak for the Korean dance community at large, I believe we actively hope for that. One obvious manifestation of this desire is the Modern Dance Promotion of Korea (MDPK), which I established in 1985. This organization has as its primary objective to increase, through cultural and artistic exchanges, mutual understanding between nations and international cooperation in dance. Toward fulfillment of that goal MDPK sponsors creative performances and scientific research in dance, supports programs that guide and educate young people through dance activities, and publishes dance literature. We might think of MDPK as the institutionalization of a burgeoning nationalism and optimism among Korean dancers. Because we are developing a dance form that is deeply rooted in the Korean spirit and the philosophy of modern Korean society, we feel that we have something unique to offer, and in exchange we look forward to continuing to learn from our neighbors in the world community.

Chapter Twenty-Four:
Toward a New Form of Dance in Korea

Lee Young-lan

Lee Young-lan is a dancer, lecturer, and, most recently, an actress. She is a graduate of the Dance Department of Ewha Women's University, and received her M.F.A. from New York University. Ms. Lee has served on the faculties of Seoul Art College and Ewha Women's University, and her monodrama "Lone Room" enjoyed a long run in Seoul.

Since the end of the Korean War there has been a great deal of interest throughout Korea in everything Western. This interest permeates everyday life, and especially influences such things as the educational system. Specifically in the dance field, people started going abroad to study after the war. Initially they went more or less exclusively to America, though more recently Germany and Japan have become popular. I think this recent change is a reaction against the fact that the first wave of influence was all Graham technique, promoted single-handedly by Ms. Yook of Ewha University. Now people are beginning to teach other things.

I teach what I call Physical Acting. To understand what that means you need to know something of my background. I started studying Korean traditional dance at age five, and then modern dance and classical ballet at about 13, in middle school. That was part of the curriculum of my school, and for Dance majors there were other, extra-curricular activities as well. Teachers were invited to create pieces for us for the annual dance festival, so we were on stage at least once a year. Then, at Ewha University, we had to learn three fields: Korean Dance, modern dance and ballet. At the end of each year we participated in the annual festival, and for the graduation ceremony we showed a piece of our own choreography. So you see, I have been dancing all my life.

When I was a junior at Ewha I got involved in a musical theater production; also, by that time I was sick and tired of always dancing the same kinds of movement patterns. In both Korean and Western dance the teachers would give us certain movements to do, and we would just practice them endlessly in front of the mirror, making ourselves beautiful! Maybe I was different, but I was very frustrated always practicing the same routine. I didn't want only to be a technician; I wanted to just explode, to say something through me. So when I auditioned and got selected for the

classes at NYU were very good for me, but the academic courses, theory and such, were hard because of the language.

E: Are you still doing those annual visits to New York?

PMS: Yes, though I didn't go this year, because I went to Poland, Hungary and Italy instead.

E: To study dance?

PMS: No, to look for companies to bring here, to Korea, for our Year of the Dance Festival.

E: And did you find any?

PMS: Just one company from France. I would like to bring some of the Germans, like Pina Bausch, but their fees are too high.

E: How have you used what you learned in New York in your teaching?

PMS: For the first three or four years I taught pure Graham technique, some Cunningham, and some Luigi-style jazz. More recently, however, I have begun to develop my own style. It is very Oriental, based in Korean tradition; it is contemporary Korean dance. I have come to realize that the Western styles are not right for us, because we are Korean. The technique is not ours; the exercise is good for the body, but not for the mind. I teach my students many styles, and I bring in good dancers and choreographers to do workshops, but for my own work I now use my own style. At my school, Kyung Hee University, in addition to the American techniques we also teach Korean traditional dance, and folk dance, and the special *Ki* dance, which is a Korean version of *Tai Chi*. That's good technique for the Korean dancer. It is all very "inward," whereas the Western styles are all "outgoing," open. For us, quiet stillness is all important. I like to use Korean music, composers, and instruments because they promote that quality in our work.

E: Have you completely discarded your Western training?

PMS: No, I continue to acknowledge its importance in strengthening the body. Graham technique is especially useful, but it is too rigid. We also need something to develop the flowing quality. I want my students to be exposed to the greatest possible variety of movement styles. Then I encourage them to throw all that away and create their own style. In teaching choreography I try to stimulate their imaginations by bringing in lots of images from the other arts, especially sculpture and painting. I like to use American post-modern art, because it gets them thinking in abstract terms. Also, we have some interesting things going on in Korean sculpture using materials that aren't so common in the West, like paper. Sometimes we start with realistic, everyday gestures, and abstract from there. Other times I have them make videos of everyday occurrences, and choreograph from those.

E: What is your own choreography like?

PMS: I recently did a piece for 70 dancers that was an hour and a quarter long, based on wedding and funeral ceremonies. The wedding was very sad, and the funeral quite light. It was intended to show a circle, like life and death.

E: Do you think of that cyclical idea as being particularly Asian?

PMS: The idea might be Asian, but the scenes, the movement, the costumes, were all abstract.

E: Are you trying for some kind of fusion?

PMS: Nowadays I have been thinking a lot about "What is dance."

E: And have you come to any conclusions?

PMS: Dance has to show some special message to the audience. I don't like too much talk, and similarly, in dance too much technique is not good. After long stillness a small movement can produce a great shock. Stillness is the hardest thing to do on stage. Young dancers don't understand that at all; they just want to jump around, like in jazz dance. But jazz is inappropriate for Korean people. Again, the Western techniques are good for training the body, but they do not speak to the Korean soul. On the inside Koreans are very different.

E: If you only see the "outside" of the technique, are you really understanding the movement?

PMS: That is why I worry about my students. They only like technique, without thinking about *why* they do what they do. It is like the difference between Japanese classical dance, *Noh* and *Kabuki*, and Korean traditional dance. The Japanese are very good at "wrapping" things, at making decorations, but the Korean dance has to do with what is inside. The Japanese smile a lot, but behind that they are not smiling. We don't smile so much; we are the same front and back. The Korean mind is "sticky"; we call it *chung*. It is like love. We have lots of love, and when we love someone it is for a very long time; it is never broken. These differences and similarities among cultures are very interesting to me. Especially in dance, the means of expression may be quite different, but the thinking, the messages, the feelings, are the same. The costume, the hair, the method are all different, but in dance we have to show something universal. If the choreography is excellent, everyone will feel the same way about it.

E: Where do you think Korean dance is going now?

PMS: I don't know. Nobody knows. That's why I am struggling with this question, "What is dance?" I think everybody is confused now, searching for direction.

E: I suppose the artist is always involved in that search; otherwise the arts become quite static. The problem is that you also have to teach, which means providing your students with a sense of direction. It's a big responsibility; bigger than the one you take on as choreographer, when you are only responsible to yourself.

PMS: Sometimes I would like to give up. I just want to be a performer: I am not a teacher, an organizer, an administrator. I don't like being President of the Modern Dance Association.

E: Why did you take on that job?

PMS: The committee members selected me.

E: But you had to agree to serve.

PMS: In Korea it may be different from what you are accustomed to in the States. It is a little like the military! We are all like brothers and sisters in the organization, because we all graduated from the same university. If they say they want me, I can't refuse.

E: In that job you again assume responsibility for providing direction—to the community at large, as to some extent you control what they will see in terms of dance. How do you decide what dance to bring here?

PMS: I like to show to the Korean artists, and the public, very different ways of making art.

E: For example, why did you select Doug Varone to bring to Korea?

PMS: Because his style is very American, unlike Germaine Acogny, for instance, who is from France, but was born in Senegal, so her art is mixed. She uses ancient, traditional influences mixed with modern technique; it is good for our people to see that. The three Japanese choreographers I have brought are all technically very proficient, but they have their own "color," or style. I look not only for technique, but for different approaches to making dances.

E: Do you have any influence on who comes here with ADF?

PMS: No, I'm not much interested in ADF. It is a very famous program, and well organized, but it doesn't change enough from year to year.

E: Doesn't it expose the students to a lot of things in a very short time?

PMS: Yes, but now our students are also going to study in many other places. That is much easier now than before. Every summer and winter vacation they go out.

E: Do you think that's good?

PMS: Not always.

E: Even though you yourself went out many times?

PMS: I already had my philosophy. For young dancers it is dangerous. They can learn a lot about technique, but it is very difficult for them to learn anything about the "soul" of dance. Ten years later, looking back on my own experience, I felt it was largely a waste of time.

E: If you hadn't had that experience, would you be able to make that kind of judgment now?

PMS: It is true that most of the Korean dancers of my generation don't feel the way I do. They still like the Western styles very much. They are very Americanized.

E: And is that good or bad?

PMS: "Good" and "bad" are not important. It is useful to know what is happening in other parts of the world, because that gives us ideas for our art. I like to travel a lot because I know the people and events I encounter will find their way into my dances.

E: What kind of dances are your contemporaries in Korea making now? What are they interested in?

PMS: Very light, comic, jazzy dances.

E: What is the "New Korean Creative Dance" like?

PMS: It is essentially dance-theater, using lots of voice, sometimes painting the face, the body; it uses very little dance technique. Often it is somewhere between drama and environmental sculpture, with minimal movement. There are also people doing continuous movement over long periods of time. It spans a wide range; generally it is quite cerebral, with little emphasis on technique.

E: Young Korean dancers like doing technique in class, but not in their choreography?

PMS: I think they have not yet figured out how to mix technique and idea; there is no middle, no balance.

E: Has your own work found that balance?

PMS: I'm trying. For the last four years I have been working on a very abstract piece based on Korean mythology. It is quite dramatic, with love, and political in-fighting, and mythic themes. The music was composed by Park Il-kyu (he is a prize-winning musician as well as dancer and choreographer). I would like to perform it in North Korea.

E: Is there much agreement in the Korean dance community concerning what makes for good dance?

PMS: That's a hard question. We have three "sections": ballet, modern, and Korean dance. I suppose they each have different ideas about "what is dance." Many people want to maintain the purity of those categories eternally. I don't agree with that; I tell my students "you have to know and use all those styles," but when I say those things in public they are very unpopular. So, I must continue to struggle with these issues.

Chapter Twenty-Seven:
New Trends in Korea*

Judy Van Zile

Judy Van Zile holds M.A. degrees from the University of Colorado, Boulder and the University of California, Los Angeles, and Advanced Certification in Labanotation from the Dance Notation Bureau. She is Professor of Dance at the University of Hawaii, specializing in dance research and ethnology. Her books include **The Japanese Bon Dance in Hawaii,** *and she has authored many articles, dealing especially with aspects of Asian dance. Ms. Van Zile was Editor of the* **Dance Research Journal** *from 1989-1993, and she is a frequent presenter at scholarly conferences both in the United States and the countries of Asia.*

On October 16, 1990, I sat in the Munye Theater watching a performance that was part of the 12th Seoul Dance Festival. Initially, I was struck by the stage set—a backdrop of three-dimensional, quite realistic trees. At first they swayed gently; then they became agitated, as if rustling in a winter storm. The lighting changed to red while crackling sounds contributed to the effect of a forest fire; and finally, all became calm again.

A lone male dancer, clad in pants and jacket clearly inspired by the attire of aristocrats of former times (*yangban*), appeared to wander through the forest. His movements could have come from anywhere—England, the United States, Japan— but in a moment I was very definitely in Korea; the meandering stopped as the dancer placed both feet together, torso tilted forward a bit and knees slightly bent. As he

* This chapter is based on an article that originally appeared in *Korean Culture*, Vol. 12, No. 3 (Fall, 1991). The research from which it is derived was carried out in Korea during four residencies over the eleven-year period from 1979-1990. Grateful acknowledgment is made to the following organizations for providing funding assistance for research: Korean Culture and Arts Foundation (Seoul); Academy for Korean Studies (Seoul); Korean-American Educational Foundation (Fulbright Program); and International Cultural Society of Korea. Acknowledgment is also made to individuals who provided invaluable translation assistance at various stages in the research process, including Alan Heyman, Joo Yun-hee, Kim Sung-ja, Lee Chun-hye, Lee Young-lan, Gary Rector, Ryu Ran, Um Hae-kyung, and Tim Warnberg, and to individuals who provided valuable comments on early drafts of the manuscript — Karen Jolly, Jane Moulin, Judy Rantalla, and Barbara B. Smith.—J.V.Z.

faced the corner of the stage, he straightened one knee and lifted the other forward, ankle bent and toes turned up. With one hand he delicately grasped the edge of his jacket and pulled it back just a little. The other arm reached forward, creating a counterpoint to the lifted leg that forced the torso to twist. The movement was held in animated suspension. Amidst the contemporary realistic stage set and geographically non-specific movements I was suddenly in the heart of older Korean dance, watching a movement that can be seen again and again in *Sungmu*, often referred to in English as the Monk's Drum Dance, and *Salp'uri*, a type of dance rooted in shamanistic ritual.

Later in the week I attended another festival performance. In the first piece a lone male in a costume of a design derived from the attire of Korean Buddhist monks executed prayer-like gestures. Then a group of similarly clad women entered, performing the same gesture, but walking *en pointe* as in classical ballet. Throughout the piece there were shifts between prayerful movements, pointe work and the long lean lines of ballet, and the occasional interjection of rounded, suspended movements of traditional Korean dance.

The second piece opened with a tableau of male and female dancers in varied relationships, the men in tights, snug-fitting bolero jackets and ballet slippers, the women in dresses of various lengths and pointe shoes. There was no geographic fluctuation here—I could have been at a ballet theater anywhere in the world. My Korean colleague said the two dances were part of an afternoon of ballet.

The next day I braved the crowded Seoul subway to go to Chamshil, on the south side of the Han River, for an afternoon at the Seoul Nori Madang. This delightful outdoor amphitheater comes alive in the afternoon with performances that seem to have quite popular appeal, usually mask-dance dramas.

I watched the center of the performing space as the musicians and dancers of Kosong Ogwangdae danced around the periphery of the circle in an opening processional. This dance-drama form originated in the city of Kosong, near the southeastern tip of the Korean peninsula. Primarily through satire, it tells of contempt for the privileged *yangban* class, an apostate monk, and the triangular relationship of a husband, wife and concubine.

As the drum rhythms became more accentuated and the dancers each took their turns in an introductory solo, my gaze shifted to the audience. There was a sharp contrast to the viewers I had seen at the Munye Theater performances. There the audience members were mostly college age girls, with a sprinkling of young men. The few older people were identified by colleagues as primarily dance teachers. At the Nori Madang, on the other hand, the audience almost seemed to be a random sampling plucked from the streets, subways and buses. Or perhaps not quite so random; this time older people, particularly men, predominated. There were many faces darkened from outdoor lives and creased with the lines of age. The audience was dotted with men and women in traditional Korean attire (*hanbok*).

What initially pulled my eyes away from the central performing space, however, was not the composition of the audience but its movement. As the drum rhythms became more incessant, some of the older members of the audience were drawn to dance. They began to lift and lower their shoulders in time to the drum beat, a movement that is one of the most prevalent features in almost all Korean dance (*okkae ch'um*). Gradually, the dancers lifted their arms sideward, wrists relaxed and hands softly pointing downward. One woman took out a handkerchief and gently manipulated it in a manner reminiscent of the long flowing scarf used in *Salp'uri*. Some people left their seats and ventured into the formal performing space. An elderly gentleman braced himself momentarily and then lifted one knee, a novice's attempt at the same movement performed by a trained dancer at the Munye Theater?

The movements of these people were a treat to watch. They were not as polished as those of the Ogwangdae performers or the dancers at the Munye Theater, but they were genuine, sincere, joyful. These people were dancing because the drum had called them; not because the curtain had gone up or the time had come to start the performance, but because, for whatever reason, they wanted to.

As I watched these and many other performances I became aware of the remarkable variety of dance that can be seen today in Korea. I began to question just what it is that delineates one type of dance from another, and what makes a dance uniquely Korean. The varieties of dance that are performed today range from those that have a very distinct Korean identity to those that do not. Individual dances can be placed along this continuum and tend to cluster around several specific categories identified by Koreans.

TRADITIONAL DANCE

Koreans categorize a rather wide range of dances under the heading of *chont'ong muyong*, a phrase meaning "traditional dance." This classification embraces dances originally performed in the royal court as part of rituals and ceremonies or as entertainment at royal banquets; dance dramas (usually masked, and known in Korean as *t'al ch'um*) and farmers' band music and dance (known as *nongak*) originally performed in villages, and also intended for rituals, ceremonies or entertainment; dances originally performed by Buddhist priests or shamans as part of rituals; and a number of dances choreographed in the twentieth century specifically for theatrical presentation that are said to be based on dances in one or more of the previously mentioned subcategories.

What binds traditional dances together are their roots in Korean culture. Although historically Korean dance has been influenced by other cultures, most notably China and Japan, traditional dances are considered to be indigenously Korean; they are part and parcel of the cultural fabric of Korea. Over the years these Korean elements have come to be displayed in the dance through costume, music, stories or thematic ideas, and movement. Hence, traditional dances are those that are easily identified as being Korean. They are the dances performed today in formal concerts of "Korean music and dance," at official government events, and at tourist venues for visitors to Korea. They are performed in other countries by dancers officially representing Korea, and are depicted on tourist posters and other items intended to quickly identify Korea as their source.

The Korean Traditional Performing Arts Center (Kungnip Kugak Won, referred to as KTPAC and until recently known in English as the National Classical Music Institute) traces its roots to the end of the fourth century via a royal music institute in the palace. Establishing its headquarters in Seoul in 1955, the center's goals originally were to preserve and transmit court dance, but recently they have been broadened to foster all forms of traditional music and dance as well as new creations. It is in the area of court music and dance, however, that the center is best known. Every Saturday throughout most of the year the center presents an hour and a half program of excerpts from the traditional music and dance repertoire. It is only here that, on a regular basis, one can see the slow stately movements of brightly attired women in dances that have been reconstructed from old documents describing court festivities. With arms frequently extended sideward, they walk, almost as if floating, while gently bending and extending their knees. They trace elaborate geometric floor patterns to the accompaniment of a live orchestra led by a musician playing the *pak*, an ancient instrument whose six slats of wood, fastened at one end with a leather thong, are spread apart and then snapped shut to provide a loud clap that signals transitions between sections. With each dance being only about ten minutes in duration, the regular Saturday performances include only samples of what is believed to have been performed in the court; it is thought that former performances were lengthy, with some dances lasting as long as an hour. Full-scale performances are reserved for special programs sprinkled throughout the year.

The preservation of the court dance tradition has been led by Kim Chon-hung. Kim studied music and dance at the court training academy and danced at the 50th birthday party of Sunjong, last ruler of the Choson Dynasty. Because of political battles and changing philosophies, there were many disruptions in the continuity of performing arts in the court. The dances performed today are based primarily on the memories of older dancers such as Kim, and on attempts, at various times, to reconstruct dances from information in selected historical documents. The KTPAC dance staff continues to search through these documents in their efforts to revive dances performed in the palace in former times.

Audiences for KTPAC performances are quite mixed: schoolchildren whose attendance is required as part of classwork, family and friends of the performers, old and young, men and women, and a handful of foreigners, many of whom have braved an almost one-hour trip on the crowded buses and subways to get to KTPAC's distant location south of the Han River, a factor that perhaps contributes to the small audiences.

The Seoul Nori Madang, completed in 1984, is a small outdoor amphitheater—geographically, and perhaps psychologically, juxtaposed alongside Lotte World,

Korea's answer to Disneyland. Performances at the Nori Madang provide a distinct contrast to the plastic, mechanical activities of its neighbor. On Saturday afternoons from April to October spectators can watch amateur and professional groups perform music and dance forms originally done out-of-doors, mostly in villages.

Figure 48 Buddhist priest performs *Para ch'um*, the Cymbal Dance.
Photo by Judy Van Zile, courtesy of the photographer.

Mask-dance-dramas, which previously afforded an opportunity for satire and outspoken comment on the upper classes or clergymen and made light of things that were taken much more seriously in daily life, are presented regularly. (Today's performances sometimes interject commentary on contemporary life and events.) Groups from throughout Korea are invited to take a turn in the performing circle, thus ensuring a variety. *Nongak*, or farmers' music and dance, is also represented in its myriad variations.

In October, 1990, as part of the 17th World Fellowship of Buddhists General Conference, a lantern festival was held. On a small stage set up in a large park bordering the Han River, Buddhist religious leaders from around the world addressed a gathering of thousands of devotees and casual spectators. Remarks were followed by excerpts from several dances. Korean Buddhist priests played and manipulated large pairs of cymbals as they turned, raised and lowered their arms, and gently bent and extended their knees in *Para ch'um*, or the Cymbal Dance, a dance generally performed on religious occasions. Other Korean priests then performed excerpts from *Nabi Ch'um*, in which they delicately moved their arms to manipulate very long sleeves in a dance known in English as the Butterfly Dance. They also used intricate movements to play a large drum in a standing frame in *Popgo ch'um*, the Drum Dance. An excerpt of the Cymbal Dance was performed again in December of that year, this time at Pongwan Monastery on the occasion of the raising of the central roof beam of a new building in the temple compound. These dances are accompanied by ancient chants, many in Sanskrit, with meanings only vaguely understood today. Although these dances were traditionally performed by priests at religious events, they are also danced today by priests on non-religious occasions and in dance concerts for purely entertainment purposes. At the concerts they are done, sometimes with modifications to the movements, by non-Buddhists as a way of making a dance statement that represents Korean Buddhism.

The performances at KTPAC, the Nori Madang, and the Buddhist gatherings are said to comprise repertoire handed down from Korea's past or, at least, attempts to reconstruct such repertoire. Although influenced at various times in history by contact with other cultures, this repertoire is consistently identified as "Korean dance."

CONTEMPORARY DANCE

At the opposite end of the continuum from traditional dance is what the Koreans categorize as *hyondae muyong*, or "contemporary dance." Contemporary dance seems to pride itself in having come from outside Korea—from the movement known in the United States as "modern dance." Dances easily identified as contemporary dance do not generally reflect any recognizable aspect of Korean culture.

Contemporary dance in Korea owes much to Yook Wan-soon, former Professor of Dance at Ewha Women's University. She went to the United States to study modern dance at the University of Illinois, and eventually moved on to New York City, where she studied with Martha Graham. Yook returned to Korea in the mid-1960s and earned the first doctoral degree with an emphasis in contemporary dance from Hanyang University. She introduced the Graham style into the dance curriculum at Ewha, and the program has subsequently become the spawning ground for most of the contemporary dance performed today. Credentials of contemporary choreographers and performers almost always include study at Ewha, and a large percentage of contemporary dance faculty members at the countless universities and high schools that offer a dance curriculum studied, at some time, at Ewha. Graham technique has become the standard for contemporary dance in Korea. At the same time, however, the Korean contemporary dance world includes individuals who have tried to go beyond this mold. These are people who have studied in university dance programs throughout the United States, a few who have studied in Europe, and several who, despite their Ewha training, have made conscious efforts to break away from the Graham style.

No dance can be devoid of the cultural roots from which it springs. However, while the court dances performed today consciously make the statement "This is the regal splendor of the Korea of former times," a contemporary piece like Nam Jong-ho's *Children, What's Behind the Mountain* seems to try to make a more universal statement in its costuming, movement, and ideas. Following dance studies at Ewha University, Nam pursued further training in France. She is presently a member of the dance faculty at Kyongsong University, and according to another contemporary dancer is famous in Korea because her work is "different," meaning that it breaks away from the Graham style. In the first section of the piece, for example, a group of uniformed children go through the rigorous disciplines of a school day. An austere teacher "calls them to order" through movement, and they mechanically perform their classroom routines. The moment the teacher leaves or turns her back, however, the children become playful and mischievous. The dance movements are not literal or pantomimic, nor do they incorporate the movement vocabulary found in many of the traditional dances. Rather, they are abstractions of regimentation and repetition interspersed with spontaneity and enthusiasm. Both the theme and movement vocabulary of the dance make a statement that could as easily have come from a German, British or American choreographer, representing the youthful days of children in Frankfurt, London or New York City.

Meeting, by An Ae-sun, is an abstract portrayal of various encounters. Although the theme is universal, the scenic design with set pieces that create dynamic shapes and long strips of elastic stretched across the stage, against which the dancers press and twist to alter the straight lines, bears the clear stamp of the late American choreographer Alwin Nikolais. Currently a member of the dance faculty at Ewha,

Figures 49-50   An Ae-sun's *Meeting*. Photos courtesy of An Ae-sun.

An received virtually all of her dance training in Korea, taking only a few classes with Jennifer Muller during a brief performance tour to the United States in 1987. Although Nikolais' company has never performed in Korea, Shin Sun-hee, An's set designer, studied in New York for 15 years.

CREATIVE DANCE

It is often easy to label a dance as traditional or contemporary and place it at one end or the other of the Korean/non-Korean continuum, but not all dance performed today in Korea can be so easily classified. A category has emerged that seems to reflect a desire both to retain elements of traditional dance and "Korean-ness," and to develop new forms. This category, known as *ch'angjak muyong*, "creative dance," falls somewhere between the Korean and non-Korean ends of the continuum.

Despite the fact that most Korean dancers talk about *ch'angjak muyong*, they do not all agree on precisely what it is. The differing views of what constitutes this category focus on such things as the training of the choreographer, elements of

Figure 51 Kim Yong-hee submits a prayer from earth to heaven in *Rice Plant,* choreographed by Moon Il-chi. Photo by Chae Yong-mo, courtesy of Korean Traditional Performing Arts Center.

Figure 52   *Rice Plant,* choreographed by Moon Il-chi. Photo by I Yong,
courtesy of Korean Traditional Performing Arts Center.

costuming and movement, and the ideas that form the basis of a particular dance.
For some, creative dance is any new choreography by someone trained in
traditional dance, as opposed to contemporary dance, which is choreographed by
someone trained in the modern dance of foreign countries. For others, it is dance
in which the costumes and movements are related to those found in traditional
dance but where the idea and choreography are new and innovative. What binds
these dances together is that although for one reason or another they are not
considered traditional, they *are* identified as being Korean. In looking at two
dances that are placed in this category we begin to see some of the things that
different people associate with Korean-ness and that serve, in dance, as symbols
of Korean culture.

Moon Il-chi is a choreographer at the Korean Traditional Performing Arts Center
who earned the first doctorate from Hanyang University with an emphasis in
traditional dance. She premiered an evening-length work entitled *Rice Plant* in
October of 1990. Based on a poem of the same name by Lee Song-bu, the theme of
the dance is purely Korean. According to a *Korea Herald* article, Moon says that she
tried to capture the spirit of life among the Koreans of former times: "The scene of
paddies standing against each other in the rice field brought up the image of ancient
Koreans who lived leaning against each other in closely associated communal
societies." Costumes are a mixture of traditional Korean attire and garments very
strongly based on traditional attire. Although movements replicate, or are based on,

Figure 53 Kuk Soo-ho's *Myth of Mount Paektu.*
Photo by Jo Dae-hyung, courtesy of photographer.

those found in traditional dance, they are drawn from a variety of forms rather than adhering to a single dance style. Despite the fact that the theme, movements and costuming are clearly Korean, the mixing of things from different forms of Korean dance and the modification of movements found in traditional dances are choreographic innovations that place *Rice Plant* in the creative rather than traditional category. Because the dance can be so easily identified as being Korean, it would be placed closer to the Korean end of the continuum than the non-Korean end.

Another performance identified as creative dance is *The Myth of Mount Paektu.* In the style of the elaborate extravaganzas of film director Cecil B. de Mille, the production has been described as an "epic spectacle" and compared to Beijing opera and Japanese kabuki. The script, by philosopher Kim Yong-ok, is based on the legend of the founding of the Korean nation: A supreme being becomes a mortal in order to civilize man, protect his people from evil invaders, and eventually give birth to Tan'gun, the progenitor of the Korean race. With a cast of almost 200 performers and a 50-member orchestra, the work incorporates dance movements found in traditional forms as well as ones that have no relationship to any Korean dances. In one section the stage is almost entirely filled with performers who are seated or kneeling. A small drum is placed on the floor in front of each performer, who strikes it using stylized movements in a manner that produces a powerful and dynamically varied rhythmic interlude as well as a visually spectacular dance. The beating of drums in a way that emphasizes both sound and movement is an integral part of many traditional Korean dances, in which the performer functions as both musician and dancer. In a section symbolic of the birth of the Korean people, performers crawl, writhe and reach as they work their way over a hill created on the stage. Movements in this section have no relationship to traditional dance forms.

Kuk Soo-ho, whose training is entirely in traditional dance forms and who is currently a member of the dance faculty at Chungang University, is responsible for the choreography and stylized movement in this mammoth theatrical undertaking. In this case, the performance incorporates many traditional movements as well as purely creative ones to tell a traditional Korean story. Although there are many Korean elements in the performance, the use of many non-Korean elements places *The Myth of Mount Paektu* closer to the non-Korean end of the continuum than *Rice Plant*, but still within the category of creative dance.

BALLET

Ballet sometimes rests at the non-Korean end of the continuum with contemporary dance, and sometimes slips closer to the middle, where creative dance lies. Clearly rooted in an imported dance style, ballet in Korea continues to demonstrate its classical European origins, as well as Korean influences. Standard repertoire items from the West, such as *Giselle* and the *Nutcracker*, are staged by local or visiting choreographers, with perhaps the only Korean element being that they are performed by dancers from Korea. The work described earlier, however, which combined Buddhist-inspired costumes, prayer-like gestures, and pointe shoes, reflects a mixing of Korean and non-Korean components. When I asked a Korean colleague why she classified this dance as ballet, she replied that the use of pointe shoes and ballet movements placed it in this category, despite the acknowledged Korean theme and Korean-inspired costumes and movements.

Another "mixture" identified as ballet is a work entitled *Shim Ch'ong*, performed by the Universal Ballet. Choreographed by American Adrienne Dellas, founder of the company and its original artistic director, the ballet tells the traditional Korean story of a faithful daughter and her blind father. With its wicked sailors, mythical underwater scene, trials and tribulations of a poor country girl who eventually marries a king, and grand palace celebration, the story lends itself perfectly to the fairy tale tradition of nineteenth century ballet. Although the designs of many of the production's costumes are based on traditional Korean attire, the performers are easily recognizable as a poor country girl, fairy tale underwater creatures, or members of royalty—whether they be Korean or not.

The movement, on the other hand, is drawn almost entirely from the codified vocabulary of ballet. Shim Ch'ong dances her concerns and joys using the long, outwardly projected lines of ballet and pointe shoes; the wicked sailors perform an athletic display of strength using the elevation and intricate footwork of ballet male *allegro*; and Shim Ch'ong and her lover express their feelings toward each other in a typical ballet *pas de deux*. In only two brief sections is there a conscious attempt to incorporate Korean dance movements: Entertainment for the court is provided by five dancers attired in costumes and executing movements taken from the Pongsan masked-dance drama form, and when sight is restored to all the village blind men their dance of joy uses movements traditionally found in dances portraying young male aristocrats.

Members of the cast were both Korean and non-Korean; the Universal Ballet seems to try to live up to its name by including dancers from a broad spectrum of ethnic and national backgrounds. With a Korean story as its basis, an American choreographer, performers of varied ethnic backgrounds, Korean-inspired costumes, and movements drawn almost entirely from classical ballet, *Shim Ch'ong* is described as "ballet with a Korean story," and falls near to, but not at, the non-Korean end of the dance continuum.

DANCE IN KOREA OR KOREAN DANCE?

The diversity of dance that can be readily seen in Korea today reflects a tolerance for a broad range of approaches. Indeed, it is possible to find dance to satisfy almost every interest and taste. There is a concern with perpetuating the dances of the past that bear an unmistakable "Korean" stamp; at the same time, however, there is a desire to try out dances that are not Korean—a fascination with the foreign. Together with purely Korean dance and foreign dance, there is an interest in experimentation and creativity.

What is perhaps most interesting today are the dances that do not lie so conveniently at one end or the other of the Korean/non-Korean continuum, and the ways in which they are identified by Koreans. These dances and their classifications reflect the kinds of things that are conceived of as being representative of Korean culture—as symbolizing, via dance, Korean-ness. Such things are generally quite concrete; they relate to costumes, themes, and movements. They usually take on a form from the past: clothing worn by people during the early days of the Choson dynasty, stories relating to myths of origin or traditional Korean occupations and values, and movements found in older dances. However, the clothing worn in Korea today is not the same as it was during the Choson period; although traditional stories will always remain, there is much contemporary literature that deals with modern concerns; and today's younger generation can be seen in discotheques doing the same popular dances as their non-Korean counterparts. Although a brief exposure to a city like Seoul brings to mind images of New York City or London, a longer stay makes one realize that there is something Korean that pervades the city, despite skyscrapers, men in Western-style suits, and young girls in mini-skirts. With so many changes in the concrete things from the past that easily identified Korean-ness, what are the signs of identity that apply today? Are there non-concrete elements that can serve as such markers?

A dance entitled *Transformation* tries to deal with the contemporary and non-concrete ingredients of Korean-ness. Choreographers Kim Bock-hee and Kim Wha-suk both received training at Ewha Women's University and both are currently dance professors, the former at Hanyang University and the latter at Wonkwang University. As I watched *Transformation* I was continually struck by the powerful visual images. Early in the piece my attention was fully engaged by the three dancers in amorphous costumes. Continually linked by either physical contact or extraordinary movement focus, they progressed slowly from one side of the stage to the other, reaching, gliding along the floor, and manipulating themselves over and under each other in order to transport the totality of the trio from one place to another.

Sun Jae-hoon, in a *Korea Times* article, wrote that the Kims "are reputed for their dance works full of Korean images and emotion displayed through modern dance techniques," and choreographer Kim Bock-hee says, "Our primary aim ... [is] to develop dance techniques and motions full of Korean emotion and taste." The choreographers and at least one Korean writer felt that the underlying motivation for the dance was Korean sentiment, and that there were images, emotions and qualities, non-concrete things, that specifically conveyed Korean-ness. Without the concrete components that so quickly spoke to me of "Korea" in other dances, I, too, focused on less tangible things. I saw a rather extraordinary statement about the body in motion—the remarkable beauty of the shapes the human body can create and the spaces it can outline for the eye of the beholder. Was this statement, however, "Korean"?

Transformation raises questions regarding both the contemporary definition of Korean-ness and its portrayal in dance. Was my failure to recognize something specifically Korean in the dance because I am not Korean? Was it prompted by the difficulties of trying to depict certain kinds of qualities or essences in dance? Or was it because of the difficulties of trying to extrapolate essences from some of their more concrete manifestations, or trying to use new forms to express the very heart and soul of Korea? Are there particular qualities and feelings that are culture-specific, or are such elements universal in nature?

The fact that the full range of the Korean/non-Korean continuum can be seen in dance today reflects a concern with holding fast to something that makes a Korean statement while at the same time experimenting with new modes of expression. Contemporary Korea is changing rapidly. Commentators have noted technological and economic advances, changes in rural conditions, and increases in contact with other cultures as Koreans travel and study abroad more frequently than in the past. These changes give rise to a struggle to re-define just what it means to be Korean. As this struggle works itself out, the varied forms of dance will reflect individual statements of Korean identity.

Part VII:

Philippines

Chapter Twenty-Eight:
'Cross-Cultural Exchange Has Always Been a Way of Life in My Country'

Nestor Jardin

Nestor O. Jardin, born in Lucena City, graduated from the University of the Philippines in 1973 with a Bachelor of Science degree in Zoology, and in 1983 finished the Management Development Program at the Asian Institute of Management. He was principal dancer with the Filipiniana Dance Troupe from 1969 to 1972, and soloist with Ballet Philippines from 1974-1989. Previously he was stage manager and company manager of Ballet Philippines, instructor at the Cultural Center of the Philippines Dance School and at the YMCA, editor of **Dance Philippines***, and Chairman of the Presidential Commission on Culture and Arts National Committee on Dance. Mr. Jardin is a recipient of several grants and scholarships, including the National Science Development Board Scholarship, the Goethe Institute Grant, the Asian Cultural Council Grant for Arts Administration , and the US International Visitors Program Grant. He is currently Associate Artistic Director for the Performing Arts at the Cultural Center of the Philippines, and Director of the CCP Coordinating Center for Dance. He is also a trustee of the Philippine High School for the Arts, and Vice President of the Asia Pacific Dance Alliance.*

I would like to start with what seems a very basic observation, and perhaps this can serve as a premise for the points we will be taking up later. Let me go back very briefly into the history of the Philippines, as a way of showing that cross-cultural exchange—artistic, cultural, social, political—has always been a way of life in my country. This will explain a lot, especially in comparison to countries like Japan and China. The history of the Philippines is such that we have been exposed to many cultures, even prior to the arrival of the Spaniards. I say "arrival of"; they would say "discovery by." I don't agree with the point of view that the Europeans discovered the Philippines; there were already many societies functioning in the Philippines when the Spaniards arrived. They were indigenous and had their own culture, their own language, their own art. The Chinese, the Indians, the Malays, and other Asian people came to settle or trade, and each of those subsequent exchanges left its permanent mark on how we think, speak, and act. So cross-cultural exchange really began even before the Spaniards. Then there is the fifty years of American colonization, which has had a greater impact than the 400 years of Spanish influence, because the Americans modernized our country's education and communication systems, among others. Even the Japanese, who occupied our country for only five years during the war, left a mark on our society.

If we look at the historical panorama of the Philippines, what we see is that although we did not have a nation before the Spaniards came—we didn't have Thailand's kingdom, for example, or China's dynasties, which unified the country— there was a great deal of cross-cultural fertilization. This explains, perhaps, why assimilation is a way of life for the Filipino people, and also the non-existence of barriers to influences from the outside world. Very briefly, that is why Western art has been successfully integrated into our culture.

Concerning the transplantation of an art form from one culture to another: I think the major issue is the manner and the frequency with which the art form is introduced, and how it is taught. Also, we need to consider the development of appreciation for it among the people, first in the artistic community, and then among the larger public. This three step process will lead into other issues. Once you have accepted the art form, you might go any of three ways: If I am an artist and I have accepted the Western form, let's say Post-modernism or Minimalism, I might simply copy it as it was introduced, I might transform it into my own interpretation of it (and there will be some local coloring in that process), or, the most important option, I might assimilate it. In that last case I make it a part of my heritage as a Filipino artist, so I present it as a new form amalgamated with the other aspects of my being as an artist.

*   *   *   *   *

The main dance program with which I am associated is housed in the Cultural Center of the Philippines (CCP). We work on the premise that we are evolving a national culture with, for, and by the people. Because of our colonial past, the fact that we have 7,100 islands with various native cultures, with all the cross-cultural influences from the West and East, it is necessary to develop a national, unified culture. It is our dream that this culture will be evolved by the people, with the artists perhaps serving as a catalyst. And with this come our various goals. We need to develop an awareness of art and culture in the Philippines. We need to develop good international relations with other countries, because we at the Cultural Center believe in two-way exchanges, inward so we can learn from other Eastern and Western cultures, and outward so we can project our own identity. We have had numerous programs that promote cross-cultural exchange in dance, either bi-lateral (that is, through formal agreement between the Philippines and another country), or informal, on an institution-to-institution or individual artist-to-artist basis. These programs are sometimes supported by the government, or by the private sector.

CCP is unique in that it is a non-municipal, not-for-profit organization. It is overseen by a Board of Trustees which approves its policies, and is governed by the accounting rules of the government, yet has its own Charter which makes it independent in the pursuit of its vision, mission, and objectives. It gets no direct financial support from the government, though all of its assets are owned by the government. CCP manages on its own. We have a Cultural Development Fund that has grown through the years, as we invest it in the money market. We spend only the interest, which comprises about 80% of our budget each year. The other 20% is earned income: We have restaurants in the complex, we rent out space, there are ticket sales, donations, and sponsorship of projects. We are involved in so many things besides dance: music; drama; production design; film; literature; visual arts and broadcast arts. We maintain a library, museums, and seven theaters. Our scope of operations is national. We have 18 regional arts councils, independent of us but supported by us. We use this network to promote our programs.

Under the CCP program we have the CCP Dance School, which is the primary unit for classical ballet and modern dance. The School is independent; it is part of Ballet Philippines, and Ballet Philippines is the resident company of the Cultural Center. The School is involved primarily in training and education, developing talent, and earning money for the company.

Most of the teachers are local, but on a regular basis there are foreign instructors who are with us during the year or for the summer workshop—mostly Americans and Europeans, some Chinese, some Japanese. They are usually recommended by other teachers who have been at CCP, or by Filipinos who have been abroad and become acquainted with their work. The more effective ones are those who really stress discipline in their teaching. Some teachers are very lax, and provide a great deal of individual freedom; others are strict, and want students to follow the prescribed method. Filipinos today tend to be quite reserved in their response to something new; they may like it, but it takes time for them to open up. If you want to get a reaction from them, you have to be a little patient.

Our dancers are quite advanced in classical ballet. For modern dance there aren't many practitioners; in fact, it isn't really taught, except through CCP. There are some people who have been trained at CCP who are capable of teaching modern dance, but they can't afford to do it because modern classes don't get enough enrollment.

Modern dance is a focus of its own in the School, particularly during the five weeks of the summer program. In the past we have invited such teachers as Norman Walker, Pauline Koner, Garth Welch, Takako Asakawa, and David Hatch Walker. Each of those teachers either created pieces for the Company or restaged earlier works. It is an on-going process, this inviting of guest teachers, and it provides the trainees and the members of the Company with exposure to various styles. Outside of the School, the Cultural Center sponsors workshops and lecture demonstrations by visiting teachers in ballet and modern dance for all students and professionals in Manila and in the regions. Teachers from the local regions are often invited to take part in these workshops.

We also have a resident modern dance faculty. The main teacher is Agnes Locsin. She is Graham trained. Among the choreographers it's Denisa Reyes, who got a degree in dance in New York. Although these people are from the Philippines, because they were trained in the States they are really American dancers. Modern dance in the Philippines is quite America-oriented.

The CCP was founded in 1969, by Mrs. Marcos. About six months later the Ballet Philippines began its residency. That was really the beginning of organized modern dance programming in the Philippines, although modern dance was introduced earlier through performances by touring groups. Ruth St. Denis was the first, in 1926. However, it was not until the Cultural Center was established that modern dance was really popularized, mainly through Alice Reyes, who was the catalyst. She was the founder and first Artistic Director of Ballet Philippines; she founded the CCP Dance School, and she established the first modern dance training program in the country. Her own training was in Colorado. Soon after her came the younger choreographers, who are taking over now.

During the regular school year the modern dance enrollment is much lower than that of classical ballet, but each summer all the modern classes are full. I believe that is in part because the students are out of school and looking for something to do.

In terms of cross-cultural exchanges, we also have begun promoting extended residencies by foreign companies. Before, we had companies coming in briefly, perhaps doing two performances and a lecture-demonstration. While this provided wonderful exposure, it didn't have as much impact as we would like. So last May we had a three-week residency of a French company, the Jeune Ballet de France. They brought the fine French choreographer Claude Bumarchon, who worked with a mixed cast of company members and local dancers. They did four performances. The effects of this type of programming, we think, will be more lasting.

Our ability to do such cross-cultural exchange is largely dictated by money; who can afford to come. From the United States, the USIS has been very active in sending teachers to the Philippines, or helping local teachers or choreographers get funding for their training in the US. Unfortunately, I think they have had budget cuts recently. The New York-based Asian Cultural Council has also funded the trips of some teachers in the past.

*   *   *   *   *

Finally, a word about what problems and rewards are encountered by dance administrators in the field of cross-cultural exchange. The first issue is understanding; it simply takes time to understand anything foreign that is being newly introduced. The second issue is compatibility. While the Filipino people are inclined to accept outside influences, if such influences do not jibe with their beliefs, or with

Figure 54 French balletmaster Jean Marion conducting a class for Ballet Philippines

their "being," they will slowly let them go. Then there is process: it always takes time to adapt to new things. For example, the students may find it difficult to adjust to new teachers, or the teachers may become frustrated until they have had time to understand something of the culture. On the first day both teachers and students are often quite shocked. Then they have to work out a process for meeting half way.

We have never had a total disaster, but some of the teachers who came to work with our students were quite recalcitrant; they would get so frustrated, not realizing that it takes time to achieve discipline, that they would simply walk out. But those are rare exceptions, primarily involving Eastern Europeans, who may have had special communication problems. The Americans seem to have a relatively easy time.

Professionalism in dance is still a new phenomenon in the Philippines. The professional dancers are prepared to work: they put in long hours, they are on time, they listen to corrections and adjust immediately. But the concept of professionalism is not necessarily a part of our system as yet.

Fortunately, the English language is not a major barrier for us, and I think the universality of dance language smooths out all the others. When you are choreographing, of course, it's more difficult than when you are teaching.

There is always the issue of finances. In the Philippines when we talk about " the West" we mean the American continent and the European continent, both about half way around the world. We are so far from everything, and the Philippines is a poor nation. When you translate dollars, or francs, or Deutschmarks to pesos it tends to be a staggering amount. We always need to look for grants.

Lastly, there is the issue of audiences. Ours is still a small dance audience, particularly for contemporary dance. It is growing, but still a problem.

The rewards of cross-cultural dance training far outweigh these problems. Dance students inevitably improve their technique and artistry in one way or another. They tend to discover new ways of using or pushing their bodies to the limit. Teachers gain a lot from the experience as well, working with students with Asian physiques who have been basically trained by Filipino teachers. Choreographers have often found it challenging to work with our dancers, who in general may not yet possess the technique that Western dancers have, but move in a unique and exciting way.

Regarding the future of cross-cultural dance exchange in the Philippines and the Pacific Rim region generally, I want to close with a word about the Asia Pacific Dance Alliance. APDA struggles because of its vastness in scope. Funding is a perennial problem. We have officers who don't even appear for the annual meetings. There are always communication problems. All of this is quite typical of international organizations. Yet, once it has its own base and systematized operations I think APDA can accomplish a great deal toward promoting cross-cultural exchange. The greatest barrier to cross-cultural exchange is often lack of information regarding what is available in other countries. Perhaps APDA will eventually provide that kind of information.

This has much to do with "networking." I am unsure how to compare the magnitude of networking effort here with what is ongoing in the States or in Europe. There are many intra-regional events here. For example, the Association of Southeast Asian Nations (ASEAN, which encompasses Brunei, Malaysia, Philippines, Singapore and Indonesia) sponsors regular gatherings. However, APDA is the only attempt to organize the whole of Asia and the Pacific Rim. We anticipate that it will grow because of the dynamism of the area, and the fact that the West is recognizing that the Asia-Pacific Rim region will be a force in the near future.

Part VIII:

Taiwan

Chapter Twenty-Nine:
Dance and Society in Taiwan: A Culture in Transition

An Interview with Lin Hwai-min and Ping Heng

Lin Hwai-min *studied ballet and Peking Opera movement in Taiwan, modern dance at the Martha Graham School and Cunningham Studio in New York, and classical court dance in Korea and Japan. In 1973 he founded Cloud Gate Dance Theatre, the first and still the only fully professional modern dance company in Taiwan, for which he has choreographed more than fifty works. As a result of Cloud Gate's extensive tours in Asia, Europe and the United States, Lin Hwai-min has received critical acclaim from many international dance critics.*

In 1982 Jaycee International named Lin Hwai-min one of the ten outstanding young persons in the world for his artistic achievement. In 1983 he founded the Dance Department at the National Institute of the Arts in Taipei. Mr. Lin has been the recipient of the most prestigious arts awards in Taiwan. He is also a critically acclaimed writer, who holds an M.F.A. from the Writer's Workshop at the University of Iowa.

Ping Heng *holds an M.A. degree in Dance from New York University and is a certified Labanotation teacher. She returned to Taiwan and founded Taipei Dance Workshop in 1984. The Workshop provides professional training for dancers and performing space for young dance troupes as well as experimental theater groups (more than 400 performances of dance and theater in the past seven years).*

Ms. Heng is a full-time Instructor in the Dance Department of the National Institute of the Arts, which she also chaired from 1989 to 1991. She is a dance notator for the Research Project on Taiwanese Aboriginal Culture, Institute of Ethnology, Academia Sinica. In 1989 she started Dance Forum Taipei, a burgeoning dance company that enjoyed its first US tour in January, 1993.

student—might easily react badly. There is a risk in such a situation of real psychological damage. That's on the individual basis; on a broader cultural level this is a potentially subversive thing you are describing, if what we are talking about is the product of a society that values passivity, docility.

LHM: That may have been true even five or six years ago, but nowadays "I do what I do as long as I like it" is a popular slogan among the young. I don't think this is any longer a Chinese land, a land of Chinese culture. That's only in books. Look at the traffic: I mean those drivers, aren't they individualistic!

PH: The whole political situation is changing, so the kids have to pick up something new. Until the end of martial law the young people were kept very ignorant of events here and in the rest of the world, especially in China. There is still a great deal of manipulation of the media—all three television stations are sponsored by the government, and the owners of all of the major newspapers are ex-military people—yet the populace is getting smarter. For the young people there seem to be three main options: to become strongly anti-government and protest everything; to get very comfortable and accept everything; or to become entirely Right Wing in the interest of security. The majority are probably in the third category.

E: Is that coming out in their art? I don't just mean are they making political dances, but are they able to respond in different ways because of their new values?

LHM: Well, attempts are made, but sometimes it's hard. They do crazy things, and that is an expression of freedom in itself, but that doesn't mean they are commenting on what's going on in the society. The line between imitation and genuine statement "from the gut" is not always clear. Through exploring their own works they are actually exploring themselves, and that's important. So yes, they are doing things, but not as crazy as American kids.

E: They probably don't have the years of risk behind them. We like to say that American kids are willing to take risks, though I must admit the ones who come to me now have to be encouraged all the time. They don't understand that if everything is under control it can be very boring. I get concerned about students who won't risk anything, who hold onto their technique at all costs. It all starts in technique class, where you want to break up some of the patterning.

LHM: I teach choreography, and it's very hard to know what to teach. Every class is different. For certain classes you have to take them apart and encourage them to be free. You say "give me junk." Then there are classes that are really creative, but they don't know how to put things together. The discipline is required. Really, somebody has to teach them the skills; you don't just inject some Van Gogh into these kids. But it's easy to get carried away: a kid thinks he's being creative, and really, without even knowing it, he is imitating. If you make the mistake of saying "that's very creative," he's suddenly a big shot. That's dangerous. When later he realizes what is happening it's already too late for the craft.

In terms of choreography, there is a new thing that has crept in either through the influence of foreign teachers or people like Ping Heng and me who have been "corrupted" by the West. That is *abstraction*. In the past, naturalistic theater was very strong. Even now people want a literal translation of each movement in the dance. When there is no plot involved they are lost. Interestingly, they don't seem to have this problem in Guangdong, where they just want to do modern dance, and are curious about everything new. I'm reserving judgment about Guangdong; I don't know what kind of thing they are ultimately going to do.

E: They are getting a lot of exposure; they're performing all over.

LHM: They are and they aren't. China is a big country. They are performing in Canton and Beijing; they show whatever they are doing at the moment, whether it's student works or masterpieces. It's wonderful to have something new and modern and free going on. My god, that's wonderful!

E: I should think they're in the second stage now; that's what has everybody worried. They are through the first stage, the first four years, when they brought in the Western artists. In theory that had to do with opening up the dancers themselves, so they could make work of their own—so the Chinese dance would be an expression in movement terms of the Chinese psyche, the Chinese culture. Now they have brought in Willy Tsao as Artistic Director, and moved on to another stage.

LHM: What work of Willy's? Jazzy? Pop?

E: Yes. Willy says very self-consciously: "We need to do a program that sells to the public, so they will come to see the other work." What we saw was a great potpourri of modern, ballet, and jazz; as many steps as you could get into as little time as possible, and one more spectacular than the next. Those dancers *killed* themselves for an hour and a half. It was all a local audience, and they loved it.

LHM: They have to do that for several reasons: to be accepted by the society, to make money, and to show that they are politically safe.

E: Yes, but to anyone with an eye there were several sections that were quite dramatic in their political statement; all these young people struggling for identity, in a rock music format. When I asked Willy about it he admitted to wanting to make a dance about the need for freedom.

It was very moving to see those dancers rehearsing the next day. They were in the studio at 9:00, because Willy wanted to go over something that had gone wrong the night before. There they were in freezing cold, with no heat, wearing their overcoats and socks because they don't have any dancing shoes (they have to save their one pair of ballet shoes for performance).

PH: And at the same time Willy is working with City Contemporary Dance Company in Hong Kong?

E: Yes. He goes back and forth between the two companies.

LHM: He's the great provider. And he's worried, too, because if he doesn't step in it could all be over.

E: Really?

LHM: In a way, because Willy is a bridge with the world outside China. But I hope dancers in Canton eventually will be able to draw from the rich resources in China and create something new.

E: That line of reasoning also makes your experience and Ping Heng's of particular interest: Are you now Western dancers, or Taiwanese dancers, or some sort of hybrid.

LHM: We're not Chinese and we're not New Yorkers. We live in Taipei, and we speak some English, and that makes a whole lot of difference. When you start speaking the language you might get corrupted—and liberated at the same time. It's pure confusion! It's frustrating. It's crazy.

E: How are you, as artists who leave Taipei to study elsewhere for a while and then return, changed by the experience? And also, how are you different from artists who do the same thing in Guangdong or Hong Kong?

PH: In Asia the Taiwanese are very special—more so than the people of Hong Kong, for example, because in Hong Kong there are no roots. The Taiwanese are a loving people; they love their country, or more than that, they love their *land*, from the bottom of their hearts.

LHM: Yes, people really do "take root" here.

PH: To me, when I am in New York I know I am just visiting. I know I will be coming back, so I can enjoy that environment wholeheartedly.

E: What do you do there?

PH: As a student (at NYU School of the Arts) I spent most of my time doing notation work, which I enjoyed very much. Perhaps that is because of my Chinese heritage; it gave me a lot of homework, and a sense of achievement, and made me feel that I have some talent. I felt we could really do a lot with notation work here; especially we could reconstruct a lot of repertoire, because that's one of the principle ways we learn about Western technique. There are also many things here that need to be notated, like our aboriginal cultures, and the pieces from the Peking Opera, and the repertory of our early choreographers. But since I came back, in '84, what I have done is only some notation work with the Institute of Ethnology, and some elementary education work in the schools.

E: It concerns me that many of the Asian dancers who come to the States are invited into companies—they seem to have a work ethic that appeals to Western choreographers—and stay on.

LHM: There may be some falling off of commitment to place among the young. Each time I am away and come back I am shocked because the change is so rapid. When I first met Ping her family was living in the middle of a rice field, and now that is one of the most expensive areas in Taiwan. And there's no rice! I just get lost in this city; it's getting to look like *Hong Kong!*

E: When we first walked into the hotel lobby here, I was struck by this thought: "There is nothing here that is distinctively Taiwanese. It's like Hong Kong, and much of it would not be out of place in New York City."

LHM: But this is tourist Taiwan. If you had time you could go to the old parts, experiencing the temples, which are wonderful in this New Year season. Also, there has been a strong renewal of the aboriginal songs and dances just in the last few years. Aborigines were looked down upon in the old days. Then the dancers of our last generation took the liberty of recreating those materials, outside of the cultural context, and presenting them in clubs.

E: What else do you think is lurking in the background?

LHM: I'm not sure, but the challenge is to make this generation of students aware of what is possible. We have to make them see that when you bring in the foreign teachers, with their new styles and techniques, you also bring along a whole set of aesthetics. You can do all the imitation you want, but you also need to understand the cultural context behind each style. That is a special problem here, because our educational system promotes the idea that everything is to be memorized and repeated on examinations, and after the examinations you just forget it. But that doesn't mean it's not "in the blood."

E: You have an advantage, because if these young people *do* carry a sense of tradition in them it can be brought out by cultivating the aesthetic sensibility.

LHM: The risk when you bring in coca cola and pizza, Michael Jackson and Russian *Swan Lake*, is that these new things are "hot," while Chinese tradition is taken for granted or neglected. We try to combat this by introducing the students to museums, inviting them to participate in religious pilgrimages, attending aboriginal festivals. We hope they will find these things more exciting than disco, and start questioning what they see. We hope they will want to know more, and that their pursuits will bring out something they already have but are unaware of.

E: Do you see reflections of this kind of thing in the work of your young choreographers?

PH: I see young artists still trying to find their own personal vocabulary. Some lean toward philosophy; others are more interested in making political or social statements, as in the '30s. Most of them have been to the States for several years, and now they are trying to find out what they have to give. It takes time to develop individuality as a choreographer. I think what I am seeing now, especially in the generation of dancers that is 30–40 years old, is the emergence of some who are finding their direction. Each has different interests: some are more like dance theater, others like *Butoh,* and still others are "dancey dancey." This has just been happening over the last five years or so; it might take another five or ten years to mature.

Figure 56   Students of the National Institute of the Arts
performing an Ami Village Festival Dance

E: It's nice to see that variety of voices coming out. This emergence you speak of corresponds to a period of heavy cross-cultural exchange with the West. Is there any inclination to deny that influence?—to assert that "We are Taiwanese"?

PH: I think these choreographers have a strong awareness of their cultural identity. Recently people like Frances Tao (Fu-lann) or Lo Man-fei have begun to choose a different type of music that is more closely related to the Taiwanese or Chinese. Also, having their own dance groups in itself makes a statement about their desire to understand what is happening in Taiwan. There is actually something of a break with China; relations are ostensibly more open now, but when you get in touch with those people you find them really quite different.

E: I think the people from Hong Kong are also quite concerned with those differences; they too are caught between China, the West, and the need to assert themselves independently. It's a terrible delimma.

PH: The most important thing is to know why you are doing what you do—not blindly to imitate.

E: Where do the choreographers you have been referring to come from?

PH: Basically two sources: First, there is Cloud Gate, still the only professional company in Taiwan, and second, from the States. I am thinking especially of those Taiwanese dancers who go to the States to study and then come back here for brief visits, during which they get some dancers together and do a piece or two. I'm not sure how valuable that experience is; those "companies" are together such a short time, and if the choreographer comes back again next year it's a question of starting all over again with new people. My concern is not with this 30-40 year old generation, but with not having enough people under 30 to keep the work going. One problem appears to be that because they are so much better trained than the earlier generation they simply take everything that has gone before for granted.

LHM: You can say the polish is not yet perfect, but really they are looking for a movement identity. It took Martha Graham so long to find that, and the people we are talking about have only been choreographing for perhaps five years. One must reserve judgment. Some years from now we can say "Hey, we have this and that."

PH: The modern choreographers here have to struggle so to find time and space for the dancers to rehearse together; often they might have to settle for something like 9:00 on a Sunday night. But if they work with my company, it's a different experience. There we have a group of dancers that takes class every day, and often they have three hours set aside for rehearsal, so they are ready for the choreographer. The local choreographers have trouble providing this kind of continuity. If they work with my company they have 20 sessions—60 hours—to finish a 15-20 minute piece. Then they leave it with the company so we can perform it in different cultural centers. Even that is a new experience for them.

E: Are you able to pay your dancers?

PH: I provide half-pay for five hours/day rehearsal time, plus performance pay.

E: And Cloud Gate?

LHM: We always pay. The monthly budget for Cloud Gate is $80,000 US, for keeping the office and everything together. We have approximately 45 people involved, staff and dancers. In Taiwan, unlike in the States, we have to carry a team of technical staff, because most of the theaters here don't have a professional crew. In fact, Cloud Gate had to run workshops for several years to train the tech crew, and the designers. We continue to train about 20 technicians a year. Also, in New York you can get a publicity person to do PR for you. Here you don't get that.

PH: My monthly budget is $8,000, and I do 30 performances over an eight month season. Fortunately, I don't have to pay for the space; I use my father's space, and he pays for all the utilities. It saves a lot of money.

E: By "space" you mean Crown Studio?

PH: Yes. I had the studio for five years before I started a company. I have lots of classes for both adults and children. That helps to support the company, but I also need sponsorship from the government, and we perform to get funds from the different theaters.

E: Does Cloud Gate get government support?

LHM: Yes, but not on a regular basis. We never know how much it will be.

E: Is that why you recently suspended operations for three years?

LHM: That was one of many reasons. You see, for its first 15 years Cloud Gate was the only professional company in Taiwan, and you know what kind of struggle that means. We went on 14 foreign tours, all over Europe, the States, Australia. In those 15 years we gave more than 600 performances. We were tired. Since we came back four months ago we have done two "seasons"—two separate programs—almost 30 performances. And soon we will do 50 performances in Taiwan in less than two months (10 in Taipei alone). We have to keep performing in order to survive.

E: There's enough audience for all those performances?

LHM: For Cloud Gate, yes. In the past we have sold out six performances each season in Taipei.

PH: They perform in the National Theater, which seats 1,500.

E: You can sell out 1,500 seats for six performances?

LHM: This company is almost 20 years old; we're not talking about some "downtown" company. I envy Ping's position [with the "semi-professional" Dance Forum Taipei], but it's almost impossible for me to go back to that.

E: Whose choreography do you perform?

LHM: Mostly mine; now we are enlarging our repertoire. We have one Paul Taylor piece, *Aureole*. It is important that we get works from masters like Paul Taylor; if we are going to do works from the West we only want the best. I only trust the best. It's expensive, but you don't get a second-rate substitute.

E: Do the company members choreograph at all?

LHM: We encourage them to choreograph, though the schedule hasn't allowed us to do any of their works recently. They have produced two concerts of their own over the last two and a half years.

E: Who choreographs for Dance Forum Taipei?

PH: Each season we involve at least four different choreographers. Two are always local, the others are guests. So far we have had Jim May—he was Artistic Director for the company in the first year, and did a piece—and several choreographers from Hong Kong. One was Sunny Pang: He got his Bachelor of Arts degree from Adelphi College, and was originally a ballet dancer. He also has a strong background in Peking Opera, so his is a unique aesthetic. Our company also does lots of lecture-demonstrations.

E: Does it have a greater educational role than Cloud Gate?

PH: Cloud Gate did that a lot too, for the first few years.

LHM: We just don't have the time for that now, and everything Cloud Gate does is too big.

E: Do you have a business manager to help with things like travel?

LHM: We have two managers. Still there is too much to be done. You have to do everything for yourself in Taiwan. Among other things we are going into villages where no one has ever been before, so of course we have to figure out how to convert school auditoriums into legitimate performing space, that

Figures 57-59 Cloud Gate dancers in Lin Hwai-min's *Tale of the White Serpent*.
Photos: Hsieh An and Wang Hsing

kind of thing. We always have to set up and do it right; otherwise people are not happy.

PH: Over the last five years Lin Hwai-min has also been Chair of the program at NIA.

LHM: Suddenly, as committed as I was, I didn't know what the whole society was doing. Taiwan has a population of what, 20 million? At least six million were involved in the stock market. It was really something!

E: Sounds like Hong Kong.

LHM: Oh no, Hong Kong is very, very stable. Here there were no rules; it was all new; it was crazy.

PH: The stock market started at about 2,000 points and went over 10,000. A lot of people made a lot of easy money, so they just quit their jobs and became "professional" market players. When people make money that easily they don't know what to do with it. They might get better clothes, that kind of thing, but it doesn't mean better quality of life.

E: What we call the *nouveau riche.*

LHM: They don't even pretend!

E: There's a certain snobbishness about it?

LHM: In Hong Kong you have snobbishness, people who really "show their presence." I don't find that yet in Taipei.

E: Social phenomena are always interesting to watch. In China it was the noise that struck me; I couldn't believe the noise level. During the dance performance we went to there, for example, everyone was talking, and shouting, and eating. It was astounding! And when the performance was over people just stood up, without much applauding, and left, except for some who ran up on stage to congratulate their friends! It was very strange for us, because we never saw behavior like that in a theater.

LHM: You have to realize that theater in China was traditionally a different thing. It was a part of life; it wasn't something you had to sit quietly and respect. We have a lot of adjusting to do. When Cloud Gate gave its very first performance in Taipei I shut the door punctually at the time the performance was to begin. They said "The Vice President isn't here yet." I said "To hell with him! We're going to start our concerts on time." Then I stopped one of the dances because somebody took a flash picture.

PH: I think generally speaking the Taiwan audience is quite warm—certainly warmer than Hong Kong.

E: We just saw an interesting concert in Hong Kong by La La Human Steps. Do you know that company?

LHM: Crazy company. Wonderful company. I wish they were here.

E: They performed at APA in Hong Kong. Some people walked out, but on the whole the audience loved it. It's as intellectually negative a performance as anything I have ever seen.

LHM: That's why they liked it.

E: What kind of audience comes to Cloud Gate?

LHM: Young people are in the majority. Now we have those who grew up with Cloud Gate, and their children. Cloud Gate attracts people from all walks of life, like cab drivers and sidewalk food stand owners. When we returned from our three year hiatus, at our debut performance, there was the President in his box, and then the full house, and then 20,000 people sitting outside, in a plaza, watching on TV monitors.

E: What made you want to start up again? Did you know when you suspended operations that it was just temporary?

LHM: We actually didn't know how long it would be. When I came back I found the society getting a little better in Taipei, though there still wasn't anything to do in the villages. In a village of 30,000 there may be no bookstore, no coffee house, no film theater; instead there's gambling, pinball machines for the kids, and porno-video for the adults. That's more or less standard. I wanted to address such problems. Also there were lots of good dancers out of work, so we started all over again.

Figure 60 Sunny Pang's *Pipa-ing,* performed by Dance Forum Taipei.

Chapter Thirty:
Dance Education in Taiwan

Chou Su-ling

> *Chou Su-ling has been on the faculty of Tsoying High School, Kaohsiung, Taiwan, since 1977, first as an English Teacher, then as Director of Extracurricular Activities, and since 1983 as Director of the Dance Division (the first such program in Taiwan). She was Project Director for the "Seven Year Report on Dance Programs in the High Schools of Taiwan" (1988), which was subsequently published in book form. Her Master's thesis at the City College of New York is a first-of-its-kind comparison of dance training in the high schools of the United States and Taiwan. Ms. Chou directed the Tsoying Dance Group that performed at the Hong Kong International Dance Conference/Festival in 1991.*

We start in 1981, when the Education Ministry of the Central Government in Taiwan decided to set up special programs for particularly gifted students in dance, music, and the visual arts. They began with nine programs, five in the elementary schools and four at the junior high level. One of those was in Kaohsiung. Three years later, when the first junior high class graduated, they found that there was nowhere for those students to go, so the government looked at the four senior high schools in this city. One of those was only for boys, another only for girls, and a third was already committed to Visual Arts, so Tsoying got Dance by default. We received the announcement that we were to build a dance program in June, and school was to start in September, so we had to do everything to set up the first high school dance program in Taiwan, including auditions, during the summer.

I had been at Tsoying since 1977 as an English teacher, and also Director of Extracurricular Activities. In 1984 I was asked to be Director of Dance too, and since 1986 I have concentrated only on the Dance Program. This has been an interesting career change, because I am not a dancer; I have never taken a dance class. In college I was very active in all kinds of extracurricular activities, so when I came to Tsoying the Director of Extracurricular Activities at that time asked me to assist him. I accepted. It just so happened that there was a national dance competition that year, and Tsoying was asked to participate. I had always been interested in dance, so I thought "All right, maybe we can do something." I went out and auditioned some students, none of whom had any technical training, and I choreographed a piece, and we did it just for fun. Fortunately, we won the first prize, and the next year we won it again. Two pieces, two first prizes! Several of the students who were in those pieces went on to NIA, which had just opened its Dance Division, so the program here and I myself became a little famous.

After that I went to dance performances and classes; sometimes I would go all the way to Taipei in the morning and come back at night. I learned what I could that way. Also, we had a connection with Cloud Gate Dance Theatre and with Lin Hwai-min through my students who went to NIA, so when the Dance Program opened up here it was natural for him to help us. He became a special consultant, and he came down from Taipei to oversee the establishment of the curriculum, the studios, equipment, teachers, everything! He invited a very good teacher from Cloud Gate, Rae Yueng, to be the first ballet and modern teacher here. She was already living in Kaohsiung, where she had a private studio and directed the Kaohsiung Contemporary Dance Company. So in that first year I was the "Lead Teacher"—that is, I took care of all of the students' extracurricular needs—and she taught the classes. Then, of course, in subsequent years we brought in other teachers.

We had one big room on the 4th floor, which was designed as an "Experimental Theater." We used two-thirds of it as studio and the rest for office space. There were about 26 students that year. Then, as the second and third generation students came in we built two new studios. Also, when the first class graduated we started a performance series for them here and in Taipei, and that was the first time we were able to see high school students performing in public. Furthermore, many of our graduates went on to the National Institute of the Arts or the Cultural University; that was considered a great success.

From the beginning, with the aid of Hwai-min, we set up a curriculum based on ballet, modern dance, and Chinese Opera movement. This heavy emphasis on Western dance may seem strange for students who have grown up in Taiwan, but I would explain it this way: ballet is a very popular language throughout the dance world; everybody who wants to dance automatically starts with ballet. But ballet isn't enough; the students need to know what else is going on, so we have modern dance too. Also, Cloud Gate is very important in Taiwan, and it is a modern dance company (Graham technique); that has a big influence. Finally, being Chinese, we must naturally have our own Chinese training, although few of our students will go on in Chinese Opera because opera performers also have to sing. Still, I want them to know what is really *inside* the opera movement. Then maybe they can use that in their choreography, so that while it might look like modern dance, it will really be Chinese.

For the most part our students won't be ballet dancers either because they are already too old; most of them start dancing with us at age 15. If they want to be ballet dancers I tell them not to study here but to go abroad right away, probably to the US. I think of ballet as just a training regimen for them. In modern dance they might be

Figures 61-63   Chinese Opera training, students of Tsoying High School

a performer and/or choreographer; this is a way for them to learn that dancing isn't just technique. That's why I have begun to invite teachers from many different modern techniques, to let them know that dance isn't just how high your leg can lift, but has to do with emotion, impression, spirit—with what is in your brain.

At present we have eight faculty: one each in ballet, modern dance and Chinese Opera, one for improvization, and four accompanists. All are part-time, and all are Chinese. We also have as many guests as possible. For example, there is a very famous Chinese Opera artist and choreographer who lives nearby, and I have invited her to come twice a week. She will teach Chinese Figure Movement, and set a piece on the students. In 1984 I started the Summer Dance Program, and it is then, for the most part, that we have Western teachers in; this summer there were five. If there are interesting Westerners teaching at NIA we invite them here for weekends—just to come in, do a workshop, and go right back to Taipei. That is how Leon Koning started here. He came down for a number of weekends and got on very well with our students. I invited him to do some choreography for us, and then to be Artistic Director. Last year, when I had to go to New York, his role here grew even more. That is what we like; in order to have a real impact on a place like this you have to make a long-term commitment. Many Westerners come and go, but it is those people who have stayed on that really make a difference.

Because of our success, in 1985 the government built a second high school program in Taipei, and subsequently four more have been added. My school, as the first dance program, has always taken the lead in advising the others; we invite their faculty here, so they see, for example, that it is good to have the students all wear black rather than colorful leotards, because that makes them look clean and beautiful. Also, they see that we use live accompaniment, so they think "Oh, we need musicians instead of just tapes." We used to go to their schools as well, to give lecture-demonstrations. I would lecture on "What is Dance," and we would show a short piece, *Dragon Boat Festival*. Because they know what the dragon boat is, when they saw it they could understand that dance isn't just disco, just pop. They could see that dance is an art form, and dancing can be a profession. I think this was a great educational service, but for the last two or three years we just haven't had time to do it. Many schools still come here to observe us, especially when we have a Western guest teacher.

I was sorry to give up this much-needed performance opportunity. Most of our students can do very well at the barre, but when they go to the center to dance 80% of what they seem to know about movement drops out. I believe that is because we don't have many performances. So I have now recontructed the Experimental Theater, to get them used to the stage. If they have some idea from the improvisation class, for example, they can try it out there. We have lights and a curtain. They can show their piece at 5:30 after classes end, and invite their family and friends. Then they can sit down and discuss what they did. I think that is good for the choreographer and for the dancers. This also gives them some experience with technical theater and

Figures 64-65 Tsoying High School students in modern dance technique demonstration

design. They do everything for themselves; it's good practice for them. Soon I expect to buy a sewing machine, so they can make costumes too.

*   *   *   *   *

I end on a personal note, because it represents another aspect of cross-cultural exchange. I have recently returned from my first trip to the United States, where I went to work on the M.A. Degree I need in order to advance further in the Taiwanese school system. It was my intention to study at New York University (NYU), but almost immediately I transferred to the College of the City of New York (CCNY), for the following reasons.

I arrived Sept. 2, and went to the Galatin Division of NYU, where the Director came to meet me and give me my file. She suggested that I call my adviser and arrange my schedule with her; I had some problems because I wanted to complete the coursework in just one year. When I telephoned the adviser I found she was out of town. I went back and asked what I should do, and was told I might as well take my English examination first. I did that, and they said "Your speaking and reading are very good, but your writing is a little weak." Still, they didn't recommend that I take a writing course, and I was much relieved because that would have slowed me down. But I still didn't know what courses I should take, so I went back to the Galatin Division, asked for any literature that might help, and read everything they gave me. I decided that Arts Administration might be good for me, so I asked where to go for that and they said "Oh, it's in X Building on the corner of W. 4th and Broadway." But, where was West 4th Street?—I had no idea. I kept asking everybody, and some people were very nice, but others were rude. They talked so fast, and used terms that I just couldn't understand. I felt frustrated and depressed. Finally I found the class and entered, but I couldn't understand what they were talking about. All I could say was "I'm a foreigner; I have only been here two days. Please help me." Some of my classmates were nice and tried to help. At the last minute, my adviser appeared. I went to see her and found that the English Program had cheated me; I needed to take a writing class after all. I don't believe I had misunderstood them the first time, and I was so angry, but what could I do? I went to register, and the computer man said to me "What is your ID number?" and I said I didn't know. He said "Well, you should," and he just threw the papers at me! Then I went to another computer person who looked a little nicer and she pushed a button and there was my ID number; it was so easy!

This went on for two weeks, and during that time I was crying on the phone almost nightly with my friend Yun-yu Wang in Colorado. She got in touch with Jill Beck at CCNY, who she thought might help. I went to see Jill Beck on a Thursday, and she made many calls for me. She sent me to the Registration Office, and the man there said "Yes, you can register. No problem." I said "are you sure?" and he said "Yes, don't think everyone is NYU!" So I went back on Friday; in one-half day I was registered, and on Monday I started classes at CCNY.

Figures 66-67   *Chinese Legends,* students of Tsoying High School

Those classes were wonderful; everyone was extremely helpful. During second semester I asked Jill Beck and Dawn Horwitz to sponsor me in doing a survey of American arts high schools. I wanted to compare them with what we are trying to set up in Taiwan. They saw that that would be good for my work, and were most cooperative. I visited five schools on the East Coast, and sent questionnaires to 26 others (seven answered, a good response rate). I have now written up that study, and found it to be very useful. Also, I took courses in stage lighting, and was able to do designs for a number of student projects, so that was helpful both to me and to my fellow students.

I think that NYU may have very good teachers, and facilities and equipment, but in a new place, new surroundings, a good *person*, a sympathetic person, is the most important thing. If everything there is good, but the person is not helpful, it's no use. Even though I could speak English, this was my first trip to America, there was a great deal of culture shock, and I was very frightened. If people were impatient, or gave me a dirty look, I couldn't understand what they were talking about, and I just gave up. After I had been in the States for a month or two I got some confidence and started traveling all over by myself. I began to feel calmer, so I was able to think, and watch, and hear. Before that it was just as if I were deaf, mute, and blind.

I'm sure if I go back the shock won't be so great. Now I know why, where and how, so travel in America will be easy for me. What I would say is that the way of thinking, the whole philosophy, is different: I think this way, you think that way. It's not just the language that causes problems; even if we can communicate with language that doesn't mean we can cooperate together. We will have to learn to do that through increased exchange.

Chapter Thirty-One:
Ballet in Taiwan

Leon Koning

> **Leon Koning** *was for many years a member of the Netherlands Dance Theater and Dutch National Ballet companies. He has performed in the works of virtually all of the great ballet choreographers, and many modern dance choreographers as well. Since 1984 he has lived and worked mainly in Taiwan, where he has served as ballet master for the Cloud Gate Dance Theatre and the dance program at the National Institute of the Arts, which he helped to create. His own choreography includes classical-style ballets and modern dances, solos as well as works for 100 and more dancers, works for professional dance companies and for students.*

I was sitting down one day with my Artistic Director, Rudi van Dantzig, and he was talking about how, when he choreographed *Monument for a Dead Boy,* he was invited to be Director of a company in America. He said "If I had done that, it would have changed my entire life." Then we got to talking about what countries it would be interesting to be in; what might be our wish. I mentioned Mainland China, and he said that wouldn't be attractive to him, even though he is a Communist. A few weeks later our company got a call from Lin Hwai-min, who had made a connection with us through Joachim Schmidt, the European dance critic. Schmidt had seen the Cloud Gate Dance Theatre in Germany, been much impressed with it, and met Hwai-min. Just at that time Hwai-min was thinking to make ballet a stronger part of training in Taiwan, because to that point they were learning modern dance almost exclusively. He came to my house, we talked 'til four in the morning, and he said "You ought to come over." I said "Yes." He said there would be a workshop that summer (it was '83), and so I went. We had more than a hundred students. I shared teaching and choreographing with some of the Cloud Gate members, and I loved it.

I extended my stay to six months, at the end of which I told Hwai-min that I wanted to work there. He said: "You have to be very careful. This isn't Europe. It's not a developed country. In one way we are 'Coca-cola,' but in another we're still 'green tea.'" So I went back to Holland, and immediately I got a letter from the Dutch National Ballet that I was in my last year, because we get "fired" at the age of 38 (they don't want to get stuck with old dancers who hang around). I thought to myself, "If I sign a contract for one more year, *they* end my career; if I don't sign, *I* end it," so I telephoned Hwai-min. He invited me to come. In the fall of '84 I started a combined job as Ballet Master/Teacher for Cloud Gate and Teacher at the National Institute of the Arts (NIA).

When I came to Taiwan for the first time it wasn't as though I were entering a different world. The circumstances were different, the "color schemes" were different, but when I went to the museums it was still the same development that Europe went through—from bronze, to pottery, to glass, to extremely sophisticated handicrafts. Because it was my first teaching job I didn't think too much, in the beginning at least, about what I should do; I didn't want to preoccupy myself with the fact that I was teaching people from a different cultural background. It was essentially "jump in and swim." Then I began to find out what the deficiencies, the necessities, and the strong points were; the situation developed to where I saw what they needed and they saw what I knew.

I was pleased to find that an interest in ballet was already well established; if you asked the students at the Institute what they wanted to do, 99% of them would say "I want to be a ballet dancer." At that time they had seen practically no live ballet; there were no theaters in Taipei then that were suitable for ballet performance. Their image of classical ballet was from video. Hence, what they saw in ballet was not what is standing at the edges of the picture, but what is dancing in the *center* of the picture. *That* was their dream. I would say "Why do you want to be a ballet major," and they would say "It's so pretty. When I look at *Swan Lake*, the girl in white is so beautiful." So I would say "What about the blood and tears in dance? Do you know anything about that?" Of course they were dumbfounded. Things started to change slowly; for some of them, as we say in Chinese, "their dream was broken." There is still no ballet company in this country, so if you are a ballet major, even if you're good, you don't have anywhere to go.

These students were under a misconception because what they had seen were mainly the big classics. They had no experience of works in which you need a strong foundation in the style of a Jiri Kylian, or a Joffrey, or a Robbins, to say nothing of Balanchine. I said to Hwai-min: "Look, let's start with two-hands barre, so they get a really strong base and can go on from there." Some of them had prior training, but they tended to be placed very badly, and the musicality wasn't there because none of the schools in Taiwan had accompanists. That was perhaps my greatest innovation; I made it a condition of my coming here that I would only teach if I had an accompanist. But there weren't any, so I had to train them, and I am responsible for practically all of those that are around now.

The students were a little impatient; they didn't understand how classical training can make you say "Hey, now I can do this which I couldn't do yesterday," like two *pirouettes* for example. Some of them were a little reluctant to start from the basics. I think maybe that was our fault. We began by focusing on dance training at the university level, whereas we probably should have started in the junior high schools. Then we would have avoided the problem we are fighting now, nine years later; the kids we are producing from the junior high schools can dance circles around the university students. When those well-trained younger students catch up with the poorly trained older ones you have to: 1) divide the class, which causes hellish scheduling problems; 2) put the good ones back to two-hands barre, although they can already do extensive *adagio*, *allegro*, and simple pointe work; or 3) move ahead and sacrifice the weaker ones. Three years hence, at the end of high school, the same problem reoccurs at the university level and we are back again with two-hands barre!

A related problem: In this country at least, and perhaps in all of Asia, parents do not see dance as a profession. They know that NIA produces a piece of paper at the end, like the other universities that train doctors or lawyers, but they also know that it is different. Their child's English course at NIA is only two years long, and if the grades aren't too good it doesn't matter as long as she can lift her legs. They really don't know how to assess that. Now, if we had a good follow-up from junior high school on we could say to those parents at some point: "Papa and Mama, this child of yours is so talented that I can guarantee you if she goes to Europe after graduation a job will be there."

There are a number of other local issues that we have to contend with. One is body type. In Taiwan almost everyone has hyper-extended knees and elbows. That is beautiful, but it can also be dangerous. If the ballet students really push to stretch the leg rather than pulling up the front of the knee—but not totally stretched so the bone is locked—they can't get into 5th position. Also, that causes rolling in, and twisting the knee, and pushing the butt out; it affects the whole alignment. The advantage to this ligamentous laxity is that the hip sockets are very free; most students have good turn-out. The other thing I have found is flat feet, yet when the foot is stretched, there *is* an arch. My guess is that this relates to the plastic slippers worn by the children here. In the West we get our children into real shoes, which provide support, as soon as possible. Here you see the kids flip-flopping around at least until they go to school.

Of course we pitch our expectations lower as far as male body types are concerned—unlike Mainland China, where they audition 2,000 candidates from the provinces and only take 20. Most of us don't have that luxury, so we make do with what we get. It is interesting that Taiwan is just now switching over from all-male and all-female schools to co-education, and the boys' work is improving because of the competition. There is a strong "macho" thing here: "No girl's going to be better than me." Anyway, we have been able to get some very good boys out of the schools. The tragedy is that just as we get them ready, right on the edge of a career at age 19, we lose them for two years to the compulsory military service. Here the military has a department for singing and dancing and music, to entertain the other soldiers, but of course a ballet dancer can't maintain himself doing that kind of thing.

Reports are that because of improved eating habits young people of both sexes are taller and heavier than ten years ago. I remember thinking when I came here in '83 that the women of Cloud Gate were noticeably small. That is no longer so; they are not exactly Balanchinesque yet, but they have plenty of size.

The major problem in Taiwan is that we still have no professional ballet companies. The dance system in this country was not truely well thought out. When Tsoying High School started its dance program in 1984 Lin Hwai-min went there to advise them, and then he sent me there to help them grow. Subsequently, the government has opened five more schools of this kind, although there are not enough quality teachers to go around. What this essentially creates is a dead-end system. These schools are reticent to cut out the weaker students, because they feel that will give them a bad name, so cumulatively they are graduating 120-150 dance majors each year, most of whom want to go to universities that can provide only half that number of places. Five years later, we have 25 or so graduates coming from each university and there is no place for them to dance.

There has been talk about changing this. Undoubtedly the government would like to have a resident company in the National Theater, like any large opera house in the world. I'm not terribly optimistic, because I think they have the wrong image. I'm afraid the people would get lots of *Swan Lakes* and *Sleeping Beauties*, and they don't really need that. Ballet provides a nice technique for expressing many things, but the Taiwanese dancers are equally well versed in Chinese dance and modern dance. I don't think they should restrict themselves to classical ballet. By way of analogy, rather than creating an American Ballet Theater I would like to see something like the Nederlands Dans Theatre or Ballet Rambert here. I think that would give the dancers more of an opportunity to create new works—to express themselves within their own culture. I don't believe in spending a lot of money on Western repertory; I think that is uninteresting.

My own choreography is much influenced by being made in Taiwan. I am seeing things through Chinese Opera, through certain indigenous effects on the stage. For example, I choreographed a work *On Mozart*, which uses a piece of music about a sleigh ride through snow. In Chinese Opera they have a way of using sticks which means "riding on horseback," so I had four girls doing that. The audience immediately understood my vocabulary. Other examples: I did a *Firebird*. The Firebird is basically a Mongolian princess, so I included the Chinese Opera *port de bras* in the prince's part. I did *Romeo and Juliet*, and rather than using weapons in the dueling parts I used movements from the martial arts. In *Pulchinello* I used the Chinese clown make-up.

I also let myself be influenced by things I see outside the theater, in society. For Tsoying High School I did a piece called *One Plus One Is Two*, about the life of the school children here. The dancers were in uniforms, and the dance used all kinds of Taiwanese school situations. There was no music, just spoken words and singing, all in Chinese. I want to make the piece into a trilogy, and I have already done Part II,

Figure 68 Leon Koning coaching a major in Chinese Opera for his graduation
concert at the National Institute of the Arts, Taipei

called *Home Sweet Home* (they sing that song here, with Chinese words). It is based
on the typical domestic situation in Taiwan as I have observed it when visiting my
students' homes. The third part will be *Outside Life*, the public life of the streets.

People who have seen these last two works have said to me "How is it possible
that someone who is not Chinese can create something that seems to capture the
essence of Chinese society?" In the newspapers here they often ask "Why aren't
there more choreographers doing this kind of cross-cultural thing," and I think they
are right: you *can* do work in which the traditional culture is recognizable, yet there
is something within it that is new. Unfortunately, there are very few choreographers
here making use of their Chinese-ness; most of what they do looks very American-

ized. In painting the traditional forms are still strong, but not in dance. The folk dance here, for example, is very watered down, because it is all imported from the Mainland. They have to get someone from the Mainland here to teach it well, and the political situation makes that extremely difficult.

It is our hope when we bring Western dance to Taiwan that the Taiwanese will reinterpret and make use of it. First, though, they need to understand fully where it comes from. Just looking at the videotapes of American Ballet Theater doing *Giselle*, for instance, doesn't mean anything unless you know that the setting and the costumes are from 1841, that it was one of the first pointe shoe ballets, and at that time, under the influence of Romanticism, death was very much associated with nymphs and sylphs who appear at night. Only when you know that and a good deal more can you incorporate classical technique for your own use; you can't just learn it from the outside. This kind of incorporation simply takes time, and if you don't do it systematically, with a great deal of patience, and consideration, and taste, you get only the worst of it. In Taiwan we started just nine years ago, and we are only beginning to get a sense of what the mingling of these cultures means.

Chapter Thirty-Two:
Great Expectations:
The Training of Taiwanese Dancers

An Interview with Lo Man-fei

> *Lo Man-fei holds a B.A. degree in English Literature from Taiwan National University and an M.A. degree in Dance from New York University. She is working on a doctoral degree in Dance at Temple University.*
>
> *A former dancer with Cloud Gate Dance Theatre of Taiwan, Ms. Lo has performed extensively in Asia, Europe and the United States. She has worked with many professional companies and in the Broadway musical* The King and I. *Her choreographic works have been presented in Taiwan, Hong Kong and the United States.*
>
> *Lo Man-fei is currently a guest soloist and choreographer with Cloud Gate Dance Theatre and the Chairperson of the Dance Department of the National Institute of the Arts.*

Editors: How do you feel about taking over as Chair of the Dance Program at the National Institute of the Arts?

Lo Man-fei: I've been postponing this for many years. Lin Hwai-min started, and then it was up to Ping [Heng] and me as next in seniority, but I was still performing and I was very interested in choreographing. As time went by I saw the growth of the school—this is now its tenth year—and our goals really became clarified. Now I think those goals are more important than my own private ones. Of course I want to see myself grow, but it's more important that dance in Taiwan should grow. It's interesting: when you see new things coming out of practically nothing you want to help it happen.

Hwai-min obviously can't contribute any more right now. He's too involved with Cloud Gate, and you can't over-estimate the importance of Cloud Gate to our dance community. Without it what would our students aspire to? How could our school continue? What would we teach them? You train dancers; you want them to be professional, and then, five years later, they don't even have the hope of a job. It's not that they are all going to find work with Cloud Gate, but at least that's a goal they can work for.

Figure 69   Lo Man-fei performing Lin Hwai-min's *It is June 8, 1989, 4:00 pm.*
Photo: Liu Zhen-xiang

E: And that is the expectation of every student who comes through?

LMF: Not necessarily a place in Cloud Gate, but employment with some profes-
       sional company. So far Cloud Gate is the most visible and stable option; the
       Dance Forum is another, although it offers only half-time work for its
       dancers. We need more companies like that. And then, of course, the
       Taiwanese dancers want to get experience abroad. We think that's very

important; we encourage that. I, myself, joined Cloud Gate in 1979, when I was 22. That was fine, but I always knew I needed to go to New York in order to feel fulfilled. I am a modern dancer, and at that time all of the dancers I liked and admired came from the US or Europe. I started dancing at the age of eight; in those days we did a lot of folk dance—modified, modified, modified "Chinese Dance." It was fun for a kid, but as an art form it was not very satisfying to one who might want to be an intellectual. As I matured I decided not to study dance, but to become an English Literature major. While at college, I began to see more modern dance, and that attracted my whole attention. I started studying with Dr. Liu Feng-hsueh, who was the Director of the whole National Theater complex (and a Ph.D. from the Laban Center in England). She is a very important figure in Taiwanese dance—in her 60s now, and still choreographing. She had a studio then, and I joined her company. She was performing modern dance, but with a strong Chinese identity—using Chinese themes, or some elements of Chinese movement, or costume, or music—but if you wanted to classify it you would call it modern dance. Also at that time the Graham Company and Alwin Nikolais and many other foreign companies were coming through. That naturally "blew my mind." I saw Cloud Gate then, and took some of their classes, which were Graham influenced (I got some of that from Liu too, though she was probably closer to the Germans).

E: Did you have any Western ballet?

LMF: Yes, when I was quite young, but it was much diluted. That was nearly 30 years ago, and at that time all the studios were most concerned with preparing works for the Chinese Dance competition. That's why many people in my generation had a lot of resentment for Chinese Dance—because what we were taught then was some kind of hybrid that really had no basis in Chinese tradition. In my grandmother's generation they didn't go to the theater to see Chinese Dance, because there was no such art form. They went to Peking Opera or one of the other "Operas," in which dance was one element. I didn't know very much then, but I did know that most of the dance of that sort was not very good.

E: Are you saying there *was* a classical Chinese Dance, but it was lost...

LMF: Not lost, but absorbed into the opera. For example, in the Tang Dynasty (about 600-900 AD) they had lots of court dance, some of which originated in China while others were imported from the Middle East, India, etc. They actually gave name recognition to those foreign influences, but it was still considered a part of the glory of China. At that time the Chinese people felt very strong. They were very confident, so they weren't afraid of foreign influences; they took what they liked and make it their own. Later, when that confidence began to wane, they either accepted everything foreign as better than what they had, or clung to everything of their own and rejected

Figures 70-71   Lo Man-fei's *Seams of the City.*
Photo: Liu Zhen-xiang

everything foreign. We always think of the Tang Dynasty as a healthy time.

E: And where are you now?

LMF: In dance we want to "do our own thing;" like modern dancers generally, we want to express our own society, our own feelings. We don't want to just hang on to a past China that seems very distant from us. We want to say things that are connected to *now*. My generation is starting to worry less about the collective identity—"Is this Chinese?"—and more about "Is this *me*?" Living in this rapidly changing society we are exposed to a lot of Western influences; as long as we acknowledge those influences they shouldn't be a handicap. One aspect of this is a new interest in exploring what is here, in Taiwan—for example, Aboriginal Dance. Before, people never went to the sources, although they were always here, and now people are really beginning to explore them .

E: Is that one way of defining your Taiwanese identity?

LMF: Yes. Before, the government wanted us to feel that we were Chinese first— that the whole of Mainland China was ours, although the government had moved to this island. It encouraged Chinese dance competition, including Mongolian Dance, Northeastern Dance, everything. Now, in my generation, we realize that we don't really know those people and their traditions; China is so huge and so different. We think that it is better to start trying to understand what is right here, locally, in Taiwan. Here we have not only the remnants of the Aboriginal cultures, but lots of folk traditions that relate strongly to the local Taoist ceremonies. We are just now learning how to study these cultures properly, so they maintain their integrity and we present what we take from them—their dance forms, for example—in a proper context.

E: Let's return to you for a moment. At what point did you go to New York?

LMF: After I graduated from college. I studied at a number of studios, including Graham and Ailey, for about a year, and then I came back here.

E: Can you describe what it was in the work you did in New York that appealed to you?

LMF: In the work of artists like Graham and Ailey I found universal themes that touched me. The dance I had done before was just "decorative;" this was different. It was like literature; it touched you through its meaning. Nikolais just "blew my mind," because I had never seen anything like that before. That's why I say it is "universal;" because you can somehow "touch base" with those artists without necessarily knowing much about their culture.

E: When you came back to Taiwan you went immediately into Cloud Gate?

LMF: Yes. Hwai-min invited me to become a company member, and that was a great breakthrough for me because I had never before worked as a professional dancer. I stayed with the company for about four years. We toured a lot—the US, Southeast Asia, Europe—and I owe a lot of my performing experience toCloud Gate. It also offered us a lot of good training: not only ballet and Graham techniques taught by Hwai-min and others, but also Beijing Opera movement and *Tai Chi*. I had never thought of those things as dance. Our curriculum at NIA is based on that mixture of training. We regularly have people coming to teach the Beijing Opera form, which has a systematic, step by step training regimen. Naturally we just learn the movement part, not the voice.

E: Are these classes similar to the ones you take in order to learn Graham technique, for example.

LMF: Similar in the sense that they are very strenous and highly disciplined. They have their own progression, which is very important. In order to do the acrobatic things you have to start from a good base.

After four years with Cloud Gate I felt I had gone as far as I could with that, and also I began choreographing. I worked hard at that, but I felt the work was terrible, and I didn't know how to make a breakthrough. I felt stifled; I felt I needed more experience. So I went back to New York, and this time I knew what I wanted to pursue. Primarily, I wanted to get into the Paul Taylor Company, because I loved it so much. I did study with members of the Paul Taylor Company, but other things came along. I did *The King and I* on Broadway, and worked with lots of small modern companies, where I made many friends. I got to see how people struggle and grow in New York; that was very important for me. I learned how much devotion and integrity you need in this profession; it was no longer just a romantic fantasy for me. Even Paul Taylor's dancers sometimes need to collect unemployment compensation!

I decided to go back to school—to NYU, Galatin Division—because I thought an M.A. would be useful for me. Also, I had developed an interest in dance medicine and proper body mechanics (I had to have surgery for an injury that I knew was the result of poor alignment). So I studied with Irene Dowd. At the same time I had a scholarship to work with Jennifer Muller, because I was interested in Limón technique, and took classes from Zena Rommett. NYU essentially provided all that for me, and with the degree I was able to go back to Taiwan and become a faculty member at NIA.

Teaching really helped me to put my ideas together; as a result of teaching I became a much better performer. Also, teaching at the Institute provided a great environment for me as choreographer. The students were right there, available to me, and like it or not they had to come to rehearsals! So I started organizing concerts on my own, using the students as perform- ers. Those years were most important to me, because I really began to feel grounded. I no longer think that I have to go somewhere else to look for anything. Still I think that experience of going out and then coming back to work is very important: Most of the young dancers will go through it, and

Figures 72-73 Dance Forum Taipei dancers in Lo Man-fei's *Dialogue with the Landscape.*
Photo: Liu Zhen-xiang

only then will they settle down to the serious business of developing something of their own. Fortunately, most of our graduates—even those who go immediately into Cloud Gate—have a desire for "the foreign experience."

E: Where does the impetus to get that experience come from? What do people expect from that kind of experience?

LMF: For myself, when I was younger I didn't know what there was out there, but I thought it was a lot, and I had to go see for myself. The desire to work with the Paul Taylor Company was a strong impetus for me. I had to be there, waiting for the call to audition. That didn't happen for me (there weren't any auditions held while I was there), but looking back I don't think that's important. It would have been great to work with the Company, but if I had I wouldn't be the same me now. I probably wouldn't have come back, at least not so soon, and then I wouldn't be involved with Taiwan. I really treasure the work here, and if I had gone with Paul Taylor I certainly wouldn't have had the opportunity to choreograph which I so much value.

E: How do you describe what you got when you were in the United States?

LMF: Exposure. I think that was very important: I saw so many types of dance; I took so many different classes; I got to meet many people and see how they work, how they live. Downtown New York is very significant for me because it was there that I saw how people grew as artists. Here in Taiwan we don't have little theaters, only the big, state-owned ones. People work for two years to put together a show for one night on that huge stage that might not even be appropriate for the material. You don't accumulate experience; you are put on the big stage too soon. In New York I learned how to start with small things. Ping Heng was with me at that time (we were roommates), and she learned the same things. Now her studio and her company are very important to the dance scene here, because they provide the opportunity to work on a relatively small scale. Her father said: "Here is this space. How do you want to use it?" We took him to New York and showed him some of the downtown loft studios, and he thought that was very interesting. He went back to Taiwan, and then came a letter saying "OK, the space is ready," so we came back and started to produce. A part of that was inviting some of the teachers we had met in New York as guests—like Doris Rudko, and Jim May. Then one friendship led to another, and soon all kinds of people were coming, and Taipei was a very busy place. All of that was made possible by the exposure we had in New York. Now, our students get much more exposure here than was available to us.

E: When you bring in foreign teachers, what do you expect of them? What do you want them to contribute to your students? to your program?

LMF: Sometimes we bring different types of technique teachers, and the intention is always to enrich the students' experience by expanding their perspective.

Many of the teachers we bring in now teach techniques other than Graham. Beyond that, we need people who will stay on a long-term basis—people like Leon Koning and Ross Parkes—to establish a foundation. Otherwise the education becomes too fragmented.

E: What about improvisation and composition?

LMF: Frances Tao (Fu-lann) has been teaching improvisation, and I share the responsibiltiy for beginning composition. Hwai-min has been teaching the more advanced composition. Whenever a guest comes, as when Doris was here, we assist, we translate, so we also learn. We keep adding new teachers. An example is [Ku] Ming-shen, who was quite an active choreographer in Taiwan for some time before she went to New York, where she developed an interest in contact improvisation. She is working now with Steve Paxton. She will come back and start a class in contact improvisation here next semester. We try to make as many contacts as we can, and then we see if we can find the financial resources to bring people here. We have a strong core faculty, and we try to augment it whenever we can.

E: Are you concerned that bringing in foreigners interferes with your students' search for their Taiwanese identity?

LMF: Oh no! We are constantly exposing them to their Taiwanese heritage. When they have foreign teachers it's just "other things." By the way, we are starting to have guest teachers other than Westerners; two years ago, for example, we had a Balinese teacher, and next year Sal Murgiyanto has agreed to come to teach Javanese dance. Our students are also very interested in the Aboriginal dance. There's so much for them to do; they have to choose what their career path will be. Most of the students will choose modern dance, but we want to feed their appetite for other forms as well.

Chapter Thirty-Three:
On Teaching Choreography in Taiwan

Doris Rudko

> *Doris Rudko studied with the famous educator Margaret H'Doubler*
> *at the University of Wisconsin, and subsequently with many of the*
> *greats of American dance, including Hanya Holm, Doris Humphrey,*
> *Charles Weidman, Martha Graham, José Limón, Merce*
> *Cunningham, and, in composition, Louis Horst. She has served on*
> *the Dance Composition Faculty of The Juilliard School since 1969,*
> *and in guest residencies at many other schools and summer pro-*
> *grams, most notably New York University and the American Dance*
> *Festival. Her international credits include stints in West Germany,*
> *Sweden, Italy, Switzerland, Greece, Taiwan and Hong Kong.*

Taiwan is quite westernized, on the surface at least. In contemporary dance, the Martha Graham technique and Russian ballet are strong influences, in addition to Chinese Dance and the Martial Arts. This is particularly true at the National Institute of the Arts (NIA). It is really quite impressive how disciplined the dancers are in perfecting the physical form of Western dance idioms—sometimes, perhaps, in a too codified way. I'm not saying there aren't fine artists who have absorbed Western influences into their own personal language. I think of Lin Hwai-min's dance, *Legacy*. Although his work has been influenced by the Graham aesthetic, this dance is an inspired creation, and deeply sourced from his Taiwanese heritage.

I do not know if the Graham technique was taught in Taiwan before Hwai-min formed the Cloud Gate Dance Theatre. Most of the leading professional dancers in Taiwan have at some time in their careers performed in the company. Liou Shaw-lu and his wife, Maura Yang, have established their own school and dance company, Taipei Dance Circle. Lo Man-fei is a beautiful dancer and talented choreographer, and there are many other active choreographers in Taiwan.

A great deal of credit also belongs to Ping Heng. When she opened her Taipei Dance Workshop in the mid-80's she invited many guest teachers to give intensive workshops in ballet and modern dance (mainly in the Limón and Cunningham disciplines). Jazz classes and creative dance for children were also offered. Ping invited me to teach choreography for five consecutive summers, first on a basic,

Figure 74　Dance Forum Taipei performs Sunny Pang's *Cadaverous Capers*.
Photo: Liu Zhen-xiang

introductory level, and later intermediate and advanced workshops. Although improvisation and choreography classes were part of the curriculum at the newly established NIA, I am quite sure my dance composition workshops were the first formal courses of study open to the general dance sector. Jim May was also a regular guest, teaching both technique classes and Anna Sokolow repertory. Informal demonstrations of the choreographic process and works from Anna Sokolow's repertory were performed in Ping's studio/theater, and were open to the public. Ping Heng's semi-professional dance company, Dance Forum, developed directly from the performing experience of Taipei Dance Workshop's most talented dancers. Jim May was the company's first Artistic Director. Repertoire consisted of new works choreographed by him and two very talented Taiwanese choreographers, Frances Tao (Fu-lann) and Ku Ming-shen. Sunny Pang, a young choreographer from Hong Kong, created some delightful works in the more abstract vein.

　　I always taught through an interpreter. Ping was very good in this role. She has her M.A. in dance notation and knows dance. When I teach dance composition I do not use the vocabulary of the technique class; I incline more to an aesthetic language closely related to the fine arts and music. It is therefore very important to me that I be able to trust the interpreter to impart the particular nuance and meaning I have in mind. Frances Tao was also excellent; she studied with me each summer and I often coached her, was her objective eye, while she was working on a new dance. Nonetheless, I found working through an interpreter somewhat frustrating in Taiwan—more so than in Europe, where most dancers speak some English. In Taiwan the main language spoken in the home is Taiwanese. Mandarin Chinese is the official language and the second language taught in the schools. Having to have almost everything I said translated into Chinese slowed down the pacing of a class tremendously. Also, my inability to speak Chinese prevented me from coaching the students spontaneously, one to one. In my fervor I would often forget that what I was saying had to be translated, because the dancers would gather in and watch me so intently. They would nod their heads in seeming agreement and I would talk on and on, until finally the interpreter would gently nudge me and we would all laugh. We learned to understand each other artistically and culturally, to appreciate our differences, and to enjoy one another's company.

I tend to gambol about improvisationally in a composition class, indicating that there are many movement possibilities inherent in a given problem, and at least as many ways to solve it. I think this was rather liberating to the Taiwanese dancers because in Taiwan's academic schools the students are expected to follow the prescribed way. Naturally, I incorporate dance theory in my composition classes, but I do not discuss concepts directly. I give the students as many movement experiences as I possibly can, some in the form of tightly defined improvisations, others through short exercises and dance studies that focus on a particular choreographic concern. This process brings them, ultimately, to the artistic sensibility I am after.

I also try to relate movement to the human condition, to our collective identity. Dance is a universal language (if I might risk that cliché). Each country may have its own stylistic differences, but human expression, not a stylized dance form, is the real source of artistry. We all smile when we are happy and cry when we are sad, yet, the specific meaning in each smile and each cry is unique to itself. It is revealed in the gesture's telling details of design, space, rhythm, and dynamics. When we are "uptight" or distraught our body expresses this in its jagged patterns in space, its uneven rhythm, and its taut energy. I try to help dancers relate the movement they produce to their instinctive behavior rather than to any codified form of expression.

A very important part of my work is developing a heightened kinesthetic sense. I call this "the dancer's sixth sense." In both the East and the West there are dancers who do not sense meaning in their motion; who do not allow movement to communicate back to them as they are moving. I find this often happens when dancers are so involved in mastering the visible, concrete form of the movement as to lose the simultaneous, neuromuscular experience of it. Many of my exercises focus on movement awareness and help dancers as well as choreographers sense what is inherent in their movement, in its feeling and its form.

I believe, however, that in every country one finds choreographers who are creative and in touch with their instinctive intelligence, with its secrets and memories that go back to the beginning of time. Students who do not possess this potential for creativity usually depend on contrived classroom steps and patterns that vaguely represent something but do not evoke any specific images in the beholder. I use improvisation to lead dancers into spontaneous movement. This forces them to avoid intellectual planning. They gradually come to realize that, as in life, their inner motivation is the force that produces movement. That force can be anything in a composition class: a mood, an emotion, music, a formal concern, the point of concentration within a limited but not limiting choreographic problem. I find that when dancers are no longer self-conscious but are aware of themselves moving they are often surprised and excited by the movement they create. It is like a spiritual awakening. The composing, the crafting, comes after they have found movement that excites them. It is then that they elaborate, develop thematic material, edit, create new movement, phrase and structure the dance—i.e., begin the process called composition. To quote Louis Horst, "to c,o,m,p,o,s,e: to put in order."

Margaret H'Doubler and Louis Horst were my mentors. I assisted Louis for many years at the Neighborhood Playhouse School of the Theater and the American Dance Festival. I find that there is a widespread misunderstanding surrounding Louis' work: It is generally thought to be about musical forms. To me, it was and is about the aesthetic principles of form to which all arts pay homage. The ABA, ABCBA, Theme and Variation, and Rondo forms covered in Louis' *Pre-Classic Dance Forms* were his means of teaching that which is basic to all forms of expression—thematic manipulation and development in both its content and its form.

Louis' format is the same for each dance composition: (A) the statement of a concise, germinal movement theme which is manipulated and extended into one or two longer phrases; (B) the statement of a secondary theme consisting of a contrasting choice of movement vocabulary. This thematic material is varied and leads to a restatement of the initial A material. Through the utilization of various techniques of repetition and variation the choreographer develops the dance to its logical conclusion.

I relate the ABA form to the circular form of nature: morning/ noon/ night; born/ live/ die; beginning/ middle/ end. In my classes, however, I do not follow Louis Horst's exact methodology; rather, I incorporate his teachings in my own way. From them I acquired a "choreographic eye," and the conscious realization that there is a craft to the art of choreography. I encourage choreographers to be both objective and subjective. I also focus on mastery of craft, but through an intuitive route. This approach is directly related to my early dance study with the well-known educator Margaret H'Doubler.

No one can tell a choreographer how to choreograph, any more than one can tell a dancer how to dance. They both learn through their own efforts. In the process of choreographing phrases of movement and short études choreographers come to the conscious realization that the basic materials with which they work are space/ time/ energy and their constant interaction and interplay while moving. It is the rhythmic, dynamic, and spacial structures of the dance that provide its power to express.

In Taiwan, particularly with beginning students, it was a rather difficult task to bring the dancers to intuit movement rather than see pictures of movement. Within any improvisation it quickly becomes obvious which students are dictating dancing steps and patterns as they are moving and which students are totally involved in the act of dancing within the guidelines of the exercise. Taiwan dancers quite naturally fall into the characteristic attitudes, steps, and patterns of traditional Chinese dance. Inexperienced choreographers are also more inclined to lean on a story for their motivation.

Very often as soon as I finished presenting an exploratory exercise the dancers would run to their notebooks to write it down. I would say, "Oh no! Please wait until the end of class. Then review the exercises and what you discovered about movement and write *that* down." I found (and this pertains to other parts of the world as well) that whenever I succeeded in inspiring the dancers to forget themselves and become deeply involved in the improvisation or exercise, the movement they created was very beautiful. It was their very own. The difficulty is in remembering these gems of movement, in all their uniqueness.

One exciting difference for me from what I have grown accustomed to in the States was the Taiwan dancers' choice of movement vocabulary. They fell quite naturally into wonderful articulations of the hands and fingers. In the West our hands are primarily extensions of the arms. Before going to Taiwan I had not seen quite such articulate and expressive hands. Somewhat conversely, the Taiwanese dancers do not gambol through space with their legs and feet as we Americans do; indeed, I would often have to stretch their traveling vocabulary to include more than walking and running steps. The men's vocabulary was usually very strong and acrobatic, no doubt from their training in the martial arts.

The narrative form, too, is very prominent in all Taiwanese arts. I have no quarrel with this form of realism, except when the choreographer transcribes the story quite literally into dance, following the narrative line at the expense of allowing the dance to find its own organic structure. Because I do not speak Chinese I found it extremely difficult to help the Taiwanese choreographers cope with this problem. I would point out that movement follows the logic of one's muscles; that their heads must not get ahead of their bodies. They were inclined to think what movement to dance next before the body had completed its existing movement. Because of this, the flow of the phrase was lacking. Direct transitions were often awkward, or in the case of connecting transitions from standing to kneeling or from the floor to standing, the transition contained no choreographic information other than kneeling and rising. One of my favorite sayings is: "Listen to your body. It will tell you when, how and where to go."

Dancers in Taiwan possess a space consciousness, as do dancers everywhere; we all create reality in that emptiness we call space. I do think, however, that there is a shift of emphasis in the Chinese dancer's identification with space. In the Chinese Opera, in particular, the actors, who are also beautiful dancers, can evoke within a very limited space the illusion of walking through a door, going out to the garden, entering another room, or traveling a long, long journey in ways similar to yet quite different from a pantomimist's creation of the real world on stage. I think our Western use of space involves a broader, more abstract canvas. We create our reality by relating to space as volume, full of lines and forces, pulls and tensions.

In my classes in Taiwan I urged students to move through space, in space, and with space. To me this is a very important area of investigation. I keep tucked in my teaching pocket many movement experiences designed to make the choreographer aware of the emotional enrichment a space consciousness brings to movement. Some of my exercises teach them to extend their thematic material and develop it in space, and some help them to be sensitive to aesthetic properties of the stage space as a three-dimensional canvas. I often have student choreographers view a beautiful design from different perspectives in space. They are usually surprised to discover that this shift in spatial detail brings to the design a slightly different nuance of meaning, similar to a different inflection in speech.

I also grapple with rhythm. Inexperienced choreographers need to be made aware of the vitality a conscious use of rhythm brings to movement. Developing a personal sense of timing is also essential. The kinetic timing of motion is sometimes sensed as abstract patterns of energy release, and sometimes it emanates from the dancers' inner connection to the ebb and flow of feeling. Rhythmic exploration also encompasses the full spectrum of energy coloring. We have all the colors of the rainbow in our medium of movement. One of my favorite teaching techniques is to suggest that the dancers focus on rhythmic coloring during their improvisation: a small vibration in some part of the body; a series of staccato accents; arrested motion; interesting rhythmic patterns in their torso; or traveling combinations. Thus choreographers begin to grasp that dance is poetry in motion.

The cultural differences in Taiwan do not affect *what* I teach as much as *how* I teach. Students in Taiwan are very focused. They come to the studio with an eagerness to learn. I might have to nudge them in a happy-go-lucky way to be more daring, not to take my exercises too literally. I might remind them that in our vast movement vocabulary there are as many different ways of expressing oneself as there are people in the world.

The Taiwanese students are taught from elementary school on to respect the teacher; also, to the Chinese age is associated with knowledge. I was always treated in a respectful manner, with a gentle dignity. In the US teachers often have to prove that they are knowledgeable before the students submit themselves wholeheartedly. Students in Taiwan are less judgmental, and hence more open. This gives me wings to fly; I can feed off the positive energy in the class. Of course, being a guest teacher from another land is a factor too. I think in general our American vitality and individuality appeal to the Chinese students, and on a personal basis they seemed to enjoy my passion for the dance, my energy, and my enthusiasm.

Chapter Thirty-Four:
New Beginnings:
Taiwan and the United States

Wang Yun-yu

Wang Yun-yu, M.F.A. from the University of Illinois at Champaign-Urbana, has taught at Illinois Wesleyan University, the University of Georgia, and (currently) Colorado College. She began dancing in her native Taiwan, and was a founding member of Cloud Gate Dance Theatre, with which she performed internationally for nine years. Ms. Wang returned to Taiwan in 1989 to serve one year as Chairperson of Dance at the National Institute of the Arts, and she has been very active in coordinating the exchange of artists between that country and the United States.

I was a member of the fifth graduating class of the Chinese Cultural University, the first college-level dance department established in Taiwan. At that time a typical entering class was approximately 60 students, of which about half would graduate. For my first three years at that school I was not thinking of becoming a dancer. Dance was not really thought of then as an art form, and there was no possibility of pursuing it as a professional career in Taiwan. Then, in my senior year, Lin Hwai-min came back from the United States, with his background in both dance and creative writing, and the first class he taught was mine, which ultimately produced four of the founding members of the Cloud Gate Dance Theatre. That is when I became seriously interested in dance training. Mr. Lin was dedicated to dance, and he made us believe that it could be a performing career.

After we graduated, about 12 of my classmates and I studied with him in a studio he had rented, but initially there wasn't any pay involved, so gradually all except four of us drifted away. I stayed with Cloud Gate for nine years, though I also had to hold another job, and my parents were worried about me because I didn't have any boyfriends like the other girls of my age. With those first generation Cloud Gate dancers I felt that even though there was sacrifice and suffering involved I had to do the work, just as our Chinese ancestors did theirs.

Before going to college I had had virtually no dance training. There were no dance classes in the public schools at that time, though most schools produced a piece each

313

year for the annual Chinese Dance competition. Through high school I mostly studied accounting. In this country the parents generally don't want their children to study dance. In my time it was thought of as a mere entertainment at best, and it had even worse connotations. I think it is one of the reasons that the Graham technique Mr. Lin taught appealed to us; we recognized it as something you had to be "hard enough" to do. The dance required not only physical but mental involvement with the movement, in such a way that it was not at all like entertainment .

As Cloud Gate members we had modern dance class every day with Mr. Lin (for the first six years or so), a Western ballet class, and a class in Chinese Opera movement taught by guest teachers. We started at 9:00 every morning and did two or three classes, and then we would rehearse until 11:00 or 12:00 at night. Mr. Lin really was not a fast choreographer. He had to see how the movement looked on each dancer's body and then re-work it many times until he felt satisfied, so things went slowly. We all had so much confidence in him (and so little experience of our own) that we just cooperated with whatever he asked. From what I have learned since, we really should have complained! On the other hand, because of the "spirit" or "soul" we got from him we learned a lot about the dedication required to be a dancer.

He often took us to exhibitions of paintings, to historical buildings, music concerts, and many Chinese Peking Operas. He would encourage us to take calligraphy and *Tai Chi* classes. He found people to teach us classical Chinese literature and history. When we were setting a piece, like *Legacy*, he would take us on weekends into the countryside, and we would sit down there by a river for the whole day and talk about our ancestors—how they crossed the black water to come to Taiwan. Because of that I learned a great deal that I would not otherwise have known about how I became who I am. I don't believe the more recent generations of Cloud Gate dancers are given that kind of experience. Most of the current generation are tall and have beautiful technique, but the society they live in has changed; the needs are different. The spirit of that first generation of Cloud Gate dancers could never be sustained or replicated.

In my last three years with Cloud Gate (1978-1980) Mr. Lin started to invite many guest teachers from the United States and other countries. He also had the company tour Asia and the United States; we did 30 or more performances in the US and Canada in one and a half months. That contact with outside guest teachers and the foreign tours started me thinking it was about time to seek a change in my career. When I finally notified Mr. Lin that I was ready to leave he was quite upset. That surprised me, but in retrospect I see that for all those early company members Cloud Gate was very much like family; although there was only four years difference in our age, Mr. Lin and I were close to being as father/teacher and daughter/student in our working relationship. We had a slight argument when I left, and for a while things were difficult between us, but ultimately we regained our trust and I have benefitted in many ways from the relationship in my dance career.

I also would like to mention Mrs. Liu, who was one of the major influences on dance in Taiwan. She is less well known than Mr. Lin because initially she was more in dance education than performance; also, she never went out of her way to seek publicity. She studied in Germany, and had her own studio and company, later called New Classical Dance Company. The company is an off-and-on affair, but it is not without influence; Mrs. Liu herself has strongly affected the field of education in Taiwan. When I came back from the United States two years ago to take over as Chair of the Dance Department at the National Institute of the Arts I was concerned to see big separations of power between performance and education, traditional dance and contemporary dance. I felt the need to unify these elements for the sake of dance generally in the country. Unfortunately, little came of that in the short time I had available to devote to it, but the point remains that we should not overlook Mrs. Liu as someone who has been quietly influential in determining the course of dance in Taiwan. She develops her students in the area of education, while Mr. Lin's whole emphasis is on producing performers and choreographers.

There is a major problem in our country that is of concern to everybody: The people who graduate from NIA—or virtually any of the other university-level programs—are not formally qualified to teach in the public schools. That is a part of what I was trying to do two years ago—to get a certification program into the curriculum at NIA. Although I did not have time to finish that job because of my commitments in the United States, I believe there are many people still working on it. Mrs. Liu is equatable to a dance teacher in physical education in the United States; a lot of people from her school, National Normal University, are trained in the P.E. Department with an emphasis on dance. Their teaching credentials are the only ones that officially qualify anyone to teach full-time in the public schools. As dance continues to grow in this country—as of last summer there were thirteen programs in the elementary schools, thirteen more in the junior highs, and seven at the high school level—we will need more qualified teachers. I know that Mrs. Liu and Mr. Lin acknowledge this need and are trying to bring about more cooperation between the organizations involved, but people of an earlier generation in some related areas are very conservative, and so things change slowly.

*　　*　　*　　*　　*

In 1981 I was awarded two concurrent scholarships from the University of Illinois, Champaign-Urbana. I went there as an M.F.A. candidate, and got my degree two years later. I was, I believe, the third Asian student to complete the program. Although I was fortunate to be there I was not very happy for a variety of reasons. During most of my time at the University my advisor, who was also Chairperson of the department, was very kind to me, and I had lots of performing opportunities. However, the performances in the school situation really paled by comparison to those of Cloud Gate. Also, I was entirely tied up in course requirements, so that I was unable to do many of the things that interested me, like choreographing and taking

Index

Other titles in the Choreography and Dance Studies series

This book is part of a series. The publisher will accept continuation orders which may be cancelled at any time and which provide for automatic billing and shipping of each title in the series upon publication. Please write for details.